KATE CHOPIN
A CRITICAL BIOGRAPHY

PUBLICATIONS OF
THE AMERICAN INSTITUTE
UNIVERSITY OF OSLO

PER SEYERSTED

KATE CHOPIN

A CRITICAL BIOGRAPHY

UNIVERSITETSFORLAGET, OSLO
LOUISIANA STATE UNIVERSITY PRESS, BATON ROUGE

PUBLISHED IN NORWAY
BY UNIVERSITETSFORLAGET

PUBLISHED IN THE UNITED STATES OF
AMERICA AND CANADA
BY LOUISIANA STATE UNIVERSITY PRESS

Library of Congress Catalogue Card Number 77-88740
SBN 8071-0915-0

Printed in Denmark
by P. J. Schmidt, Vojens

To
Brita Lindberg-Seyersted

Contents

Mr. and Mrs. Thomas O'Flaherty

Kate O'Flaherty 1869

Kate Chopin 1870

Oscar Chopin 1870

Kate Chopin with four of her sons ca. 1877

Kate Chopin ca. 1886

Kate Chopin 1899

Kate Chopin 1894

The Storm

A Sequel To the 'Cadian Ball

I

The leaves were so still that even Bibi
thought it was going to rain. Bobinôt, who
was accustomed to converse on terms of perfect equality with his little son, called the
child's attention to certain sombre clouds
that were rolling with sinister intention from
the west, accompanied by a sullen, threatening
roar. They were at Friedheimer's store and
decided to remain there till the storm
had passed. They sat within the door on
two empty kegs. Bibi was four years
old and looked very wise.

"Mama'll be 'fraid, yes," he suggested with blinking eyes.

"She'll shut the house. Maybe she

Kate Chopin's handwriting 1898

Preface

Kate Chopin (the name is pronounced in the French way) became known to the American reading public of the early 1890's through her Louisiana tales in *Vogue,* the *Century,* and the *Atlantic.* With the collection *Bayou Folk* (1894) she gained national recognition as an outstanding short story artist of the local color school, and she seemed to be on the way to becoming an American writer of no little importance.

Mrs. Chopin had written nearly a hundred stories and published another collection – *A Night in Acadie* (1897) – when her major work, *The Awakening,* appeared in 1899. This novel about a sensuous, independent woman is in many respects an American *Madame Bovary.* The critics termed it a brilliant piece of writing, but they were horrified by the heroine's self-indulgence and the author's objective treatment of it, and they admonished her to go back to the description of "sweet and lovable characters."

Deeply hurt by the reviews and by the fact that she was ostracized and her novel banned in her own city, St. Louis, Kate Chopin wrote very little more, and after her death in 1904, her writings were quickly forgotten. Father Daniel S. Rankin performed an invaluable service when he saved her manuscripts from possible destruction; interviewed those who had known her, and in 1932 brought out a biography of her. Like most of the critics, however, he concentrated on the regional aspects of her writings, brushing aside *The Awakening,* for example, as "morbid." In the *Literary History of the United States,* where Kate Chopin is highly praised as a local colorist, the novel is not even mentioned.

When Cyrille Arnavon in 1953 translated it into French, meanwhile, he introduced the book with an important new appreciation of Mrs. Chopin's courageous realism. Since then, others have joined him in a re-evaluation and revival of the author, notably Kenneth Eble, Robert B. Bush, Edmund Wilson, Larzer Ziff, and George Arms, who have very perceptively discussed various aspects of her surprising accomplishment. *Bayou Folk, A Night in Acadie,* and *The Awakening* – recently republished – are today read in many university courses. With the appearance of the *Complete Works of Kate Chopin,* her total *oeuvre,* including about fifty previously unpublished or uncollected stories, finally becomes available.

In spite of this rediscovery and growing reputation of Kate Chopin, little has yet been written about her, and Rankin's biography – long out of print – has remained the only full-scale treatment of her. An extensive re-examination of the author would therefore seem to be long overdue. Previously unknown Kate Chopin stories and letters, besides a very important diary, have recently come to light. Much in the material now available points to a new reading of both her life and work. Mrs. Chopin appears to have been a more ambitious person, and especially a much more enterprising and purposeful author, than we have hitherto known. She was ambitious above all in the ever-increasing openness and the growing artistry with which she described woman's sexual and spiritual self-assertion. The aim of the present study is therefore to give a new portrayal of her life and career, and particularly to attempt a fresh approach to the most significant – and still largely neglected – aspects of her realism and her artistic achievement.

I might never have thought of undertaking this study but for Cyrille Arnavon's suggestion that I expand a paper which I had written for him in 1959 on Kate Chopin. My foremost debt of gratitude therefore goes to the critic who was the first to point to her real stature.

In 1962, Edmund Wilson urged me to write a book on the author and edit her work. His comments on my manuscript and his preface to the *Complete Works* are but two examples of the active support he ever since has given this project, and I am deeply grateful for the generous and truly inspiring interest he has taken in it.

I wish to express my sincere gratitude to Father Rankin, who patiently answered endless questions about Mrs. Chopin. We would know much less about her life but for his pioneer effort, and my own indebtedness to him is particularly evident in my first two chapters. (It should be noted that Rankin's complete set of notes for his sparingly annotated book was accidentally lost, and that a considerable part of his material is beyond checking.)

Unfortunately I can name only a few of the great number of persons who have helped me in so many ways during my years of research on Kate Chopin. Her many grandchildren were truly generous in their assistance, and my sincere gratitude goes to all of them when I mention only Mrs. Marjorie McCormick; Mr. Fred Chopin; Miss Gladys Breazeale, who furnished a wealth of information; and especially Mr. Robert C. Hattersley, who kindly looked in old trunks and came up with the important unknown diary.

I also wish to express my sincere thanks to Professor Katherine Bridges; Mrs. K. D. McCoy; Professor Max Putzel; Miss Margaret Ruckert; Mr. Herbert S. Stone, Jr.; Miss Elizabeth Tindall and her colleagues at the St. Louis Public Library; and the late Mrs. John S. Tritle, all of whom spared no effort to put me in contact with important material.

The ready cooperation of the Houghton and Widener Library staffs at Harvard University greatly aided me in my work. Since the day I began the study of the Kate Chopin papers in the Missouri Historical Society, its officials have facilitated my use of them in every possible way. I am greatly indebted to the Institution and its staff, and particularly to Mrs. Ernst A. Stadler, its Manuscripts Librarian, who in her expert assistance went far beyond any call of duty.

I am indebted to the Missouri Historical Society; Mr. Robert C. Hattersley; Miss Gladys Breazeale; Mr. Herbert S. Stone, Jr.; the Harvard College Library; Manuscript Division, the New York Public Library, Astor, Lenox and Tilden Foundations; and the West Virginia University Library for their kind permission to use the Kate Chopin material which they are holding, and to the University of Pennsylvania Press for their permission to quote from Rankin's biography.

A Fellowship from the American Council of Learned Societies enabled me to spend two fruitful years in the United States, and another from the Norwegian Research Council for Science and the Humanities made it possible for me to complete this book.

I record my gratitude to Professor Daniel Aaron and to Professor Kenneth S. Lynn, who both read the work in part and offered very perceptive comments and suggestions. Professor Arlin Turner directed me to important sources of information; gave invaluable advice in the field of textual criticism, and offered highly constructive suggestions when he read the manuscript at various stages of its composition. I am deeply indebted to him for his assistance, and also for his unfailing support of the Kate Chopin project in general. I am indebted also to Mr. Sam B. Armstrong, who suggested many stylistic improvements in the book.

Professor Sigmund Skard has followed and encouraged the undertaking from its earliest stages. The manuscript has benefited greatly from his suggestions, especially in the field of organization and focus.

Finally, and most particularly, I wish to thank my wife, fil. dr. Brita Lindberg-Seyersted, for her constant encouragement and her very perceptive advice.

I

St. Louis' Littlest Rebel

1. *Kate O'Flaherty: French and Irish*

"The first time I ever saw St. Louis I could have bought it for six million dollars, and it was the mistake of my life that I did not do it."[1] In this statement, Mark Twain reflects the spectacular quadrupling of St. Louis from the early 1850's to 1882, the year he went back to look again at life on the Mississippi. When Katherine O'Flaherty was born in the city on February 8, 1851, it still counted only 75,000 inhabitants, but, calling itself the "Gateway to the West," it was confidently looking forward to a rapid expansion. At the same time St. Louis was also very proud of its past, in which the forefathers of its still important French Creole aristocracy – the Creoles were pure-blooded descendants of French and Spanish settlers – had played such an illustrious role.

Kate O'Flaherty's roots in the French and Creole elite of St. Louis went back almost to the founding of the village in 1764. Her mother, Eliza Faris O'Flaherty, was the grand-daughter of Victoria Verdon Charleville, who was born in St. Louis in 1780. Mme. Charleville was the daughter of Victoria Richelet Verdon who owned a line of keelboats which operated between St. Louis and New Orleans.[2] These families seem to go back to French settlers who came to America around 1700.

We know from Father Daniel S. Rankin's *Kate Chopin and Her Creole Stories* that the young Kate listened spellbound to the tales which her great-grandmother Mme. Charleville told her about the enterprising men and women who had made the history of the Louisiana territory.[3] Full of Gallic joy and enthusiasm, this woman would return again and again to her endless stock of stories, in which fact and fiction were not always kept apart. She told Kate about La Salle, who took possession of the region for France. She could relate how Natchitoches (pronounced Nack-uh-tush), the oldest settlement of

French Louisiana, was founded in 1714 as an outpost against the Spanish in Mexico, and how Pierre Laclede founded St. Louis fifty years later.

Mme. Charleville could also tell how the Louisiana Purchase brought about a rapid growth of St. Louis. Having been settled largely by French colonists from New Orleans, it had a definitely, Southern and Gallic atmosphere. But the reports of the Lewis and Clark expedition soon resulted in an American influx. In a short while strategically located St. Louis was overrun by restless easterners who joined the westward movement, and for decades these settlers, traders, and adventurers gave the city a wild and rough frontier atmosphere. Shortly afterward they were joined by Irish immigrants, and the Germans followed a little later.

Thomas O'Flaherty, Katherine's father, was one of these Irish newcomers. Born in 1805 in County Galway, he was an ambitious and self-possessed boy. Not wanting to become a land agent like his forefathers, he emigrated, and shortly after his arrival in St. Louis in 1825, he started a boat store, a wholesale grocery, and a commission house.[4]

He had chosen a fortunate moment to become a merchant, for after the recent introduction of steamboats, traffic on the Mississippi was expanding rapidly. Business prospered, and Thomas O'Flaherty with it. His distinction and gracious manners and his easy command of French made him acceptable to the city's social elite, and in 1839 he married into a well-known Creole family. His wife died the next year, however, in giving birth to a son, George. In 1844, O'Flaherty married Eliza Faris, who was not yet sixteen. Early marriages were common among the Creoles, and in Eliza's family it had for generations been usual for the girls to marry at about the age of fifteen.

In the words of a contemporary, Eliza O'Flaherty was "a woman of great beauty, intelligence, and personal magnetism."[5] She loved society, and she made the spacious O'Flaherty home on Eighth Street, then a fashionable address, into a place of joy, vigor, and enthusiasm. While the Creoles could demonstrate an un-American formality and an aristocratic reticence, the Faris family showed no reserve toward their Irish relative. Mme. Charleville, for example, felt a deep affection for him, and when she became a widow in 1849 she moved in with the O'Flahertys.

Meanwhile the family grew. Thomas O'Flaherty, Jr., was born in 1848. (All we know about him is that he drowned at the age of twenty-five.) Kate's birth followed in 1851. Another daughter was born soon afterward, but she lived only a few years. Kate's half-brother George was a great favorite of hers, and she long treasured a letter he once wrote her. It was written in English, but we are told that Kate's "earliest acquaintance was with the French tongue rather than the English, French being the language spoken in her family in those days." (It should be added that though she had a very good command of French, all indications are that English was her entirely natural means of expression; in writing, she never used any other.) Another contemporary informant describes the language further as "the soft creole French and patois and the quaint darkey dialect" spoken by the many Negro servants in the O'Flaherty home.[6]

Kate O'Flaherty's spiritual heritage derived from both her parents. Her mother's poise, gentility, and "indescribable air of caste and good breeding" represented "the quiet, confident, self-possessed aristocracy" of a family "socially secure and eminent in lineage." This was reflected in the social prominence of the guests who came to the house, and in the large, attractive Southern house itself with its stately garden.

Mr. O'Flaherty's influence was also important. Kate inherited his calmness and self-reliance, his "keen mental alertness and discernment," and much of his energy.[7] His spirit of vigorous enterprise made itself felt in many fields, for example in the campaign to supply troops for the Mexican War; for this he was made an honorary Captain. He helped to bring the telegraph to Missouri. A devoted Catholic, he actively aided such organizations as the Catholic Institute of St. Louis and its library and newspaper. He continuously helped the city's less fortunate Irish, and through his efforts in this direction, he became a close friend of Archbishop Kenrick.

Kate Chopin's earliest recollections, her son Felix tells us, centered around her father, who was agreeable and understanding, but nevertheless a mystery to the four-year-old girl in that she did not know where he went every morning.

She tried but could not solve the problem by herself. She was always to be like that, a child who tried to solve questions and puzzles, and to ask the solutions only when her powers of discovery were of no avail. One day she asked her father where he went and why the carriage came home without him. He enjoyed the questioning. It indicated that she was aware of things; was interested in life about her.[8]

Against the protests of everyone except the great-grandmother, he took the elated girl with him the next day, and the mystery was solved. It was to the Cathedral he went every morning. She was disappointed, but she could never tell why. Perhaps part of the reason was that the church was emptier and Mass less exciting than on Sundays. On the other hand, she became highly excited when her father then showed her his store and the busy river front. Afterward she was always fascinated by the life along the levee, which she associated with her father and his importance.[9]

The enterprising Captain O'Flaherty was also one of the founders of the Pacific Railroad, which on November 1, 1855, opened the St. Louis-Jefferson City part of its road. With other local leaders, he was on the inaugural train. When it came to the Gasconade River, the bridge collapsed. O'Flaherty was one of the twenty-nine killed. To the cries of the injured were added the horrors of a violent thunderstorm during which lightning struck the wreck.[10] Kate, not yet five years old, probably was spared these gruesome details, but there was no way of shielding her from shock and grief and from the awesome impressions connected with this, her first acquaintance with the sudden loss of a loved one. At the funeral, she "wondered," as she later told her children. The service took place in the Cathedral she knew so well, and the Archbishop's address, which spoke of hope and peace after death, opened up for her new questions which she could not answer.[11]

2. *A Rebel Teenager*

The O'Flaherty family had suffered a heavy loss. What had been a gay, joyous home, in which the Captain's wit and humor had been much in evidence, now was a place of sorrow. There was no one to carry on his activities, and the household became more reclusive. Though piano-playing, for example, was resumed after a year's mourning, the atmosphere of subdued sadness never left the home, which was dominated by Kate's mother, grandmother, and great-grandmother, all of them highly religious widows.[12] On the basis of information from Kate Chopin's children, Rankin (p. 34) gives this description of the situation:

The sudden catastrophe turned Mrs. O'Flaherty's mind more and more to religion. An intimacy grew up between child and mother that had not existed before. The daughter had admired the father with affectionate devotion. The sadness of the mother drew the child to her. In the silence of deep distress in the mother's heart, and strange wonder in the child's, a sympathy awoke that never ceased and never grew less while the mother lived.

The grandmother accepted the situation "with quiet resignation to the will of God." When the great-grandmother also accepted the inevitable, it was, however, with a determination to be a guide to the child and to aid her "in understanding life and its vagaries."

Her theories of education were distinctly unique for the day. She would teach this girl to face life and its problems without a trace of consciousness, hesitation, or embarrassment. She insisted always on the child speaking French to her, while she supervised eagerly the daily music lesson. ... Stories told with fervor were the reward for lessons well learned. She continually stressed the nobility and generosity of the child's father. She taught her not to rely on appearances. For her proper direction in the path of virtue, she told the child accounts of the early days of St. Louis. One story that was repeated over and over, with sad and sordid explanations, was a vivid account that stirred Katherine O'Flaherty's interest in the intimacy of people's lives and minds and morals. (It was a favorite adage of the dear old soul that one may know a great deal about people without judging them. God did that.) ... That story narrated the supposed adulterous relations of Madame Chouteau with Laclede ....[13]

Rankin tells us that Mme. Charleville loved to fire Kate's mind with "enthralling stories of the characters and characteristics, often quite intimate, of the city's founders," and that her "stories of questionable nature" influenced the later writer of bold realism.[14] We do not know in what form the story of Pierre Laclede and Mme. Chouteau, the mother of his lieutenant, came down to young Kate; but Mme. Charleville undoubtedly said, as do most historians, that Madame left her brutal husband after the birth of this son and later lived with Laclede and bore his children without ever marrying him. She never took his name, and one commentator suggests that this was because "the shrewd woman wanted no trouble with the laws of church or state."[15] Another local story of the time was probably also frequent in Mme. Charleville's repertory, that of Mme. de Volsey, a prominent woman who carried on in such "open and shameless debauchery" that her husband at long last succeeded in obtaining a divorce, the first to be granted in the Catholic city.[16] Rankin comments on the effect on Kate of these stories:

The child with the questioning brown eyes and expressive face and inquisitive mind...listened with astonished attention, alert and eager.... It was the great-grandmother's influence that awoke a penetrating interest in character, particularly in independent, determined women. ... [Mme. Charleville,] grand yet composed in all her ways, ... had the greatest influence on the girl's mind and heart and life. She had determined to arouse the child's curiosity and not let it be unsatisfied. Under her care the girl grew wise and thoughtful. ... She learned to face all questions coolly and fearlessly – and grew self-contained, calmly possessed, and an enigma to her immediate elders. Neither vanity nor selfconsciousness was part of her nature.[17]

When not listening to the old lady, Kate O'Flaherty lived as did any other girl of her time and place. In September, 1860, she started her formal education as a day student at the St. Louis Academy of the Sacred Heart. There she met Katherine Garesché, a girl her own age, and they were constantly together. In what seems like a fragment of an autobiography, Kate Chopin writes of her: "It was at this time that I formed a friendship with Kitty Garesché; a friendship which lasted all through our childhood and youth and which, I will not say ended – but was interrupted by her entering the Sacred Heart Convent as a religious in 1870." And she continues: "We ... climbed together the highest cherry trees; wept in company over the 'Days of Bruce' and later exchanged our heart secrets."[18]

In 1930, Sister Garesché, too, recalled these youthful pleasures, which included "riding a pony that Kate owned, always in the care of a faithful negro servant, but principally, and certainly first in our affection, music and reading – veritable passions." She goes on: "Kate's musical talent was remarkable, she played the piano both by ear and note. Perhaps in those early days we loved reading still more."[19]

We have no information about Mme. Charleville's possible influence on Kate O'Flaherty's reading. We know, however, that at least a sound knowledge of the French classics was taken for granted in her circle. We also know something about the role literature played in the life of Mme. Marie Benoist, a contemporary and a relative, and very likely also a friend, of Mme. Charleville. Kate probably also knew her from her visits to Oakland, the Benoist family's estate near St. Louis. Mme. Benoist was described as being intimately familiar with not only all the famous French authors, but also the classical writings of antiquity, and her wide reading was reflected in her conversation which was "always interesting." [20] All the descriptions we have of these two women, both of whom grew up in Gallic St. Louis and who seem to have had a very full life, suggest that they combined the warmth of the Creole mother and the regal bearing of a French chatelaine with something of the resourcefulness of an American frontier woman and the open-mindedness found among the women of French literary salons.

The books Kate O'Flaherty read at this time were mostly British. She was an omnivorous reader from an early age and all through her life, and we know that she was introduced to Walter Scott when she was six and a year later to the works of James Hogg, the Scottish poet. [21] The long list of books she read with Kitty Garesché before 1863 included such works as *The Pilgrim's Progress, Blind Agnes,* Grimm's *Fairy Tales, Ivanhoe,* and writings by Gray and Dickens. [22] Kate may have wept over these mostly romantic books, but that she, at the same time, was not uncritical is suggested by her reactions to the poems that her schoolfriends wrote in her album in 1861. After some lines on the felicity of memory, she commented: "Very pretty, but where's the point?" After another poem which asserted that "it is the worst of pain,/To love, and not be loved again!" she wrote: "foolishness."

In this book she also inserted her "First Communion Picture." Sister Garesché recalled how they both had been confirmed by Archbishop Kenrick on May 1, 1861: "We had been prepared most carefully and fervently and I remember how we talked over together the secret emotions of that Day." The list of other things they did included, for example, riding in omnibuses, visiting the levee, going to museums, and hearing a talk on arctic explorations. The active girls also started learning Italian together in secret. At Kitty's home they played and listened to the father reading aloud, and sometimes Kate was permitted to spend the night there. When Sallie Britton, another schoolmate, extended a similar invitation, however, the request – as Kate Chopin later recalled – "was never granted, because Sallie was not a Catholic." [23]

These were exciting days in St. Louis. As a key center for trade going in all directions, the city was teeming with activity and growing at an accelerating pace. Certain traits of the old frontier had survived; Sister Garesché tells us that they could watch "the 'Indians come to town,' riding on horseback in procession, every month, from some nearby Reservation." [24] The past was also in evidence in the high-spirited, aristocratic, Southern atmosphere first brought in by the French Creoles from Louisiana and later reinforced by Americans coming from Virginia. These two groups of early settlers, who between them owned 2,000 slaves, were fighting a losing battle with the large groups who poured in from New England, Ireland, and Germany, bringing with them democratic and radical ideas. In the 1850's, cosmopolitan St. Louis was the scene of bitter fights among its national groups. The city also felt the pre-Civil War tensions. Earlier, Elijah P. Lovejoy, a St. Louis publisher, had been forced out of town and later killed in nearby Alton, Illinois, by an angry mob who resented his abolitionist campaign. Now, the city's Courthouse became the scene of the law case which gave St. Louis national attention and Dred Scott, the Negro slave, a fame nearly as great as that of Uncle Tom. Occasionally, slave auctions took place on the steps of the Courthouse. Sister Garesché later said: "I never went to slave sales, nor do I think Kate ever did, though we wanted to." [25]

We cannot guess with what feelings the girls would have gone to such an auction, but we do know that both their families took the Southern side during the Civil War. Many of their fellow St. Louisians did the same, and there were frequent incidents in the divided city, which all through the war was ruled with an iron Union hand. No one was allowed to leave the area without permission. However, this did not prevent George O'Flaherty from joining the Confederates.

Kate's love for her half-brother may have contributed to her strong Southern sympathies, which made her the "Littlest Rebel" of St. Louis. Years later, Kate Chopin recalled how she "tore down the union flag from the front porch when the Yanks tied it up there," and Sister Garesché tells us that Kate "came very near being arrested .... She was only saved by the kind, timely interference of a neighborly ... Unionist." (The Union officers never found the flag, which Kate kept for the rest of her life.) And she continues: "Another day we gathered a bouquet of flowers from Kate's beautiful garden – and we gave them to the Sentinel for the Southern prisoners in the nearby . . . Prison."[26] This was also the place to which George was sent after his capture in 1862. He was later exchanged, but on his way to his regiment, he died of typhoid fever, only a month after the death of Mme. Charleville.[27]

These new losses were crushing to the twelve-year-old girl. William Schuyler, a St. Louis writer who later became a friend of Kate Chopin, tells us that she "knew the faithful love of her negro 'mammy'," and also "saw the devotion of which the well-treated slaves were capable during the hard times of the war." However, neither this love and devotion, nor that of her grieving mother could help Kate, who apparently needed two or three years of semi-seclusion to get over these blows. She not only often stayed away from school during this period, but also kept to herself within the home. Turning to escapist literature – such as the novels of Scott – she tried to forget the world and her grief. Her favorite resort was the attic, where she would "pore over the stacks of poetry and fiction which were stored there – the shelves of the library being reserved for solid and pretentious cyclopedias of Roman Catholic religious works." In time she bounced back into life, however, and from 1866 to her graduation two years later she studied seriously. She was also active in school activities and she became noted for "her gifts as a teller of marvellous stories."[28]

There was a French air about the day school of the Sacred Heart. One sensed always a fragrance there, a former student has told us, "which reminded one of Paris – a faint mixture of spiced food and incense."[29] France was reflected also in the school's educational system, as it had been drawn up by the French founder of the order. There was nothing unusual in the fact that the Academy concentrated on religion, wanting to give the young ladies a secure "anchorage in faith" and preparing them for their future roles as "Christian home-makers, Catholic wives and mothers." It was also quite normal for such an institution to train the students in domestic skills ranging from needlework to household economy, and in social accomplishments such as languages, music, and deportment. What gave the Academy its particular French touch was its emphasis on mental discipline and intellectual vigor. The founder wanted the girls to be introduced to current events and scientific discoveries so that they could "take part intelligently in conversation," and she also emphasized the study of literature as a means of developing their judgment and reasoning power.[30]

It is difficult to estimate how fully this ideal was achieved at Kate's school. We do know, however, that Mother O'Meara, her instructor in English, was very intelligent and – in Sister Garesché's words – "most gifted for composition in both verse and prose."[31] Apparently encouraged by Mother O'Meara, Kate now wrote both poems and essays, and some of these she copied in her commonplace book, which is extant. Covering the years 1867 to 1870, this volume also includes bits of diary and excerpts, with comments, from her reading. Here, she often echoes interests and attitudes that were fairly common among her schoolmates. She writes on the careers of the Rothschilds and expresses her passion to travel in Germany, "that cradle and repository of genius." At the same time she fears that her dreams might "prove but 'the baseless fabric of a vision'." She regrets that Macaulay regards the Catholic Church as "a mere work of human policy," whereas "we (Catholics) see every evidence of a divine institution" in it. Yet, in many other instances, we find traits and views which seem to be decidedly her own.

For example, in "Memories," a poem on the commonplace theme of an old man reminiscing about the lost ones, and in "The Early Dead," a composition dedicated to the memory of one of her school friends, we find a note of pain and despair stronger even than that found in the romantic authors she had devoured. The words – such as *wail, anguish, sorrow* – are those of her reading, but the insistence with which she returns to them is definitely her own and in line with the grief she had recently experienced.

Kate's personal touch is evident also when in the pious essay on "The Early Dead" we find her first speaking of the "womanly happiness" her late friend had looked forward to, but then repeatedly referring to the sin and corruption she had been spared, this untainted "flower awaiting to be plucked"; when we find her occupied with the "loveliness and terror" of the "wreathing and recoiling snakes" on a Medusa head; and when in a composition on "Christian Art" we find her first dutifully asserting that Greek art must be inferior to that of Christianity because it is pagan and earthly, but then going on to say that music can powerfully awaken man's "slumbering passions." Here again the words are borrowed, but the emphasis is her own and characteristic of the later writer.

Two subjects – literature and education – seem to have held the girl's particular attention at this time, and her quotations from books on these matters link the great-granddaughter of Mme. Charleville with Kate Chopin, the author. When the commonplace book opens with a reminder from Bulwer's *My Novel* that "the indulgence of poetic taste and reverie does great and lasting injury" as it serves to "give false ideas of life," it might have been the old woman speaking. Her ideas are also reflected in a long quotation on Germany from a book written by an English lady. Here, German women are described as being "more *natural* than we are," and it is contended that "the moral education of an English girl is for the most part negative" as she is told not to do this, not to think that, and not to ask "Why not?" because it is unladylike to argue. And the writer goes on: "The idea that certain passions, powers, tempers, feelings ... are to be put down by the fiat of a governess ... is monstrous." In Germany, meanwhile, "the affections, the impulses ... are not so habitually crushed or disguised; consequently the women appear to be more natural, and to have more individual character."

Kate also quotes the author's statement that she is delighted to find that it is perfectly acceptable for a lady to be engrossed by the cares of housekeeping, which the English – with their "false conventional refinement" – consider vulgar: "The description of Goethe's Charlotte cutting bread and butter has been an eternal subject of laughter among the English, ... and no princess can be suffered to ... be in love except in white satin."

3. *An Enigmatic Belle*

After Kate O'Flaherty was graduated from the Academy in June, 1868, she must often have worn white satin herself. She plunged into fashionable life, and for two years she was, it has been said, "one of the acknowledged belles of St. Louis, a favorite not only for her beauty, but also for her amiability of character and her cleverness." In the words of Alexander DeMenil, a St. Louis editor who had known Kate from childhood, "there was not a brighter, more gracious, and handsomer young woman" in the city.[32] Sister Garesché also remembered her from this time:

I do not think Kate resembled her mother so much as her father. Now-a-days she would be described as an "Irish Beauty." She was not tall. Her very abundant dark hair drooped in a wave, lower on one side than on the other, which gave her a very arch, sprightly expression. Her eyes were brown, and looked right at you. She had a droll gift of mimicry. Though she was the object of great admiration, she accepted it in a matter-of-fact way and did not seem a bit vain. She had a remarkable self-possession, a certain poise of manner, though very sweet and simple. Her laugh was quiet; her voice gentle and low. It seems to me, that in her, intellect predominated and kept the passions cool.[33]

Whatever truth there may have been in this last statement about the seventeen-year-old Kate, it seems that she pursued her main interests – music, reading, and writing – with something quite close to passion. As for music, she played the piano well, and she loved to go to concerts. "Her musical memory had become remarkable," Sister Garesché observes. "She would go to the opera of one evening; then the next morning be able to reproduce by ear the parts she liked best."[34]

St. Louis had two opera companies and a Philharmonic Society, and many famous artists visited the city. In December, 1868, Kate listened to Ole Bull with great enthusiasm. In the commonplace book she first commends him for "displaying nothing of that exaggerated style most usually seen in fine violinists," and then goes on: "To describe the effect his music had upon me would be impossible. It seemed the very perfection of the art, and while listening to him, I for the first time longed to be blind that I might drink it all in undisturbed and undistracted by surrounding objects."

On the next page we find this entry: "New Year's Eve, Dec. 31st, 1868. Rain! Rain! Rain! – I am going to receive calls tomorrow – my first winter I expect a great many visits." In St. Louis at this time the number of those who called on a popular belle on New Year's Day could go into the hundreds. Kate O'Flaherty, however, was not interested in being feted: "What a nuisance all this is – I wish it were over. I write in my book today, the first time for months; parties, operas, concerts, skating and amusement ad infinitum have so taken up my time that my dear reading and writing that I love so well have suffered much neglect."

All we have from Kate's hands dating from this period is the commonplace book and a fable entitled "Emancipation," and we have no way of knowing whether what she calls her "writing" stands for something outside of this. We know a good deal about her reading, however. One informant tells us that she felt she had acquired most of her education not at school, but from her own reading,[35] and we know that she read not only the classics she found at home, but also new books as they came out. Whenever possible, she preferred to read French and German authors in the original, partly because she wanted to keep up her languages (she even studied at the German Reading Club), and partly, she said, "because French and German notions and ideas are so different from the English – that they lose all their naive zest by being translated into that [most] practical of tongues." She also kept up on magazines: "What a bore it is to begin a story – become interested in it and have to wait a week – a full round week before you can resume it," she noted in her book. "Thus have I devoured in Appleton's Journal (a new paper, by the way) 'The Man Who Laughs' by V. Hugo, devoured it to the very last word of the last number and must wait till next Saturday to satisfy in a small degree my ravenous appetite."

Her impressive reading list from this time includes such authors as Dante, Cervantes, Corneille, Racine, Molière, Mme. de Staël, Chateaubriand, Goethe, Coleridge, Jane Austen, Charlotte Brontë, and Longfellow. Her interest in the lives and the vocation of writers is seen in her reading many books on authors and such a work as Mme. de Staël's *Influence of Literature on Society*. One entry in her book in connection with lengthy quotations from Lamartine's *Graziella* suggests not only a general romantic bent, but also an interest in the question of whether the suffering an author causes others is redeemed by the literary works it engenders. First she gives the poet's description of how the girl dances "dans la frénésie ... de ce délire en action"; how she loves Lamartine even if he does not love her, and how he starts loving her after her death. Then Kate comments:

'Poor Graziella'? No rich Graziella! Happy Graziella! ... To have won not only the tears – the remembrance of Lamartine, but an offering of his rich and rare talents at the shrine of her memory. – The story is doubly enhanced when we think that it is really an episode, and a cherished one in the life of the gifted writer. What tears of grief, of indignation does one not shed over its pages – tears all ending in forgiveness. For at the end we feel an assurance that Graziella has conquered – since her heart's idol – years after her death – weeps at her remembrance.

Kate O'Flaherty seems also to have been greatly interested in Mme. de Staël's two novels *Delphine* and *Corinne,* the one dealing with a

woman who finds her passion for her lover more important than what
the world says of it, and the other with an English poetess, who settles
in Italy in order to live and work unhampered by the narrow English
moral laws. In view of the fact that these books have some bearing on
the works of the later Kate Chopin, it is worth while to quote, as Kate
did in her commonplace book, an essay on Byron's conversations with
the French novelist.[36]

Byron observed, that he once told Madame de Staël that he considered
her *Delphine* and *Corinne* as very dangerous productions to be put in
the hands of young women. [He went on:] "She endeavored to prove
to me, that, *au contraire,* the tendencies of both her novels were super-
eminently moral ... . [I then said] that all the moral world thought, that
her representing all the virtuous characters in *Corinne* as being dull,
commonplace, and tedious, was a most insidious blow aimed at virtue. ...
I continued saying, how dangerous it was to inculcate the belief that
genius, talent, acquirements, and accomplishments, such as Corinne was
represented to possess, could not preserve a woman from becoming a
victim to an unrequited passion, and that reason, ... and female pride
were unavailing.

"I told her that *Corinne* would be considered, if not cited, as an excuse for violent *passions* ... . She told me that I, above *all people,* was
the last person that ought to talk of morals, as nobody had done more
to deteriorate them. I looked innocent, and added, I was willing to plead
guilty of having sometimes represented vice under alluring forms, but
so it was generally in the world, therefore it was necessary to paint it so;
but that I never represented virtue under the sombre and disgusting
shapes of dulness, severity, and *ennui,* and that I always took care to
represent the votaries of vice as unhappy themselves, and entailing unhappiness on those that loved them, so that *my moral* was unexception-
able."

As Kate's first season wore on, her personality asserted itself more
and more and in a way which increasingly made her an enigma to
those around her. In many respects she still seemed like a conventional
society belle; her entertainments were those of many another romantic
young girl (she speaks, for example, of a "visit to the churches by
moonlight"); she had the perfect form and poise that went with
her self-possession, and she showed – particularly with those she
trusted – the abandon and gaiety that was part of her Irish heritage.
She seems, furthermore, to have agreed with a statement she quotes

that "Society is a sphere that demands all our energies and deserves all that it demands," and that for example the man who deserts it for the challenge of a monastery is deceived because there "the conflict is less, the reward nothing."

At the same time, however, she apparently identified herself with a picture of an independent woman which she quoted from Byron: ". . . quietly she grew,/And kept her heart serene within its zone./. . . Her spirit seemed as seated on a throne/Apart from the surrounding world, and strong/In its own strength . . . ." Along with her amiability and vivacity she had a certain reserve which gave her the privacy she strongly craved. Everyone found it enigmatic that she would never speak about herself, apparently not even to her mother, and a diary entry illustrates this reticence:

A friend who knows me as well as anyone is capable of knowing me – a gentleman, of course – told me that I had a way in conversation of discovering a person's characteristics – opinions – and private feelings – while they knew no more about me at the end than they knew at the beginning of the conversation. Is this laudable? Bah! I'll not reason it, for whatever my conclusion I'll be sure to follow my inclination.

What a dear good confidant my book is. If it does not clear my doubts, at least it does not contradict and oppose my opinions. You are the only one, my book, with whom I take the liberty of talking about myself. I must tell you a discovery I have made – the art of making oneself agreeable in conversation. Strange as it may appear it is not necessary to possess the faculty of speech; a dumb person, provided he be not deaf, can practice it as well as the most voluble. All required of you is to have control over the muscles of your face – to look pleased and chagrined, surprised, indignant, and under every circumstance – interested and entertained. Lead your antagonist to talk about himself – he will not enter reluctantly upon the subject, I assure you – and twenty to one – he will report you as one of the most entertaining and intelligent persons, although the whole extent of *your* conversation was but an occasional "What did *you* say" – "What did *you* do" – "What did *you* think."

While she thus used to draw people out, she even more strongly wanted to draw everything she could from the books she read. " 'Tis thought and digestion which make books serviceable, and gives health and vigor to the mind," as she quoted from (Thomas?) Fuller. When Kate was uninterested in parties – a friend later reminded her, for

example, of the night she "went to Mrs. Maffitt's party ... and slipped down the stone steps trying to get away" [37] – it was because she
wanted to be alone with her thoughts, and if occasionally she wished
to discuss the subjects which occupied her, she found her surroundings
unreceptive to her sometimes unorthodox opinions. "Very long ago I
could do nothing with them; nobody wanted them," as she later observed with a mixture of sadness and self-irony. [38] A diary outburst of
March 25, 1869, shows her dilemma:

Holy Thursday – and no sun – no warmth – no patch of blue sky, nothing to make one's heart feel glad .... In three more days Lent will be
over – and then commence again with renewed vigor – parties, theatres,
and general spreeing. I feel as though I should like to run away and hide
myself; but there is no escaping. I am invited to a ball and I go. – I
dance with people I despise; amuse myself with men whose only talent lies
in their feet; gain the disapprobation of people I honor and respect; return home at day break with my brain in a state which was never intended for it; and arise in the middle of the next day feeling infinitely
more, in spirit and flesh like a Lilliputian, than a woman with body and
soul. I am diametrically opposed to parties and balls; and yet when I
broach the subject – they either laugh at me – imagining that I wish to
perpetrate a joke; or look very serious; shake their heads and tell me
not to encourage such silly notions.

I am a creature who loves amusements; I love brightness and gaiety
and life and sunshine. But is it a rational amusement, I ask myself, to
destroy one's health, and turn night into day? I look about me, though,
and see persons *so* much better than myself, and *so* much more pious
engaging in the self same pleasures, – however I fancy it cannot have
the same effect upon them as it does upon me. –

Heigh ho! I wish this were the *only* subject I have doubts upon. One
does become so tired – reasoning, reasoning, reasoning from morning till
night and coming to no conclusions – it is to say the least slightly unsatisfactory.

Kate goes on to say that she refuses to "resume the thread of Sister
Mary Catherine Macaulay's life – which in a devout mood the other
day" she had begun – because together with the bad weather it
"would by evening throw [her] into such a fit of blue moralizing and
contempt of the species as to render [her] unbearable to the rather
large household for weeks to come – a situation not 'devoutly to be
wished'." She seemed fascinated by these last words on death taken

from Hamlet's famous soliloquy, and this quotation was one of many on this subject with which she filled the pages of her book. Death seems to have occupied her even more than might have been expected of an eighteen-year-old of the Romantic era, and we suspect that silent grief for her loved ones may have been one reason for it, and that the weight of her frustrated reasoning – which, likewise, she shared with no one – may have been another.

The problem of independence, so typical of adolescence, was one which she debated intensely with herself at this time. She lived in a milieu which was devoutly Catholic and expected her to be the same. In her social circle and in her home full of women, it was largely taken for granted that she should submit to authority and that she should become a devoted wife and mother in the traditional manner.

One side of Kate's strong personality rebelled at this: She refused to become depressed through reading religious books; she decided to "follow her inclination," and she was interested in the bluestockings whom she defined in her book as "ladies who cultivated learned conversation." At the same time, another side of her felt that she should listen to her elders, and this other Kate's view on the role of woman is suggested by the continuation of the dictionary definition she quoted: " 'Blue Stockings' soon became a title for pedantic or ridiculous literary ladies," and particularly by what she copied from a novel called *The Woman's Kingdom*:[39]

If a house with fair possibilities for home comfort is thoroughly comfortless, ... [if] the gentlemen of the family are prone to be "out of evenings" – who is to blame? Almost invariably, the women of the family. The men make or mar its outside fortunes; but its internal comfort lies in the women's hands alone. And until women feel this – recognize at once their power and their duties – *it is idle for them to chatter about their rights.* [Kate underlined these ten words, and the last one twice.]

Then on May 8, 1869, she wrote a report in her book on a three-week trip to New Orleans which shows that she had gained a new perspective on the question of what a woman could do with her life. She opens with a few pointed observations on her traveling companions – the trip was "not remarkably gay for me when one reflects that Mother is a few years older than myself ... Mrs. Sloan a walking, breathing nonentity – Mamie a jovial giggler" – and then continues:

N. Orleans I liked immensely; it is so clean – so white and green. ... One evening I passed in N. O. which I shall never forget – it was so delightful and so novel. Mamie and myself were invited to dine and spend the evening with a Mrs. Bader – a German lady. She, her husband and two brothers in law lived in a dear little house near Esplanade St. ... One of the brothers was a gay, stylish and very interesting fellow. ... [I] talked French and German – listened enchanted to Mrs. Bader's exquisite singing and for two or three hours was as gay and happy as I ever have been in my life. Mrs. Bader ... was the famous Miss Ferringer – Singer and Schauspielerin, who in order to support indigent parents went upon the stage, thereby not only retaining respect, but gaining it from every quarter. Her talents and womanly attractions won her a kind and loving husband – Mr. Bader – one of the first merchants of New Orleans and a man worth $ 600,000.

No wonder that Kate was exhilarated. She had just learned to smoke in Louisiana, which was still a rather daring indulgence for a lady,[40] and she had met a daring and successful woman artist (even if New Orleans was a theater town, it was exceptional for an actress to be accepted in society). On her return to St. Louis, she read Bjørnson's *The Fisher Maiden,* which deals with a woman artist's development and her emancipation from her narrow-minded and conventional milieu. It was at this time, apparently, that Kate wrote "Emancipation," which she subtitled "A Life Fable":

There was once an animal born into this world, and opening his eyes upon Life, he saw above and about him confining walls, and before him were bars of iron through which came air and light from without; this animal was born in a cage.

Here he grew, and throve in strength and beauty under care of an invisible protecting hand. Hungering, food was ever at hand. When he thirsted water was brought, and when he felt the need of rest, there was provided a bed of straw upon which to lie: and here he found it good, licking his handsome flanks, to bask in the sun beam that he thought existed but to lighten his home.

Awakening one day from his slothful rest, lo! the door of his cage stood open: accident had opened it. In the corner he crouched, wondering and fearingly. Then slowly did he approach the door, dreading the unaccustomed, and would have closed it, but for such a task his limbs were purposeless. So out [of] the opening he thrust his head, to see the canopy of the sky grow broader, and the world waxing wider.

Back to his corner but not to rest, for the spell of the Unknown was over him, and again and again he goes to the open door, seeing each time more Light.

Then one time standing in the flood of it; a deep in-drawn breath – a bracing of strong limbs, and with a bound he was gone.

On he rushes, in his mad flight, heedless that he is wounding and tearing his sleek sides – seeing, smelling, touching of all things; even stopping to put his lips to the noxious pool, thinking it may be sweet.

Hungering there is no food but such as he must seek and ofttimes fight for; and his limbs are weighted before he reaches the water that is good to his thirsting throat.

So does he live, seeking, finding, joying and suffering. The door which accident had opened is open still, but the cage remains forever empty!

When Kate O'Flaherty met the twenty-five-year-old Oscar Chopin at about the time she wrote this fable, she seemed ready to leave her childhood cage with its "slothful rest" and its many protective female hands and to brace her strong limbs and take the plunge into the unknown. Oscar had left his native Louisiana to work in a St. Louis bank, and he met Kate at the estate of the Benoist family through whom they were distantly related. According to one of her sons, Kate Chopin always treasured the memory of the time at Oakland when "love came to her heart." [41] On May 24, 1870, Kate recorded her feelings in her book, in a hand much larger and more forceful than that of her last entry. What she writes would suggest that she felt ready to take the leap into marriage:

Exactly one year has elapsed since my book and I held intercourse, and what changes have occurred! not so much outwardly as within. ...

All that has transpired between then and now vanishes before this one consideration – in two weeks I am going to be married; married to the right man. It does not seem strange as I thought it would – I feel perfectly calm, perfectly collected. And how surprised every one was for I had kept it so secret!

She did not touch her book again until June 8 when she wrote: "To-morrow I will be married. It seems to me so strange that I am not excited – I feel as quiet and calm as if I had one or two years of maiden meditation still before me. I am contented – a" – here she broke off abruptly. The next entry is a forty-page honeymoon diary which opens with these lines:

June 9th. My wedding day! How simple it is to say and how hard to realize that I am married, no longer a young lady with nothing to think of but myself and nothing to do. We went to holy communion this morning, my mother with us, and it gave me a double happiness to see so many of my friends at mass for I knew they prayed for me on this happiest day of my life. The whole day seems now like a dream to me; how I awoke early in the morning before the household was stirring and looked out of the window to see whether the sun would shine or not; how I went to mass and could not read the prayers in my book, afterwards how I dressed for my marriage – went to church and found myself married before I could think what I was doing. What kissing of old and young! I never expected to receive so many embraces during the remainder of my life. Oscar has since confessed that he did not know it was customary to kiss and that he conferred that favor on only a very few – I will have to make a most sacred apology for him when I get home. It was very painful to leave my mother and all at home; and it was only at [the] starting [of the train] that I discovered how much I would miss them and how much I would be missed.

II

A Louisiana Chatelaine

1. *Honeymoon in Europe*

Going east, the couple spent a day in Philadelphia. "What a gloomy, puritanical looking city!" Kate Chopin exclaims in her diary; "the people all look like Quakers." Nothing could prevent her from enjoying the "*lovely* night" with the moon over the Schuylkill River, however: "I thought of how the moonlight looked at Oakland. The moon ... filled us with happiness and love." If she here sounds like the conventional, romantic young bride, the report the next day of her encounter on the train to New York with one of the famous Claflin sisters reminds us that one side of her was attracted by unorthodox ideas about what a young wife could do with her life:

... we had the honor and pleasure of making the acquaintance of Miss Clafflin [sic], the notorious "female broker" of New York – a fussy, pretty, talkative little woman, who discussed business extensively with Oscar, and entreated me not to fall into the useless degrading life of most married ladies – but to elevate my mind and turn my attention to politics, commerce, questions of state, etc., etc. I assured her I would do so – which assurance satisfied her quite.

The Claflin sisters had done much with their lives, both before and after they had become Mrs. Victoria Woodhull and Mrs. Tennessee Bartels. They had traveled widely, telling fortunes and conducting spiritualistic seances, before Commodore Vanderbilt in 1869 launched them on a career as Wall Street stock brokers. It was apparently Victoria that Kate Chopin met, a woman who has been described as the "most spectacular figure" of the Gilded Age. Domesticity bored her; instead, her ambition was to fight for woman suffrage and to be nominated a candidate for the presidency of the United States (which she later was). She had just begun publication of a newspaper in which she urged women to become independent; soon she was also to advocate socialism, birth control, and free love.[1]

If Mrs. Woodhull specified the aspects of a married lady's life that she objected to, Kate Chopin regrettably does not report them; nor does she elaborate on her own views. Covering only the three-month trip through Germany, Switzerland, and France, the diary does not describe her later life as a New Orleans housewife, and when she writes in Heidelberg that she "staggered at the amount of unpacking and washing to be given out; which interesting occupation engaged my time till 5 in the afternoon," it is, of course, no proof of a possible distaste for woman's traditional role.

But the diary does show Kate Chopin doing a number of things that were more or less foreign to women of her time. She goes with her husband to hear "the 'Bulls and Bears' of Wall St. bellowing and grunting in the Stock and Gold Boards – proceedings which interested [her] very much." When Oscar visits "some Halle to witness these Germans' interpretation of a galop and waltz, etc.," she says: "Dear me! I feel like smoking a cigarette – think I will satisfy my desire ...," and when one afternoon he takes a nap, she goes for a walk alone: "How very far I *did* go. ... I wonder what people thought about me – a young woman strolling about alone. I even took a glass of beer at a friendly little beer garden quite on the edge of the lake." One reason why she is always attracted by lakes is her ambition to learn to row: "I find myself handling the oars quite like an expert," she exclaims in triumph one day. When the rain forces the couple to seek shelter in a peasant hut, she welcomes it because the place and the people formed "quite an interesting study" to her, and her diary here looks much like a writer's notebook.

When Kate Chopin remarks in Cologne: "What a hot, scorching day it has been, and what wild, unheard of things we do in travelling that at home we would shudder to think of," we have no way of knowing what she refers to. Certainly, with the exceptions above, the wedding-trip seems to have been conventional enough. The couple attends theater, opera, and symphony performances; they go to see Beethoven's birthplace and that of Goethe; look at art and architecture; worship in famous Catholic and Protestant cathedrals, and take in the sights on the Rhine which Kate Chopin had so much looked forward to. Seeing Rollensecke, the castle where Roland supposedly sat out his years watching the convent into which his beloved had retreated upon hearing a false report of his death, she is excited and has "no doubt" that the legend is true, and looking at the Heidelberg she had read about in Longfellow, she exclaims: "... for once in my life [I] have not been disappointed by the real versus the ideal." She raves about the German Alps, and when for the first time she sees real mountains, all her idealism is brought into play: "I should fancy such scenery – such a beautiful side of nature, would influence these people only for good deeds."

The Franco-Prussian war, which had then just been declared, and the sight of Moltke's "iron countenance" (she met him on the stairway in her hotel), do, however, somewhat qualify her conception of German goodness. As the Prussians advance, she becomes more and more pro-French, praising the "thrift and intelligence" and the "endurance and pride" which will enable France to rise again; and when the Republic is proclaimed on September 4, just as she is visiting Paris, she says: "If now they will form their batallions [sic] against the Prussian & cease their cry of 'A bas l'Empereur'!" She is apparently no republican: Seeing the "rude populace" tearing down the Imperial eagles while "shouting the Marseilles [sic] with an abandon and recklessness purely french [sic]," she comments: "It cannot but make one sad."

The war made the couple cut short their stay in France, and they hurried back to St. Louis, where Kate Chopin – in the final words of the commonplace book – "once again ... embraced those dear ones left behind."

2. Oscar Chopin, A Creole from Natchitoches

Kate Chopin had married into a French-Creole family from northwestern Louisiana. When she moved with her husband to New Orleans, she first met Oscar's father, Dr. Victor Chopin. (He was no relation to Frédéric Chopin.) Why the Doctor should have left his native France is not clear as he disapproved of everything not French. When he settled in America it was in Natchitoches Parish (the Louisiana term for county), where the pronounced Gallic atmosphere pleased him and where he married Julia Benoist of Cloutierville, on the Red River, a wealthy woman of distinguished French lineage.[2] Soon they left this little town and moved a few miles down the river to the so-called McAlpin plantation, which they had bought with its

4,367 acres and 94 slaves.³ The Robert McAlpin who had owned the property until his death in 1852 deserves a footnote in American literary history, as legend has it that he had been the model for Simon Legree of *Uncle Tom's Cabin,* a tradition which Kate Chopin was to touch upon in her later first novel, *At Fault.*⁴

At about the time the Doctor moved in, the erratic Red River abandoned its old channel between Grand Ecore, just above Nat-chitoches, the main city of the parish, and Colfax, thirty miles to the southeast and a little below what was soon to be known as the "Cho-pin plantation." The new Red River, which carried most of the water and all the traffic, ran some five miles to the east of its former course. This old stretch was renamed Cane River.

A rich, agricultural country, Natchitoches Parish counted 14,000 inhabitants, more than half of whom were slaves. The best Cane River lands had been given to French settlers early in the eighteenth century. Further lands were claimed by a number of Acadians, or Cajuns, French pioneers who in 1755 had chosen to leave Acadia (Nova Scotia) rather than swear allegiance to the British. When the Anglo-Saxons came from 1820 onwards, there were left only the poorer, wooded hill-lands which rise gently to the west. While the number of Redbones (part Indian, part white) declined, that of "free-mulattoes" – so called because they had never been in slavery – increased. Most of them gathered in a colony on "L'Isle des Mulâtres" (today Isle Brevelle), an area on the western bank of Cane River, where some of them owned considerable land and also slaves.⁵

On the eastern bank of Cane River, then as now called "La Côte Joyeuse," there were a number of large plantations, and ante-bellum life among the planters appears here to have been one of constant social activity. The Creoles were gay and easygoing, and on the Joyous Coast they availed themselves of every excuse to give a party.⁶ The Chopins could easily have entertained in the style of their neighbors and become part of the set, but the Doctor was stingy and wanted no such frivolities. He was so mean and dictatorial to his wife that she left him for some years in the 1850's, and he very likely served as model for the heroine's father in *The Awakening* – Kate Chopin's later major work of fiction – who "coerced his own wife into her grave."⁷

The Doctor seems to have been cruel also to his slaves. They con-tinually tried to escape, and neither his overseers nor his son wanted to work for him. "When Oscar was just a boy, the Doctor tried to make him overseer. To facilitate matters all his slaves were chained in a row to work in one field at a time. From sunrise to sunset the boy and the slaves toiled in the field together. Oscar, generous-hearted like his mother, did not force them to work." Soon he ran away to live with relatives.[8]

When the Civil War began, the Doctor took his whole family to France. It is still reported in Natchitoches that the people there, many of whom had lost their all, resented the fact that he came back a richer man after the war.[9] This may have been a reason for Oscar to leave for St. Louis. At the time his mother died early in 1870, he had just become engaged to Katherine O'Flaherty.

3. New Orleans, 1870–1879

When Oscar Chopin and his wife came to New Orleans in October, 1870, the Doctor was at first cool toward his daugther-in-law; he disliked her being half-Irish and he resented his son's decision to take her to live on the American side of the city. But, as Rankin says (p. 84):

His attitude changed after the first visit of Oscar with Kate. The Doctor was unable to make sarcastic remarks to his son's vivacious young wife. Her brown eyes looked too calmly at him; her clear fluency of French speech, her perfect accent astounded him. Her fair young loveliness won his admiration. [Since Kate was] always at ease, her quick change from vivacity to quizzical seriousness baffled him. He detested music. She made him listen to her as she played the piano and soothed his irritability with French melodies heard in his youth and now almost forgotten.

The Doctor died before the year was out. Wallace Offdean, a character in one of Kate Chopin's later stories, is said to be a portrait of the Oscar who had just lost his father:[10]

With his early youth he had had certain shadowy intentions of shaping his life on intellectual lines. That is, he wanted ... above all [to] keep clear of the maelstroms of sordid work and senseless pleasure in which the average American business man may be said alternately to exist, and which reduce him, naturally, to a rather ragged condition of soul.

Offdean had done, in a temperate way, the usual things which young men do who happen to belong to good society, and are possessed of moderate means and healthy instincts. He had gone to college, had traveled a little at home and abroad, had frequented society and the clubs, and had worked in his uncle's commission-house ... .

But he felt all through that he was simply in a preliminary stage of being, one that would develop later into something tangible and intelligent, as he liked to tell himself. With his patrimony of twenty-five thousand dollars came what he felt to be the turning-point in his life, – the time when it behooved him to choose a course, and to get himself into proper trim to follow it manfully and consistently.[11]

What Oscar Chopin chose at this turning-point was to enter the New Orleans world of business as a cotton factor. In an environment that was prejudiced against trade, the cotton factor, coming from a good family and adhering to strict business ethics, was looked upon as a patrician in the world of commerce. As an agent, he sold the planter's cotton; as a banker, he handled his money; and as a merchant, he supplied him with all that was needed on the plantation. Cotton factorage could be risky, but also profitable, and Oscar prospered.

When Kate Chopin later, in *The Awakening,* made the heroine's husband a New Orleans Creole business man, we might perhaps expect him to reflect the personality of Oscar. But Léonce Pontellier has little contact with Edna, his wife, and regards her as a piece of property, whereas Oscar understood Kate and respected her individuality. Their conjugal understanding is said to be represented by another couple in the book: "The Ratignolles understood each other perfectly. If ever the fusion of two human beings into one has been accomplished on this sphere it was surely in their union."[12]

All statements made about the Chopins tend to confirm this. One informant tells us that "Kate was very much in love with her Oscar," and another that she was devoted to him and thought him perfect. This may have been because her husband realized that Kate was unique and allowed her to follow her inclinations, for example in dressing unconventionally, exploring the city on her own, and shunning, as far as possible, the formal claims of society. Kate Chopin loved music and dancing; she could both dress and act like a queen when necessary, and she became a favorite in the social life she was inevitably drawn into, but she and her husband always preferred each other to other company.[13]

Oscar was genial, gay, and a good talker, and so was Kate. Her closest friends also knew her as an excellent storyteller, and at times she demonstrated her gifts as a mimic, perfectly simulating the actions, manners, and particularly the voices of those who aroused what has been called her "insatiable curiosity." To the delight of Oscar, she would also mimic some of his Creole relatives; indignant about the latitude he allowed her, these relatives rebuked him for forgetting his "duty," which, presumably, was to make her conform to their rather strict rules for the behavior of ladies. Entrenched in New Orleans' Vieux Carré among the swelling number of Americans, the Creoles were full of prejudice against the newcomers. Yet this did not embarrass Kate Chopin, who simply laughed it off with her husband.[14] But while she had a strong will of her own, she was also gentle and considerate. "She enjoyed smoking cigarettes," one informant tells us, "but if friends who did not approve of smoking came to visit her, she would never offend them."[15]

Rankin declares that Kate Chopin was "completely happy." He maintains, however, that she continued her frustrated reasoning and that the shifting moods of Edna Pontellier of *The Awakening* are those of the author: "There were days when she was very happy without knowing why. She was happy to be alive and breathing...." And also: "There were days when she was unhappy, she did not know why, – when life appeared to her like a grotesque pandemonium ...."[16]

As before, these negative moods made Kate Chopin an enigma to those around her. They were rare, however, and the exaltation shown in her bearing indicated that she was happy with her "attractive and glamorous existence, designed to the tastes of her own choice." One of the few things to cloud her gay insouciance was the duty of a weekly reception day. She seems at times to have resented this obligation, and her husband could not have stopped her had she, like Edna, decided to escape from it. That she did not go to this length was probably due to her knowing that Oscar, who had not forgotten his mother's sufferings, would have let her have her way.[17]

The young wife has been summed up in these words: "She was really just a girl completely happy with her home, her husband, and in the eager expectation of ... her first child." The many servants made the daily routine an easy one, and she enjoyed a personal freedom that was new to her, since for the first time she found herself independent of the O'Flaherty household, so full of her elders. She was glad, nevertheless, to welcome her mother, who joined the couple for the young woman's first Mardi Gras festival and then stayed on for several months after the birth of Jean Chopin, on May 22, 1871. From May to July, 1894, Kate Chopin kept a most important diary – she called the book "Impressions" – which has only recently come to light, and here she gives a description of this event, which is of interest in connection with her later fictional approach to the theme of childbirth:[18]

This is Jean's birthday. . . . I can remember yet that hot southern day on Magazine Street in New Orleans. The noises of the street coming through the open windows; that heaviness with which I dragged myself about; my husband's and mother's solicitude; old Alexandrine the quadroon nurse with her high bandana tignon, her hoop-earrings and placid smile; old Doctor Faget; the smell of chloroform, and then waking at 6 in the evening from out of a stupor to see in my mother's arms a little piece of humanity all dressed in white which they told me was my little son! The sensation with which I touched my lips and my finger tips to his soft flesh only comes once to a mother. It must be the pure animal sensation; nothing spiritual could be so real – so poignant.

Urged by Mrs. O'Flaherty, who missed her daughter, Kate Chopin made frequent, long visits to St. Louis. Occasionally Oscar would accompany her. Helped by her mother's neighbor, the capable obstetrician Frederick Kolbenheyer, Mrs. Chopin gave birth to three sons in St. Louis. But the last of her six children – Felix and Lelia – were born in Louisiana. The parents seem to have been happy with their big family. It has been said, at least, that the youngsters were "always allowed to enjoy themselves," and that the jovial and fun-loving Oscar liked to play with them. In 1874, the Chopins moved to the Garden District, a fashionable section in the American part of the city. Here they lived first on Constantinople Street, and later on Louisiana Avenue, in a spacious house surrounded by palmtrees and live oaks.[19]

✳Kate Chopin's New Orleans period has been described as one in which she was "engrossed in the manifold duties which overpower a society woman and the conscientious mother of a large and growing family." Yet whenever she could, she slipped away, enjoying her liberty to go where she wanted. At a time when women's freedom of movement was still severely restricted, she developed a walking habit, and the heroine of *The Awakening* explains the philosophy behind it: "I always feel so sorry for women who don't like to walk; they miss so much – so many rare little glimpses of life; and we women learn so little of life on the whole." [20]

Kate Chopin, feeling adventurous, explored the city and its environs. Like Whitman, she loved to ride on streetcars and observe people, and she seems to have covered the routes of all the carlines at her disposal. In the little notebook she kept in New Orleans, which is now lost, she occasionally jotted down brief remarks on things seen and done during her outings, but she added no personal opinions or reflections. Nowhere did these unpretentious notes suggest any literary intentions. [21]

But she must have gathered a wealth of impressions as her intense curiosity about life spurred her to roam through the picturesque and cosmopolitan city. In New Orleans there were Creoles and Cajuns, Negroes and mulattoes, Germans, Italians, Irish, and Americans. In this variety of nationalities and races, the Negroes were much in evidence with their songs, their racy French patois, and their superstitions which persisted even though Voodoo practices had been banned. Octoroon balls were still being given. Lafcadio Hearn, who settled in the city in 1877, describes one of them at which he observed the beautiful "serpent women," as he calls them, dancing with their present or prospective "protectors." [22]

Still dominated by the Creoles, New Orleans had a definitely Mediterranean character. The excitable Latin temperament was responsible, for example, for the sparkling Mardi Gras festivities. The climate also contributed to the city's South-European atmosphere. In the hidden gardens of the pastel-colored Vieux Carré mansions, there was a fragrance of myrtles and oleander trees. In the Garden District, the air was heady with a perfume of jasmine, sweet olive, and magnolia, which served to accentuate the dreamy quality of the white-porticoed houses. "Work ... in this voluptuous climate ... is impossible," Hearn exclaimed. But while the Creoles were languidly lazy, besides being courteous and graceful, they could also quickly flare into violence. Mark Twain describes how intensely they loved cockfights, and Hearn observes that murders were so common that nobody bothered about them. [23]

While Kate Chopin took advantage of the entertainment afforded by the New Orleans panorama of human nature, she no doubt also made every use of what the city's Academy of Music, two opera houses, and several theaters had to offer. Edwin Booth, Sarah Bernhardt, and other great artists performed here, and the French Opera House was the first in America to stage such works as *Lohengrin* and *Tannhäuser*. (Mrs. Chopin's love of Wagner was probably born here.) New Orleans newspapers, meanwhile, made an effort to keep their readers up to date on science and modern literature. Hearn's columns were particularly effective, with their excerpts from the French press and from the works of Flaubert, Gautier, Maupassant, Baudelaire, and other French writers. George W. Cable was also a columnist, but he soon turned to writing stories. When *Old Creole Days* appeared in 1879, it gave New Orleans a definitive place in American literature, even though the Creoles soon complained that he had "destroyed the Louisiana of Chateaubriand and Longfellow." [24]

During the years of Reconstruction, Louisiana was afflicted with what was perhaps the most corrupt carpetbagger government in the South, and Kate Chopin could not help becoming involved in the problems that this created, since Oscar was a member of the White League. This League was an armed organization created by Southern Democrats in order to "resist the coalition of the Radical party . . . and the colored population . . . against the white race," and it had several clashes with the Republican Radicals. Oscar took part in the most notable of these, the Battle of Liberty Place, which was fought on September 14, 1874, with a loss of forty lives. The Radicals were beaten, but they quickly resumed power when President Grant backed them with troops. The Federals were finally withdrawn in 1877, and this marked the end of both the Radical rule and Reconstruction. [25] What Hearn called the "lava-flood of . . . frauds and maladministrations" went on as before, however. [26]

The yellow fever was another affliction plaguing Louisiana. It struck nearly every year, and the epidemic of 1878, for example, took no less than 4,000 lives in New Orleans alone. Mrs. Chopin was no doubt anxious for her growing family, and she may have been fleeing from "Yellow Jack" when she and her children so often went to St. Louis and when she spent long summers with them at Grand Isle on the Gulf of Mexico.

This island fifty miles south of New Orleans was monopolized by the Creoles of the Vieux Carré. A few former mansions served as pensions, and an old sugar factory with its mill house and slave cabins had been converted into a hotel. Reached only by boat, Grand Isle was a secluded, peaceful summer paradise, with its sand beaches and its idyllic paths among acres of yellow camomile and groves of water-oaks and orange trees. The atmosphere was even more sensuous than that of New Orleans, with the "soft and languorous [breeze] that came up from the south, charged with the seductive odor of the sea," as Kate Chopin describes it in *The Awakening*. But the waters of the Gulf are also destructive; turned into a floodwave by the 1893 hurricane, they were to wipe out the island as she had known it.[27]

Back in New Orleans, Kate Chopin continued her explorations of the city. She was particularly attracted by the river front with its rows of boats, piles of cotton, and multitudes of people. The last entry in her notebook described a "journey with Oscar through the district of warehouses where cotton is stored." She saw "the whole process of weighing, sampling, storing, compressing, boring to detect fraud, and the treatment of damaged bales." She also heard everyone complaining that there was "too much rain for cotton." Indeed, the 1878 and 1879 cotton yields were so small that Oscar Chopin, who had made large advances to planters, suffered losses from which he did not recover, and after closing his business at the end of the latter year, he moved with his family to Cloutierville.[28]

4. *The Cloutierville Years, 1879–1884*

Like New Orleans, northwestern Louisiana had also been affected by Reconstruction. Certain little known events of that turbulent period have been recorded by Phanor Breazeale of Natchitoches, who served his region as a judicious District Attorney. He was also Kate Chopin's brother-in-law and told her much about the parish, and to give an idea of the background against which she was later to deal with racial problems, a few sections of his report may be quoted.

During most of the 1870's, Breazeale tells us, Natchitoches was ruled by the Republicans, with Rayford Blunt, an illiterate Negro, serving as its State Senator. The Democrats, which meant nearly all the whites, were angered by the ruling party's use of Federal troops to subdue them, and meeting in Natchitoches on September 21, 1878, they approved a motion "That this convention adjourn and disperse this Negro crowd," that is, the Republicans convened nearby. The Negroes disappeared when they saw 1,500 armed whites descending upon them, and their later attempt to free the captured Blunt by force was unsuccessful. Soon released by the Democrats, Blunt had a number of them tried. "Two white men managed to get on the jury, and they played poker all night long with the Negroes and won everything they had, until finally they said they would play for a verdict of not guilty against all the things they had won .... The Negroes lost, and the boys from Natchitoches Parish were freed." [29]

If this part of Breazeale's report offers comic relief, what followed was not comic. Some time after the Natchitoches Democrats had won the 1878 elections, their "leaders in solemn conclave decided that there were many objectionable Negroes who had to be killed. This was done by a company of patriotic Democrats ...." No action, apparently, was taken against the killers.

At the end of 1879, the violent Reconstruction period was fast becoming history, and life in this isolated, fertile part of Louisiana now in many ways seemed idyllic and reminiscent of ante-bellum days. As before, cotton was "King," the chief source of income and the main topic of conversation. On the rebuilt plantations, the bells once more called the Negroes – now mostly sharecropping tenants – from the fields at mealtime. Freight boats again stopped at Chopin and other Cane River landings, unloading supplies and taking in cotton. Show-boats were back, and dances and seeding parties had been resumed. When the Colfax *Chronicle* brought such news as that "the people of Cloutierville are to have a grand pic-nic and fish-fry at Chopin's Lake to-day," it suggests a care-free, fun-loving community. [30] The big planters were again the leaders of the parish, and the social activity within this largely Creole circle was nearly back to the pre-war level.

When Kate and Oscar Chopin came to Cloutierville, they were in a way already part of this group. The Chopin plantation, now cut in two by the new railway, was run by Lamy, Oscar's brother, and on the Baxter estate, near Grand Ecore, lived Eugenie, his sister; both had married into the Henry family which owned the picturesque Melrose plantation on Cane River. Marie, youngest of the four Chopins, was shortly to become the wife of Phanor Breazeale. Rankin writes (p. 102) that "though Kate Chopin did not live on a plantation she became intimately acquainted with the splendor and leisure of post-war Louisiana plantation life through contact with Oscar's many relatives." And he goes on: "[Her] home became the center of social life. Her inherited *esprit* or gaiety ... made her the delight of all her acquaintances." Though she was "intellectually superior to her social equals," they "affectionately admired and approved her tact [and] her musical and conversational talents." The acceptance of Kate and Oscar into the social circles of Natchitoches probably was helped by his White League record; this organization had been particularly active in northwestern Louisiana.

In a later story, Kate Chopin graphically described Cloutierville: "This little French village ... was simply two long rows of very old frame houses, facing each other closely across a dusty roadway" that skirted "the river bank, steep in places and crumbling away." At one end of the road was the Catholic church, whose services Mrs. Chopin apparently attended fairly regularly. The priest, Father Beaulieu, was a man of compassion and understanding, and according to Rankin (p. 100), he was to appear in several of her stories as "Père Antoine." At the other end was the Chopin home, a comfortable, two-story, "Louisiana-type" house. Oscar Chopin settled down to manage some small plantations he owned. On borrowed money, he bought a general store in Cloutierville, which became very popular since he was liberal in the giving of credit.[31]

Meanwhile, Kate Chopin kept up her activities. To her former habit of taking walks she added that of horseback riding. She would then wear "a fantastic affair," as a lady has described it, "a close-fitting riding habit of blue cloth, the train fastened up at the side to disclose an embroidered skirt, and the little feet encased in pretty boots with high heels. A jaunty little jockey hat and feather, and buff gloves rendered her charming." Besides being a wife and mother, she was also, as her daughter has told us, the "Lady Bountiful of the neighborhood, dispensing advice and counsel, medicines, and, when necessary, food to the simple people around her, and in this way learning to know and to love them too, for no matter how keenly they appealed to her wonderful sense of humor, she always touched on their weaknesses fondly and tolerantly, never unkindly." No wonder that these people were impressed with her regal dignity, her warmth and kindness, and her enjoyment of life. The fact that in 1880 the new Cane River packet was named after Mrs. Chopin's newborn daughter may well have been a reflection of her popularity.[32]

Kate Chopin was a magnificent, gracious, and efficient chatelaine,

and we are told that she led a "happy and industrious life." She had
her share of leisure, too. The Natchitoches *Vindicator* writes at one
point that she was to spend "several months" with relatives in St.
Louis. But, that her life was not free from anxiety is seen in the
newspaper report that Oscar, who was never strong, had been to Hot
Springs, Arkansas, to "recuperate his health." He recovered, but
when in January, 1883, he caught swamp fever, he had so little
power of resistance that he died "almost before his family could
realize that he was in danger."[33]

Kate Chopin was now "a handsome, inconsolable ... Creole
widow of thirty" – in the situation of Thérèse Lafirme, the heroine
of her later first novel. Unlike the childless Thérèse, however, she of
course had the care of a large family. Even so, it may well be herself
she described when she wrote that "Thérèse had wanted to die with
her Jérôme, feeling that life without him held nothing that could
reconcile her to its further endurance. For days she lived alone with
her grief, ... unmindful of the disorder that gathered about her."
What finally roused the heroine from her "lethargy of grief" was that
she felt it her duty to carry on Jérôme's work of running the family
plantation: "She felt at once the weight and sacredness of a trust,
whose acceptance brought consolation and awakened unsuspected
powers of doing." Again, this is very likely Kate Chopin herself who,
"having rejected all offers of assistance from kindly relatives, undertook the management of her plantations and developed much ability
as a business woman," as William Schuyler tells us. He goes on: "She
had to carry on correspondence with the cotton factors in New Orleans, make written contracts, necessitating many personal interviews
with the poorer Creoles, the Acadians, and the 'free mulattoes,' who
raised the crop 'on shares,' see that the plantation store was well
stocked, and sometimes even, in emergencies, keep shop herself. It was
hard work, but in doing it she had the opportunity of closely observing all those oddities of Southern character" which she was to describe
later.[34]

Kate Chopin carried on this work for more than a year, and
apparently with success. (She was no doubt helped by her vigor and
intelligence and by her knowledge of the value of money.) But her
mother kept urging her to come with her children to St. Louis, and in
1884, she finally yielded. Probably feeling she had proved her mettle,
she sold what Oscar had left her – with the exception of two very

small plantations – and paid his debts, whereupon she moved to Mrs. O'Flaherty.[35]

Mother and daughter were devoted to one another, and when the older lady suddenly died in June, 1885, Kate Chopin was "literally prostrated with grief."[36]

III

Growth and Literary Success

1. *1890: At Fault*

Having lost all her immediate relatives, the thirty-four-year-old Mrs. Chopin was now utterly alone with her deep sorrow. In a photograph taken at this time, she appears languid, withdrawn, and suffering. After the loss of her husband, she had visited Kitty Garesché, probably to seek solace. That she now wrote an autobiographical fragment dealing with her old schoolfriend suggests that she looked for comfort in the fact that at least this old intimacy was still alive. Kate Chopin's daughter has described the effect of the bereavements in this way:[1]

When I speak of my mother's keen sense of humor and of her habit of looking on the amusing side of everything, I don't want to give the impression of her being joyous, for she was on the contrary rather a sad nature. She was undemonstrative both in grief and happiness, but her feelings were very deep as is usual with such natures. I think the tragic death of her father early in her life, of her much loved brothers, the loss of her young husband and her mother, left a stamp of sadness on her which was never lost.

The only one who seems to have been able to help her in her grief was Dr. Kolbenheyer, who had been her obstetrician and who now was her family doctor. He became "a cordially accepted intimate friend, almost an ardent admirer of Kate Chopin."[2] His visits continued also after she moved in 1886 to 3317 Morgan Street, a house she had bought in a new, western part of the city, and their personal contacts were supplemented by frequent letters.[3]

Kolbenheyer was a man of a marked and impressive personality. His pronounced radical and republican ideas had forced him to leave his native Austria. Settling in St. Louis in 1870, he soon became acquainted with the city's journalists, particularly with Joseph Pulitzer, who later made him Vice-President of his St. Louis *Post-Dispatch*.

The Doctor had an extremely active mind and wide learning, and he was a specialist on such philosophers as Kant, Hegel, and Schopenhauer. His wit and charm and his emphatic and outspoken manner made him a fascinating talker.[4] Rankin writes (pp. 89, 106) that Mrs. Chopin's "religious opinions and philosophic attitude toward life were strongly influenced" by this determined agnostic:

[The Doctor's] insinuating conversations carried conviction to Kate Chopin, to the extent at least that she no longer remained a Catholic in any real or practical way. No doubt there were other influences. But to trace the course of this yielding of her faith is unquestionably difficult.... Whatever the combination of influences that united to exert a strong power over Kate Chopin's mind, she became, within a year after her mother's death, a Catholic in name only. She never openly repudiated the faith of her youth; she remained merely indifferent to the practical duties of the Catholic religion.

The literature Mrs. Chopin now read was another of the factors which influenced her during this crucial period. She had never abandoned her reading, not even when she managed the plantations. It seems very likely that the study of science which she had started then was now strongly encouraged by the Doctor. She was particularly interested in biology and anthropology, we are told, and "the works of Darwin, Huxley, and Spencer were her daily companions; for the study of the human species, both general and particular, [had] always been her constant delight."[5]

After some time, Dr. Kolbenheyer started reading to her the letters she had sent him from Louisiana and urged her to begin to write fiction. He did this because he was struck with the literary quality of her descriptions, and perhaps also because he knew that with six children and a rather limited income she could well use whatever she could earn. But the Doctor's main reason for encouraging her to take up writing was probably that he hoped it would give her some relief from the emptiness and deep despair to which her losses had reduced her and from her longing for the Louisiana that was so intimately connected with Oscar.[6]

Kate Chopin revisited Natchitoches in 1887, and the following year she started to write.[7] Her first effort was "If It Might Be," an undated poem which is interesting as a possible expression of a wish to join her dead husband:

If it might be that thou didst need my life,
Now on the instant would I end this strife
'Twixt hope and fear, and glad the end I'd meet
With wonder only, to find death so sweet.

If it might be that thou didst need my love,
To love thee dear, my life's fond work would prove.
All time, to tender watchfulness I'd give;
And count it happiness, indeed, to live.

"Psyche's Lament," the next poem we have from Kate Chopin's hand, is an illustration of the speaker's despair at having lost what she had loved:

O let all darkness fall upon mine eyes:
    I want no more of light!
Since Helios in the blazing skies
    Cannot make day so bright
As my lost one did make for me the night!

O, sombre sweetness; black-enfolden charms,
    Come to me once again!
Leave me not desolate; with empty arms
    That seeking, strive in vain
To clasp a void where warmest Love hath lain.

Now is no heartbeat pulsing into mine
    Since he is gone. I see,
I feel but the cursed lights that shine –
    That made my Love to flee.
O Love, O God, O Night come back to me! [8]

A progressive Chicago magazine called *America* published "If It Might Be" on January 10, 1889, and this marked Mrs. Chopin's first appearance in print. She was at that time working on two stories. The first of these was "Euphrasie," which reflected Oscar and Natchitoches; the widow thus apparently turned to what she had lost now that she was trying to reorientate herself in life and to give it a new meaning through her writing. But she put the tale aside, and the second – an "Unfinished Story – Grand Isle – 30,000 words," as she termed it – she destroyed.[9] (We know nothing more about it.) The reason may have been that her intensive reading of Maupassant at this time had given her new ideas about the craft of story writing.

In a previously unknown manuscript from 1896, significantly entitled "Confidences," she writes:[10]

About eight years ago there fell accidentally into my hands a volume of Maupassant's tales. These were new to me. I had been in the woods, in the fields, groping around; looking for something big, satisfying, convincing, and finding nothing but – myself; a something neither big nor satisfying, but wholly convincing. It was at this period of my emerging from the vast solitude in which I had been making my own acquaintance, that I stumbled upon Maupassant. I read his stories and marvelled at them. Here was life, not fiction; for where were the plots, the old fashioned mechanism and stage trapping that in a vague, unthinking way I had fancied were essential to the art of story making. Here was a man who had escaped from tradition and authority, who had entered into himself and looked out upon life through his own being and with his own eyes; and who, in a direct and simple way, told us what he saw. When a man does this, he gives us the best that he can; something valuable for it is genuine and spontaneous. He gives us his impressions. ...

He has never seemed to me to belong to the multitude, but rather to the individual. ... Someway I like to cherish the delusion that he has spoken to no one else so directly, so intimately as he does to me. [Originally she wrote: ... so directly, so secretly as he had to me when I emerged from the woods.] He did not say, as another might have done, "do you see these are charming stories of mine; ... study them closely, ... observe the method, the manner of their putting together – and if ever you are moved to write stories you can do no better than to imitate ...

Kate Chopin's manuscript breaks off here, as the next page, in which she presumably elaborated on precisely how Maupassant had spoken to her, unfortunately is missing. It is unlikely that this was her first encounter with him. The reason for the impact this time was probably that she was now looking for both a literary technique and a view of life that were congenial to her, and what she read may have been a yellow-covered volume with some of those stories about sex, solitude, and suicide which she was later to translate.[11] We know that he continued to be one of her favorite authors, and in 1894 a friend wrote that she had "a preference for the best examples of the French school of literature, at the head of which she places De Maupassant, whose artistic method she thinks has not been reached by any other French writer of the present day."[12]

4 *

Mrs. Chopin reportedly said that she had written "very diffidently at first." (In a diary comment on the reading of a self-confident neighbor's manuscript she observes that "such belief in [one's] own ability is a bad omen.") She also said that her first productions had been "crude and unformed," and that at some point she had started "to study to better her style." [13] The comment on her neighbor suggests other authors she herself may have turned to: "If she were younger I would tell her to study critically some of the best of our short stories. I know of no one better than Miss Jewett to study for technique and nicety of construction. I don't mention Mary E. Wilkins [Freeman] for she is a great genius and genius is not to be studied."

We know nothing more specific about Kate Chopin's study of literary technique, but whether or not she felt she had mastered it by the time she wrote her next story, "A Poor Girl," in May, 1889, she sent the tale to the *Home Magazine.* Her notebook sums up the editor's reply: "Objection to incident – not desirable – to be handled – remarks 'well written – full of interest' – would reconsider if changed." She then showed the story to the co-founder and able editor of the St. Louis *Post-Dispatch,* her friend John Dillon, who was a liberal, a lover of literature, and an opponent of the idea that man was intellectually superior to woman. [14] Even he gave what she in her diary later termed "damning praise," showing prejudice against her subject matter while encouraging her to continue her efforts.

Whatever it was in the "Poor Girl" that was offensive, she destroyed the tale, but her next two stories appeared in print before the end of 1889: "Wiser Than a God" in the *Philadelphia Musical Journal,* and "A Point at Issue" in the *Post-Dispatch.* The first of these is about a young woman who refuses to marry and becomes a famous pianist instead. In the second story, meanwhile, the heroine marries her suitor; they share an idealism about marital freedom, but circumstances soon force them back to a more conventional stand.

Mrs. Chopin's next effort was *At Fault,* a novel she completed in April, 1890. Once again her theme is a problem connected with marriage, this time the question of the responsibility of one spouse toward the other. David Hosmer, the chief male character, is told by the woman he loves that he should not have divorced Fanny, his wife, when he found out that she drank, but instead have tried to help her. They remarry, but he cannot prevent her from falling back into drinking. All three suffer, until the accidental death of Fanny enables the two lovers to marry.

Kate Chopin had spent nine months writing *At Fault*. She was impatient to see it published, partly because it would aid her in self-criticism – she once said that during the first years she had learned much from seeing her work in cold type – and partly because her ambition was to become known among the nationally important critics and hopefully have their encouragement.[15] In June, 1890, she discussed the manuscript with C. L. Deyo, a clever journalist friend. When the first publisher she approached refused the novel, she immediately had a St. Louis company bring it out at her expense, and in September, she personally promoted it by sending copies to newspapers and magazines. She also sent a copy to William Dean Howells, whose writings she admired and whose comedies she liked to read to her friends.[16]

The most extensive review of the book appeared in the St. Louis *Post-Dispatch*. The critic refused to go along with the author in taking people as they are and not believing it possible to make them over. He also objected to Hosmer's saying "shut up" to Fanny, and he insisted that even if it was a fact that David's sister had been engaged many times, it "ought not to be mentioned." But at the same time he gave high praise to the author, surprisingly enough even for the degree to which she had succeeded in keeping herself and all moralizing out of the book.[17] Approval also came from most of the other local reviewers, who pointed to the quiet humor, vivid portrayals, artistic skill, and graceful finish of this first novel, in which they found "unmistakable indications of strength."[18] In a somewhat similar Eastern reaction, the *Nation,* on the one hand, criticized the large number of people whom they considered morally at fault in the book, and, on the other, commended it for its graphic descriptions and skillful characterizations.[19]

2. *1894: Bayou Folk*

The praise given *At Fault* undoubtedly stimulated Kate Chopin in her efforts. She was already at work on her second novel, "Young Dr. Gosse." In January, 1891, she started it on its rounds to the publishers. All we know about this effort is that no one wanted it, though

William Schuyler in 1894 described it as "her very strongest work," and that the author destroyed it, probably in 1896.[20]

After completing this novel, she concentrated on the shorter forms of fiction, writing no fewer than forty stories, sketches, and vignettes during the next three years. Such local periodicals as the *Spectator, Fashion and Fancy,* the *St. Louis Magazine,* and *St. Louis Life* were the first to accept her writings, which now showed a marked improvement in technique. But from the outset she aspired to being published by the nationally known eastern magazines. She first succeeded in this with her children's tales, which from 1891 appeared in the *Youth's Companion* and *Harper's Young People.*

One of these tales is the vignette "Boulôt and Boulotte." It deals with two small Cajuns who have never worn shoes, but who are now sent to Natchitoches to buy a pair for each. They return barefooted. Asked why they had not put on their new brogans, Boulôt sheepishly looks down because he had not thought of it, while Boulotte is master of the situation: "You think we go buy shoes fur ruin it in de dus'?" This sketch seems to have so much pleased Howells, then an editor of *Harper's,* that he wrote the author a letter of praise and encouraged her to send more of the same kind. This letter, which is lost, apparently represented the only contact between the two, and indeed Howells' only comment on Kate Chopin.[21]

The St. Louis author's writings for adults began to appear in the East in 1892, when *Two Tales* published "At the 'Cadian Ball." On January 14, 1893, *Vogue* opened its pages to Kate Chopin and published "A Visit to Avoyelles" and "Désirée's Baby." The latter is a story about a woman who walks with her baby into the bayou when her husband accuses her of being part Negro. It proved such a success that the *Vogue* editors eagerly accepted what the author later sent them, and they were to print eighteen of her tales between 1893 and 1900.

While she found a ready market for most of her writings, she had difficulty in getting certain of her more unusual stories published, no doubt on account of their subject matter. "Mrs. Mobry's Reason" may well have shocked editors with its treatment of a case of hereditary madness. "A Shameful Affair" may have offended them with its portrayal of a heroine who violates the rules for womanly modesty when she is passionately aroused. These tales were finally published by the *Times-Democrat* of New Orleans, whose readers were somewhat conditioned to the new literary tendencies. Still another story had to wait five years before it finally reached print. This was "Miss McEnders," which deals with a young woman who wakes up to the fact that her father is dishonest and her fiancé a *viveur*.

For the most part, however, Kate Chopin's writings of this period presented no problems for the editors. That the heroine of "In Sabine" leaves her husband is acceptable because she is mistreated by him. Mme. Delisle of "A Lady of Bayou St. John" is on the point of committing adultery when she learns that her husband has been killed in the Civil War, but then devotes the rest of her life to his memory. When the hero of "At Chênière Caminada" is so infatuated with a young woman that he wants her with "the savage instinct of his blood," the expression may pass because nothing comes of his desire.[22]

Kate Chopin also wrote a small number of poems during these years. One of them is called "You and I":

> How many years since we walked, you and I,
> Under the stars and the April sky;
> You were young then; I was not older;
> Then you were shy, nor was I bolder.
> Was it love did we feel? was it life did we live?
> It was springtime indeed; but can springtime give
> The fullness of life and of love? Completest
> When living and loving and roses are sweetest!
> Shall we walk together once more, you and I,
> Under the stars and the summer sky? [23]

The speaker of "You and I" seems on the whole to prefer the full life of maturity to a return to the spring companion. In "An Idle Fellow," however, a sketch written the day the author sent her poems of this period to *Vogue,* the speaker is tired and seems to identify herself with a thrush which wants the mate that had been with her last blossom-time. The idea suggests itself that these items represent facets of Kate Chopin's duality of a longing for Oscar versus a desire for growth.

While "An Idle Fellow" found no publisher, another of Kate Chopin's writings was accepted by what was considered America's leading magazine. After having shown "Euphrasie" to Dr. Kolbenheyer in 1890, the author rewrote and renamed the story and in May of the following year offered it to the editor of the *Century.* Richard Watson

Gilder, who, in Hamlin Garland's words, "lived in the constant hope of discovering genius in every mail," replied that he might take it if she made certain changes. A few days later she returned it with this comment: "The weakness which you found in 'A No-Account Creole' is the one which I felt. I thank you more than I can say, for your letter. My first and strongest feelings upon reading it, was a desire to clasp your hand. I hope I have succeeded in making the girl's character clearer." (Euphrasie is torn between her promise to marry the Creole Placide Santien and her love for Wallace Offdean, who finally persuades Placide to let the girl make her own choice.) On August 3, 1891, Gilder accepted the story with "very sincere pleasure."[24]

Two years went by, however, without the *Century's* printing the tale, and in May, 1893, when Mrs. Chopin was again represented in *Vogue,* she could no longer contain her impatient ambition and went to New York, where she tried to interest Gilder and other publishers in her second novel and in a collection of her tales.[25] Three months later, Houghton Mifflin accepted this volume of stories, and the year 1894 was to give her all the national recognition she could have asked for: "A No-Account Creole" was printed in January; *Bayou Folk,* as the collection was called, appeared in March, and the reviewers lavished praise on it; in September, a story of hers was published in the *Atlantic,* and in December, another in the *Century.*

Bayou Folk contains twenty-three tales and sketches. All of them are set in Louisiana, mostly in Natchitoches, and many of the characters appear in more than one story. The unity thus achieved is further enhanced by the discreet humor and warm understanding displayed by the author throughout. The book was the first of importance to deal with the Cane River country, and in scores of reviews, Kate Chopin was enthusiastically welcomed as a new, distinguished local colorist. As for her artistry, the *Nation,* for example, declared that "her stories are among the most clever and charming that have seen the light," and the St. Louis *Post-Dispatch* saw "a sureness of handling" and a confidence in the book which spoke of "power only half displayed."[26] She was not satisfied with praise *per se,* however, but wanted perceptive, discriminating criticism; this is apparent in a diary entry of June 7, 1894:

In looking over more than a hundred press notices of "Bayou Folk" which have already been sent to me, I am surprised at the very small number which show anything like a worthy critical faculty. They might be counted upon the fingers of one hand. I had no idea the genuine book critic was so rare a bird. And yet I receive congratulations from my publishers upon the character of the press notices.

The few reviews Mrs. Chopin liked were undoubtedly those which suggested that she was not just another so-called "dialect writer." In St. Louis, William Marion Reedy – then just emerging as a nationally recognized critic – wrote in his *Sunday Mirror:* "[*Bayou Folk* is] the best literary work that has come out of the Southland in a long time. It is best because it is truest," he added, and better than similar work of Cable on the Louisiana Creoles because it shows no strain for effect, and because the stories "are racy of the soil; direct from the people." But then he went on to declare her talent to be "not of the quality that is confined to the portrayal of the life of a section." The *Atlantic,* too, envisaged a wider role for the author when it observed: "Now and then she strikes a passionate note, and the naturalness and ease with which she does it impress one as characteristic of power awaiting opportunity." [27]

3. *The Crucial Self-Assertion*

It was in early April, 1894, that the highly favorable reviews of *Bayou Folk* started to pour in. On April 19, Kate Chopin wrote "The Story of an Hour," a truly remarkable tale about a subdued wife's vision of living only for herself.

Louise Mallard, who suffers from heart trouble, is gently told the news of her husband's death in a railway-accident. She "wept at once, with sudden, wild abandonment"; then, "when the storm of grief had spent itself she went away to her room alone." As she sat looking at the spring life outside her window, her young face, "whose lines bespoke repression and even a certain strength," showed that something was coming to her which she tried in vain to hold back: [28]

When she abandoned herself, a little whispered word escaped her slightly parted lips. She said it over and over under her breath: "free, free, free!" ... She did not stop to ask if it were or were not a monstrous joy that held her. A clear and exalted perception enabled her to dismiss the suggestion as trivial. ...

She saw ... a long procession of years to come that would belong to her absolutely. And she opened and spread her arms out to them in welcome.

There would be no one to live for her during those coming years; she would live for herself. There would be no powerful will bending hers in that blind persistence with which men and women believe they have a right to impose a private will upon a fellow-creature. A kind intention or a cruel intention made the act seem no less a crime as she looked upon it in that brief moment of illumination.

And yet she had loved him – sometimes. Often she had not. What did it matter? What could love, the unsolved mystery, count for in the face of this possession of self-assertion which she suddenly recognized as the strongest impulse of her being!

"Free! Body and soul free!" she kept whispering. ...

There was a feverish triumph in her eyes, and she carried herself unwittingly like a goddess of Victory. ... [But Mr. Mallard had not been involved in the accident at all, and his unannounced return an hour later proved fatal to his wife:]

When the doctors came they said she had died of heart disease – of joy that kills.

This astonishing story strongly indicates that the sudden success which *Bayou Folk* brought Kate Chopin was of crucial importance in the author's own self-fulfillment. It gave her a certain release from what she evidently felt as repression or frustration, thereby freeing forces that had lain dormant in her. It is highly significant that she wrote "The Story of an Hour," an extreme example of the theme of self-assertion, at the exact moment when the first reviews of the book had both satisfied and increased her secret ambitions. It is equally noteworthy that on May 22, when her national fame was already an acknowledged fact, she confided the following reflections to her diary:

How curiously the past effaces itself for me! I sometimes regret that it is so; for there must be a certain pleasure in retrospection. I cannot live through yesterday or tomorrow. It is why the dead in their character of dead and association with the grave have no hold upon me. I cannot connect my mother or husband or any of those I have lost with those mounds of earth out at Calvary Cemetary. ... If it were possible for my husband and my mother to come back to earth, I feel that I would unhesitatingly give up every thing that has come into my life since they left it and join my existence again with theirs. To do that, I would have to forget the past ten years of my growth – my real growth. But I would take back a little wisdom with me; it would be the spirit of perfect acquiescence.

It would be interesting to know what it was that Mrs. Chopin had found when she in the late eighties had made her own acquaintance, as she was later to term it in "Confidences"; how she now by 1894 had acquired that "spirit of perfect acquiescence" which she had evidently lacked while Oscar and Mrs. O'Flaherty were still alive; and what she had in mind when she spoke of her "real growth." Did she feel she had realized unused capacities through maintaining with no assistance her large family and her plantations? Had she formed relationships during her widowhood which had widened her field of experience? Had her involvement with the new science made her believe that she could now stand on her own without the aid of the Church? Or, finally, did she have in mind her growth as a writer?

Whatever other aspects of her growth Kate Chopin may have been thinking of, her development and success as a writer was certainly of very great importance to her. "I want [*Bayou Folk*] to succeed," she exclaims in her diary, and another entry shows her reaction to a sketch that William Schuyler had just written of her for *The Writer*: "I don't know who could have . . . better told in so short a space the story of my growth into a writer of stories." She took art very seriously. When Edwin Booth's letters were published after his death, she doubted that these "expressions wrung from him by the conventional demands of his daily life" could throw any new light upon his life work. "The *real* Edwin Booth gave himself to the public through his art," she observed. "His art was his closest and most precious possession." As for herself, she clearly regretted that she was not always accepted as a serious literary artist. "How hard it is for one's acquaintances and friends to realize that one's books are to be taken seriously," she was to complain after the publication of her fourth book.[29]

Another matter of great importance to Kate Chopin was her artistic integrity. She could not use material forced upon her by well-meaning acquaintances, but had to choose her own. Except for having discussed one manuscript with John Dillon, another with C. L. Deyo, and a third with Dr. Kolbenheyer, she seems never to have asked the advice of any of her St. Louis friends.[30] She refused to make anything but minor changes in the quick first draft of her writings, and nearly all her stories were printed practically as they had first come to her; yet some of them equal those of Maupassant in their finish and artistry.

This accomplishment becomes even more remarkable when we consider that her work was done in the family living room, where the children were swarming around her. The author often wished she could be undisturbed while writing, her daughter has told us. But she loved her youngsters and never wanted to shut them out of her presence. She wanted their love, too, and to get it she gave them a good time. She spoiled them by being always available and willing to help and by making no demands on them; for instance, she never encouraged her boys to have jobs. Instead, she used her limited means to support them and to give them a gay and lively home. In turn, they adored her and felt that she understood them and gave them everything.[31] Like one of her characters, Kate Chopin "attracted youth in some incomprehensible way," and she was constantly surrounded also by the friends of her children. Gifted with sympathy and understanding, she was a stimulating listener, with a rare ability to draw a person out, and her visitors often would confide in her matters which they would never broach to others.[32]

An account of a talk that Mrs. Chopin once had with a boy suggests that one of the reasons she liked adolescents – and also poets, philosophers, and loafers – was that they had not yet become stale through conformity or hardened by disillusionment, but still retained something original and spontaneous. "We never know what illusions are till we have lost them," she had told the boy. "They belong to youth, and they are poetry and philosophy, and vagabondage, and everything delightful. And they last till men and the world, life and the institutions, come along with – but gracious! I forgot whom I was talking to." This statement reminds us of Kate Chopin's love of the spontaneity in the people of Natchitoches, who still lived in close contact with fundamentals and in relative ignorance of the great world and its institutions. When she went back occasionally to Cloutierville, it was not only to "refresh her recollections," as a friend observed, but also to be stimulated by the unrestrained enjoyment of life and the comparatively uninhibited show of emotion found among her former neighbors.[33]

Kate Chopin could show abandon and spontaneity herself. Her Irish gaiety was much in evidence; she loved laughter, and her brilliant eyes sparkled with humor as they took everything in. She had a lovely, expressive face; a delicate, pink complexion, and white, wavy hair. Now grown a little stout, the author was of a commanding appearance, which made her friends compare her to a French marquise. Although she never cared about dressing in style, she always looked well. She was patient and kind, we are told, and never ruffled or depressed; yet her diary shows that her smile could hide both wrath and despondency.[34] When she made one of her heroines suddenly imagine herself freed from the responsibilities that oppressed her, the author very likely projected a wish that she had had at times herself.[35] But she had her feet firmly on the ground, and in the Irish way she would soon bounce back and be active again with her duties.

Mrs. Chopin never dwelt upon the past morosely. She also thought it meaningless to be sentimental over oncoming age, as her "friend" (undoubtedly Dr. Kolbenheyer) had been when she remembered his fifty-first birthday "with a little gift, a sip of champagne & 'wish you luck'." Reporting this in her diary, she comments: "I am younger today at 43 than I was at 23. What does it matter. Why this mathematical division of life into years? Days are what count – not years. ... I wonder if I shall ever care if it is 43 or 53 or 63. I believe not."

As before, Kate Chopin could be not only outgoing, but also retiring and elusive, displaying the secretive element in her nature that made her an enigma even to close friends. A statement in "Confidences" illustrates her need for distance and secrecy: "There is somewhere registered in my consciousness a vow that I would never be confidential except for the purpose of misleading," she observes. And when she admits that "consistency is a pompous and wearisome burden to bear always" and goes on to talk about herself, she quickly becomes elusive again.[36] Mrs. Chopin's reserve was of the kind that attracts, and a number of distinguished men who had loved the author and wanted to marry her at this time described her to Rankin as "a woman of mysterious fascination," adding that she "attracted them by an alluring quality which they found incapable of analysis." She was "always content with her own society," they told him, and she "had her life in her own home – with her thoughts, her dreams, and her children. ... She preserved her emotional and intellectual independence" while keeping her numerous attachments with admirers and friends.[37]

According to these informants, Kate Chopin possessed "a quality of sex that is inexplicable." She was quite aware of the power of her sex appeal, and she also realized the attraction of what W. M. Reedy called her "noble character." But, according to one of her admirers, she seemed to reply to their silent declarations: "I have seen other days of life and know the mystery and lure of another's love. You cannot touch my heart." One reason she never remarried may thus have been her love for Oscar. It has also been suggested that she did not want to become dependent again and lose her new freedom and power. Yet another reason has been given by one of her daughters-in-law, who has said that she now lived for her writing and had enough with that.[38]

Since Kate Chopin spent only an average of one or two mornings a week on the physical act of writing, she had ample time for her other activities. Card-playing was one of them; describing herself as "something of a euchre fiend," she once regretfully noted that she had "missed the euchre club again." Concerts and plays continued to draw her. She played the piano and organized musicales with her friends. She also found great pleasure in thinking through a whole piece of music in her head, and even published a little composition of her own.[39] As before, she was an omnivorous reader; a casual note in her diary tells us, for example, that she had "read a few delicious comedies of Aristophanes last night." She read sitting in a Morris chair in her comfortable but simple living room; apart from a few paintings on the wall and a candle and a naked Venus on the bookshelf, there were hardly any ornamentations in it.[40] This unpretentious parlor was the regular meeting-place for some of the city's outstanding minds.

4. *A French Salon in St. Louis*

One of Kate Chopin's newspaper friends was later to write of her that she had come "closer to maintaining a salon than any woman that has ever lived in St. Louis." Describing her as no less than "the most brilliant, distinguished, and interesting woman that has ever graced St. Louis," he declared that in her home one could find "entertainment, instruction, and pleasure . . . [in] the play of wit and the flashes of culture" that savored of the true salons of, for instance, Mme. de Staël. He added that it was a place to meet interesting people and that for many years it was Mrs. Chopin who entertained literary and artistic visitors to the city. Her home was indeed always full, particularly on Thursday, which was her "day"; and admiring the author as they did, her friends may well have thought it an honor for visitors to be introduced to her. They were no doubt gracefully received, even though Kate Chopin once confessed that celebrities depressed her. We might add that, except for one meeting with Ruth McEnery Stuart, we have no details of visits with Mrs. Chopin by literary colleagues of national importance.[41]

The group that gathered around her reflected the considerable cultural activity which had invigorated the city during the postwar years. Dr. Kolbenheyer and William Schuyler provided links with the St. Louis Philosophical Society, an organization formed in 1866 by New Englanders and Germans who wanted to live out their enthusiasm for philosophy and the arts. Through its offspring, the St. Louis Movement, it had turned the city into a lively fermenting-ground for new ideas, and with its *Journal of Speculative Philosophy,* to which William James and John Dewey contributed, its school of idealistic Hegelian philosophy had made a national impact. When the movement lost momentum in the eighties, a generation of younger intellectuals, who worshiped such gods as Whitman, Flaubert, Zola, Swinburne, and Wilde, was ready to take over. The author of a recent book on T. S. Eliot's background maintains that this younger group carried on the "minor cultural explosion" which the Society had ignited and that the result was "a culture . . . favorable to the growth of a genius" like this poet, who was born in St. Louis in 1888.[42]

It was to this second generation that Kate Chopin and most of her entourage belonged. While she never pretended to be learned or aspired to be a leader, her personality and her accomplishments made her such an important central figure that the St. Louis *Star-Times* in 1898 named her first when it enumerated the four leaders of the city's "working literary colony," as the commentator called it. She was too independent to be noticeably influenced by her friends (Dr. Kolbenheyer's early influence is the only known exception), but they no doubt stimulated her both with their admiration of her and with their lively interests in various fields. William Schuyler, for example, was a writer, critic, and composer, besides being a champion of Wagner. Alexander DeMenil was an editor of genteel magazines. He was probably too conservative for Mrs. Chopin's taste; her closer friends were, in Felix Chopin's words, "pink-red liberals" who believed in intellectual freedom.[43] One of these liberals was Henry Dumay, an ambitious literary Frenchman who since 1892 had been teaching French literature, including the writers of the day, at St. Louis' Washington University. Some members of the group were lawyers. Others, like John Dillon, C. L. Deyo, and George S. Johns, were outstanding St. Louis *Post-Dispatch* editors who exposed the abuses and hypocrisy of the city's monopolistic oligarchy and fought the widespread corruption. There were a few women in the group, too; one of them was Sue V. Moore, editor of *St. Louis Life*.[44]

These people wanted to promote Kate Chopin and their city and region at the same time. But she did not wish to be written up as a regional writer. That she was a great admirer of W. M. Reedy, whom she apparently knew, was in part because he was the most unprovincial literary critic of St. Louis. As it has been pointed out, he looked not for the local in a novel, but for what could be "recognized as real anywhere," as Reedy put it. When he later was to speak of Mrs. Chopin's "true literary genius," he was perhaps thinking of this universal quality which he had observed already in *Bayou Folk*. He was a man of great humanity and a lover of life, and his unconventionality had made him somewhat notorious. In his *Mirror* he presented writings which appeared nowhere else, of both avant-garde and unjustly forgotten authors from many countries, and his intelligent, sensitive, and independent literary judgment soon made him and his magazine a national institution.[45] Some of Kate Chopin's stories were printed in the *Mirror* at the editor's invitation. When he did not ask her to write more for him, it was perhaps because of his assistant editor, Frances Porcher, who was fairly open about her literary aspirations.

Mrs. Chopin rarely displayed her ambition openly, but on the strength of *Bayou Folk* she was asked by Mrs. Moore to write for *St. Louis Life*. This was a light magazine, with society news and some fiction. Several stories and book reviews by Kate Chopin appeared in the periodical before its name was changed to the *Criterion* and Dumay became editor. At his invitation, Kate Chopin wrote a series of six essays during February and March of 1897, in which she commented on books and writers.[46] Shortly after, Dumay and the publisher moved the magazine to New York, where for a time it was a brilliant literary journal, with articles by James Huneker, Percival Pollard, and other leading critics.

Kate Chopin apparently never showed the active iconoclasm displayed by some of these writers; nor did she copy the startling behavior – except possibly for the cigar-smoking – of George Sand, whom she is said to have so much admired that she named her daughter after the author's *Lélia*.[47] On the contrary, even though one of those who knew Mrs. Chopin described her as an "advanced literary lady," she showed such dignity and was so discreet in all she did that DeMenil, for example, was led to see her as "simply a bright, unaffected, warmhearted, unpresuming and *womanly* woman [who had] ... none of the manners, airs, affectations, and eccentricities" of the bluestockings.[48] The most intellectually gifted woman in her circle, she was familiar with the topics and movements of the day and loved to be mentally stimulated by spirited discussions, particularly with her male friends. As one of them observed, on an intellectual, man to man basis, she would answer anything, never shirking a question or becoming embarrassed.[49] Yet with all her daring and vigor, she had exceedingly quiet manners. Her sharp observations were given unemphatically and with the light touch of her humor. Mrs. Chopin was unassuming and showed no trace of self-display. Sue V. Moore declared her to have "no literary affectations" and "no 'fads' or 'serious purpose' in life." [50]

Nevertheless, from 1890 to 1892 she had been a member of an organization which was devoted to a serious purpose. At the insistence of a friend, she joined the Wednesday Club of St. Louis, then just founded by T. S. Eliot's mother and forty other women, with the intention "to create and maintain an organized center of thought and action and, by united effort, to promote the usefulness of its members." They provided jobs for unemployed women; campaigned for cleaner streets, and tried to save girls from ignominy. At their biweekly meetings they treated such subjects as "The Lake Poets"; "What is Culture," and "The Dignity of Labor." On December 23, 1891, Kate Chopin read a paper to them on "Typical Forms of German Music." But the next year, when it became compulsory to belong to a specific study group, she gave up her membership.[51]

The club's work suited Charlotte Eliot, we are told, because of her Unitarian wish to improve the world and because she wanted to compensate for her thwarted poetic and scholastic ambitions by proving the value of women to society. But Mrs. Chopin was a somewhat different case. She did not much believe in idealism. Once meeting a woman who wanted to "make life purer, sweeter, better worth living," she commented: "It is well that such a spirit does not ever realize the futility of effort. A little grain of wisdom gained from the gospel of selfishness – what an invaluable lesson." [52] The concept of self-improvement was also rather foreign to her. When noting in "Confidences" that a woman had urged her to cultivate the "religious impulse" which she felt to be lacking in Mrs. Chopin's work, the author added: "My dear Madame Précieuse – I have discovered my limitations and I have saved myself much worry and torment by recognizing and accepting them as final. I can gain nothing by cultivating faculties that are not my own – I can reach nothing by running after it – but I find that many things come to me here in my corner." [53]

The author also disliked the pretentious aspects of the Wednesday Club. With light irony she observed that she had been afraid her ignorance would be detected by these serious "thinkers and disseminators of knowledge and propounders of questions." She had therefore escaped to her corner where no questions and no fine language could reach her and where she was slowly regaining her self-respect. [54]

But Kate Chopin did share Mrs. Eliot's literary ambition, and her frustration as well. On both of these points she was affected by the success of *Bayou Folk*. The local society journalists began to record the doings of both her and her children, stressing the fact that the famous writer was a St. Louisian. Though some jealous wives perhaps feared the attractive widow, she was frequently invited to the homes of socially important families who liked to court fame. [55]

The author was now faced with a dilemma. From early youth she had wished to keep away from gossipy, empty-headed, vain people, and her success had made her more impatient with them than ever. She had been reared with the Creole notion that publicity was a bad thing, particularly for a lady, and the general idea that a woman should be satisfied with her home. Furthermore, the aristocratic manners and the perfect etiquette she had inherited, which allowed her to keep distance, were foreign to some of the aggressive, "new" people around her. There were thus reasons enough for her inherent reticence to assert itself, and Rankin suggests (p. 141) that her success had no effect upon her life and that she was uninterested in publicity. But the letters and the diary we now have show how she, at the same time, was goaded on by her "commercial instinct," as she called it in her diary, and by her powerful literary ambition.

These various impulses resulted in a compromise. Kate Chopin did everything she could to further her local and national success, while retaining her womanly modesty and hiding her secret aspirations from everyone except Kolbenheyer. We therefore find her even giving readings to people she did not care for. "How immensely uninteresting some 'Society' people are!" she exclaimed in her diary after such a meeting. "That class which we know as Philistines. Their refined voices, and refined speech which says nothing – or worse, says something which offends me." When someone remarked that acting upon the stage could be done even by ladies and gentlemen, she commented: "It took quite an effort to withhold my wrath at such [a] statement. God A'mighty! Aren't there enough ladies & gentlemen sapping the vitality from our every day existence! are we going to have them casting their blight upon art."

What appealed to Mrs. Chopin was the unpretentious and the genuine, as we see, for example, from her description of two women she had met. "There is a straightforwardness, a dignity and gentle refinement about her manner that ... attracts. She draws me, somehow," she said about the one, and about the other: "[She is] a frank, wholesome woman, amiable and natural; ... with nothing of the *précieuse* offensiveness of manner to which I have become more sensitive than ever." She liked to look out of the window, she observed, because "there is a good deal of unadulterated human nature that passes along during the length of a day." (She added that she did not live in the most fashionable part of the city.) [56]

The author was paying a price for her compromise with her more reticent tendencies: "Things which bore me and which I formerly made an effort to endure, are unsupportable to me," she wrote. "My love and reverence for pure unadulterated nature is growing daily. Never in my life before has the Country had such poignant charm for me." When she wanted to escape people and the world, she went to the district around the Meramec River, south of St. Louis, and she was exultant about "the pure sensuous beauty of it, penetrating and moving as love!" [57] This was the place where she spent her summers, and it was here she wrote a diary entry dated July 24, 1894, which suggests what nature meant to her:

I am losing my interest in human beings; in the significance of their lives and actions. ... I want neither books nor men. They make me suffer. Is there one of them can talk to me like the night – the summer night? ... The night came slowly as I lay out there under the maple tree. ... My whole being was abandoned to the soothing and penetrating charm of the Night. – The katydids began their slumber song. ... How wise they are. They do not chatter like people. They only tell me: "sleep, sleep, sleep." ... It was a man's voice that broke the necromancer's spell. A man came to day with his "bible class." He is detestable with his red cheeks and bold eyes & coarse manner of speech. I hate people who teach lies. Can he tell ... me things of Christ? I would rather ask the stars: they have seen him.[58]

5. *1897: A Night in Acadie*

Such a wish to escape, coupled with what appears to be a desire to seek God in nature, was not uncommon with Kate Chopin. But most of the time she faced life actively, and if the success of *Bayou Folk* emphasized her tendency to withdraw at times, it even more encouraged her to expand. A number of the nearly forty stories she turned out between 1894 and 1897 – the year her second collection was published – reflect the new strength and the new insistence on expressing herself fully which were now released in her.

"The Story of an Hour," the first of these tales, was refused by the *Century,* probably because R. W. Gilder considered it unethical.[59] As editor of the most widely read magazine of its kind in English, he wielded an influence equal to that of Howells. He insisted that realism be softened by idealism and did not hesitate to turn down a book like Stephen Crane's *Maggie* or to temper even the writings of Mark Twain.[60] The self-assertive Mrs. Mallard must have seemed to him a hopeless case of callous egotism, but on two other occasions he indicated that he might accept Mrs. Chopin's women if she would tone them down. Eager to appear in the *Century,* she complied, first in 1891 with the heroine of "A No-Account Creole": "I have tried to convey the impression of sweetness and strength, keen sense of right, and physical charm beside," she told Gilder. And in 1897, after reworking a tale called "A Night in Acadie," she wrote: "I have made certain alterations which you thought the story required to give it artistic or ethical value. ... The marriage is omitted, and the girl's character softened and tempered by her rude experience." [61]

But even in this milder version the latter tale was unacceptable to Gilder. Zaïda, a girl who has an "overmastering and aggressive" will and who is used to deciding for others, is to wed André in secret, but he turns up drunk and she refuses him. When he tries to force her, she is defended by Telèsphore, whom she has met only that day, a man strong with his fist but so easily charmed by his belles that he has recently been on the point of proposing to several of them. The two Creoles fight over Zaïda like brute animals while she watches in her bridal gown, not lifting a finger to stop them from killing each other. In making the girl lose her will-power and meekly take orders from the victorious Telèsphore, Kate Chopin violates the logic of the story. In the original, Zaïda apparently made her defender marry her on the spot, and this final act of the strong heroine would have been much more in character.[62]

As far as we know, "Confidences" is the only further item which Mrs. Chopin changed at the suggestion of an editor. It was in September, 1896, that she was invited by Walter Hines Page to write an essay – apparently on herself – for the *Atlantic's* "Contributors' Club." She immediately wrote an article in which she had a friend putting questions to her. Page asked her instead to "set forth the matter directly," even though he appreciated, as he said with a suggestion of condescension, "the reason why [she] shrank from a direct 'confession'." That Kate Chopin did not stand in awe of even the highest-ranking editors is seen in something she added in the second version of "Confidences" (it was deleted in the third, which was the final one); here she answers someone who is clearly Page: "He appreciated what he supposed to be the underlying notion of my diffidence and intimated that he readily understood I might be ashamed of myself. In this he is mistaken. ... I am sometimes 'afraid o' myse'f' but never ashamed."[63]

In one of her *Criterion* essays she strikes back also at Gilder and his moral prudishness. She here describes how "a prominent New York editor" had returned one of her tales, which was promptly accepted by "a well-known Boston editor." "I am delighted with the story," she quoted the Bostonian as saying, "and so, I am sure, will be our readers." These were the words with which H. E. Scudder of the *Atlantic* accepted "Athénaïse," a forceful story that Gilder had refused, perhaps with a comment on its lack of ethical value.[64]

When Kate Chopin made the changes which Gilder in a few instances suggested in her stories, it was only to get them published in the prestigious *Century*. If she resented American literary limitations in general, she was particularly impatient with having to temper her own heroines. Woman's quest for self-fulfillment was a theme which had occupied her all along, and her new force is seen particularly in her heroines who live out their strong impulses. Some devote their lives to maternal and wifely cares, while many insist on freedom from traditional duties and limitations. Mme. Farival of "Lilacs" has affairs, it is intimated; Suzima of "A Vocation and a Voice" turns a boy into her lover, and Alberta of "Two Portraits" gives herself "when and where she chooses." [65] These tales demonstrate not only her new daring, but also the growing artistic mastery of an author who has learned to present her stories objectively. Nowhere does she impose herself upon the story, and when she occasionally lets her passionate heroines meet with some kind of check, she refrains from all moralizing.

Mrs. Chopin shows a similar discretion also in her non-fiction, where we find only a very few observations bearing on her own moral attitudes. Some days after writing "Lilacs," she visited a former schoolfriend whom she had not seen since she had become a nun. "I wonder what Liza thought as she looked into my face," she commented in her diary; and she continued:

I know she was remembering my pink cheeks of more than twenty years ago and my brown hair and innocent young face. I do not know whether she could see that I had loved – lovers who were not divine – and hated and suffered and been glad. She could see, no doubt, the stamp which a thousand things had left upon my face, but she could not read it. She, with her lover in the dark. He has not anointed her eyes for perfect vision. She does not need it – in the dark. – When we came away, my friend who had gone with me said: "Would you not give anything to have her vocation and happy life!" There was a long beaten path spreading before us ... [where] a little dog was trotting .... "I would rather be that dog," I answered her. I know she was disgusted and took it for irreverence and I did not take the trouble to explain that this was a little picture of life and that what we had left was a phantasmagoria.

A few days later, Kate Chopin added this observation in her diary: "There are a few good things in life – not many – but a few. A soft, firm, magnetic, sympathetic hand clasp is one. A walk through the quiet streets at midnight is another. And then, there are so many ways of saying good night!" She returned to the night, a central symbol with her, in "Vagabonds," a sketch told in the first person and obviously based on a conversation she had had with a vagabond while managing the Cloutierville store: "I called him names; but all the same I could not help thinking that it must be good to prowl sometimes; to get close to the black night and lose oneself in its silence and mystery and sin." (Mrs. Chopin tried vigorously to scratch out the last two words.) [66]

Kate Chopin was a puzzle to nearly everyone. She insisted on distance and privacy. It is typical that the personal documents she left behind consist only of the commonplace book, the 1894 diary, a page on Kitty Garesché, and a handful of letters. Even though she clearly thought it conceited to publish one's memoirs, as her comment on those of a former schoolfriend shows, it is remarkable that she was never to make literary use of her own childhood, for example, or to refer to her late husband outside of the diary entries quoted in the preceding pages. Though she could be outgoing and spirited, she was also very reticent and secretive, perhaps in part because she felt a need of hiding a passionate nature. The few personal documents we have – and it is unlikely that anything but a few additional letters may turn up later – give us no clear answers as to the author's personal life. (It might be added that Rankin heard nothing but "data beyond reproach" about the author.) What we can say, however, is that many of her prose writings, and some of her poems, such as the following "If Some Day," are full of the sensuous and the passionate: [67]

If some day I, with casual, wanton glance
Should for a moment's space thine eyes ensnare;
   Or more, if I should dare
To rest my finger tips upon thy sleeve,
Or, grown more bold, upon thy swarthy cheek;
   If further I should seek
With honey-trick of tone thy name to call
Breathing it soft, in meaning whisper low,
   Then wouldst thou know?

Is there no subtler sense, that holds not commerce
With the glancing eyes, the touch, the tone?
   Whereby alone
I would convey to thee some faintest gleam
Of what I dare not look, or speak, or dream!

This poem is closely related to one of Kate Chopin's two main poetic themes, that of the awakening of the senses in spring. That the speaker for the moment restrains an impulse to touch the companion's swarthy cheek only increases the sensuous ambiance of these lines, which is carried in such expressions as "casual, wanton glance" and "honey-trick of tone." The other common subject of Mrs. Chopin's poetry, the wish for a reunion with the lost lover, is found in many of her poems of this period. "Good Night" is a typical example:[68]

> Good night, good night!
> Good-by it shall not be;
> For all the days that come and go, dear love,
> 'Twixt now and happiness, 'twixt thee and me,
> Shall moments dark, oblivious prove.
>
> Until I look into thy tender eyes,
> And hear again thy voice, no light,
> No day will break, for me no sun will rise –
> My own, my well-beloved – good night, good night!

Even if some of the Kate Chopin diary entries we have quoted suggest that the speakers of these two poems have borrowed certain of the author's own traits, we cannot prove it.[69] We are on slightly safer ground if we want to see something of Mrs. Chopin in the heroine of the story "Madame Martel's Christmas Eve." Madame is a widow whose heart turns "savage and hungry within her for human companionship – for some expression of human love" when her children begin to slip out of her life, but who "at the same time [seems] to feel a reproach from her dear, dead husband that she had looked for consolation and hoped for comfort aside from his cherished memory. . . . How he and he alone had always understood her! It seemed as if he understood her now; as if he were with her now in spirit . . . ."[70]

This corresponds with the statement of a friend of Mrs. Chopin that one reason why she did not remarry was her feeling that she could not be as close with anyone as she had been with Oscar.[71] And Madame's wish to have the children almost locked up with her is echoed in the author's unusually warm description of her first meeting with Ruth McEnery Stuart: "I wanted to . . . set her down beside my sitting-room fire; to lock the door against receptions, luncheons, and the clamor of many voices. I would have had her sleep and rest

there for a week, for a month, for a year!" This was because she felt
that this visitor would "not inflict the penalty of speech upon sympathetic companionship"; even should she speak, her voice was like
"soothing ointment," and it was a voice of that Louisiana which to
her represented her years with Oscar.[72]

Although Kate Chopin's more and more passionate heroines hardly
were like ointment to the editors, most of her stories of this period
were accepted by the first magazine she sent them to; many by *Vogue*,
even though they considered her "daring in her choice of themes,"
and some by the *Century* and the *Atlantic*. But "Lilacs" and "A
Vocation and a Voice" were turned down by many editors before
they were finally published, and "Two Portraits" was refused by
everyone, including the *Yellow Book* and the *Chap-Book*. The author's eagerness to appear in the latter is seen in what she wrote to
Stone & Kimball, its publishers, who brought out such avant-garde
writers as Ibsen and Maeterlinck: "I would greatly like to see . . .
something – anything over my name in the *Chap-Book*."[73] But they
did not respond, and in 1895, they also returned "Young Dr. Gosse,"
her second novel.

That same year, Houghton Mifflin turned down the idea of a
volume of the "Mad Stories" by Maupassant which she was then
translating, and when Mrs. Chopin suggested a second collection of
her own Creole tales, they told her to bring the matter up later.
Instead, she offered *A Night in Acadie,* as it was called, to Stone &
Kimball, and eventually it was accepted by Way & Williams of Chicago. Later she sent Houghton Mifflin "A Vocation and a Voice,"
a group of her more recent stories, but early in 1897, H. E. Scudder
replied: "Have you never felt moved to write a downright novel? The
chance of success in such a case is much greater than with a collection
of short stories."[74] With Kate Chopin's desire for both artistic and
financial success, these words by Scudder may have contributed to
some small degree to the fact that she began *The Awakening* that
year.

While Mrs. Chopin was working on her novel, *A Night in Acadie*
was finally published in November, 1897. This collection is in many
ways a continuation of *Bayou Folk*, set in the same Louisiana localities
and reintroducing some of its characters. Published by a little-known
house, the book received less notice than its predecessor, and the
reviews, though still very favorable, also were a shade less enthusiastic

than before. The author's new openness about passion sets *A Night in Acadie* apart from the first collection, and it made the *Nation* complain that the book's sensuous atmosphere was a little too heavy, and the *Critic* – edited by R. W. Gilder's daughter – object to unnecessary "coarsenesses" in it. Reedy of the *Mirror* showed his discernment when he said that Mrs. Chopin's interest was "the same old human nature that is as old as mankind"; in general, however, the critics continued to see her solely as a Louisiana dialect writer.[75]

When these reviews began to appear, Kate Chopin was putting the last touches to *The Awakening*. She could now look back upon a highly productive decade: Since 1888, she had written three novels and nearly a hundred stories and sketches, besides essays, poems, and a one-act comedy. The author had never worked so energetically as she did on *The Awakening,* and no one could have guessed that this work was to be followed by very little more.

IV
Southern Setting, Global View

1. *The Louisiana Local Colorist*

About thirty of Kate Chopin's stories are set outside of Louisiana.
One of them takes us to France; a few others are so vague about the
locale that they could be set almost anywhere, while the rest seem to
be placed in St. Louis or vicinity. Of her Louisiana tales, some are
enacted in New Orleans or neighboring districts. Most of them, however, are set near the Red River, mainly in Natchitoches parish, which
Mrs. Chopin made her particular literary province.[1] All of the stories
she published in the *Century* and the *Atlantic* and in her two collections have an unmistakable flavor of the picturesque and in many
respects unique state which had been her home for nearly fifteen
years. It is not surprising, therefore, that she was taken for a Louisiana
local colorist and compared with Cable and Hearn, Grace King and
Ruth McEnery Stuart, with whom she shared the honor of introducing this state into English-language American fiction.

Though already past its prime, local color literature was still much
in evidence during the nineties, and Kate Chopin's work has many
characteristics in common with it. Like the authors of this school, she
concentrated on the characters of a very definite part of the country,
painting them in their physical and social setting. Though only lightly
suggested in her writings, the enchanting southern atmosphere creeps
into our senses, and though discreetly represented, the peculiarities of
the Creoles, Cajuns, and Negroes are clearly evoked. The musical and
mimic gifts of this acute observer helped her to give an entirely correct
rendering of the dialects of these groups, and the close contacts she
had had with the high and low of her region, as society woman or
shopkeeper, enabled her to portray intimately their lives and their
idiosyncrasies.

As presented in Mrs. Chopin's stories, the Louisiana Creole is
proud, graceful, and aristocratic, hot-blooded and irrational in matters

of love and honor; the Cajun simple, honest, and God-fearing (the priest's word was law in this Catholic, remote area, where we even today find Cajuns clinging to their old-fashioned French language), and the Negro superstitious, yet realistic, and lively – Kate Chopin once spoke of "that child-like exuberance which is so pronounced a feature of negro character." Common to them all is an unambitious, complacent acceptance of conditions as they find them, and a devotion to a hedonist enjoyment of life in the here and now. Creole, Cajun, and Negro alike have the talent for turning a gathering into a high-spirited, joyous affair, as we see in such stories as "Madame Martel's Christmas Eve" and "At the 'Cadian Ball."[2]

The latter tale is set somewhere along the railroad connecting New Orleans and Alexandria. The first person we meet is Bobinôt, a "big, brown, good-natured" Cajun plowing his rows of cane. He is typical of the region, and Friedheimer, the store-owner, is the only Yankee mentioned in what apparently is a homogeneous Latin country. Grosboeuf, who has given his Cajun balls for years, recalls how the Americans who built the railroad once caused the only disturbance of his parties because they "were not in touch with their surroundings." When he speaks of them as "ces maudits gens du raiderode," it shows how particularly the older Cajuns prefer not to speak English and how, at the same time, their ancient French relies on America rather than France for modern concepts. They still give their daughters such old-fashioned Gallic names as Fronie and Ozéina, however, and basically they are still the French peasants their ancestors were when they left the old country.[3]

The gap between the Cajuns and the upper-class Creoles is seen in the reaction of Clarisse, the cousin of the planter Alcée Laballière, when she learns that he has gone to Grosboeuf's party: "The 'Cadian ball,' she repeated contemptuously. 'Humph! *Par exemple!* Nice conduc' for a Laballière'." With her perfect manners and her more correct and modern French, she feels superior to the unsophisticated Cajuns. (When excited, she speaks French also to Bruce, her Negro informant, though he seems to speak only English.) Alcée has a special intention in leaving. Clarisse has rejected his advances, and a cyclone has ruined his nine hundred acres of rice. In desperation he has decided to run off with Calixta, a "Spanish vixen." Swallowing her pride, Clarisse goes to Grosboeuf's, lures Alcée away from the girl in the nick of time, and declares her love for him. (When assuming this masculine role, she properly hides her face in her arms.) Acknowledging defeat, Calixta tells Bobinôt, who is her submissive suitor, that she is now willing to marry him.[4]

This is an example of Kate Chopin's stories of young love and courtship, which make up a considerable part of her Louisiana writings. Others turn to problems arising after the lovers have married. A few of her tales deal with touchy racial questions. Occasionally there is a faint echo of the Civil War, and "The Locket" takes us to the battlefield itself. (When the *Youth's Companion* refused this story, it was perhaps because she suggested that "big black birds" prey like vultures on the dead bodies.) [5]

A number of her tales describe acts of kindness and devotion. Gilma Germain of "Dead Men's Shoes," for instance, gives away the farm he has inherited to those he feels have a better right to it, and the hero of "Cavanelle" devotes his life to helping needy relatives. In other stories, Mrs. Chopin enters into the minds of children. In "Croque-Mitaine," for example, she makes us identify ourselves with P'tit-Paul's sly smile when he finds out the real nature of the hideous ogre which will devour him if he does not obey his governess; stealing out of the house when she has gone to a masquerade, he discovers the monster on the road taking off its awful horns and wiping its face, and now he knows that "Croque Mitaine is only Monsieur Alcée going to a masked ball!" [6]

P'tit-Paul's family is able to have a governess come all the way from Paris, and most of Kate Chopin's Creoles are relatively well off. But there are also others who have been impoverished by the war. St. Ange Delmandé of "A Wizard from Gettysburg" is one example, and Placide Santien of "A No-Account Creole" another. While the former is saved in true *Youth's Companion* style through the finding of a hidden treasure, the latter has long ago had to hand over his Red River plantation to the Yankee creditors. "The war did its work, of course," as the author tells us. At the same time it is clear that the fate of the Santien property is partly a result of the family's pride and lack of energy. Having "the best blood in the country running in his veins," Placide can refuse to apply his skills (hence the title) and still be somebody.[7]

The encounter between Santien and the creditor is one of the author's comparatively rare juxtapositions of Creoles and Yankees. Another is staged in *At Fault,* in which a few St. Louisians are visiting

Natchitoches. One of them is surprised by the Latin, unashamed show of tenderness she finds there; a second Yankee, a boisterous woman, becomes "subdued and altogether unnatural" when exposed to refined Creole manners, and a third bewilders Mme. Duplan, a planter's wife, with his wish to discuss the Negro race, a theme she considers unfit for polite conversation.[8]

Like the Santiens and the Laballières, the Duplans appear in many stories. The Cajun Sylveste Bordon of "A Rude Awakening" plows Joe Duplan's fields and drives his cotton to the landing – that is, *when* he works, for, in the words of his underfed and poorly clad daughter, he is "de lazies' man in Natchitoches pa'ish." Evariste Bonamour of "A Gentleman of Bayou Têche" is an equally impoverished Cajun. He is illiterate and simple-minded, and his "homely cabin of two rooms [is] not quite so comfortable as Mr. Hallet's Negro quarters." In consequence, the Negroes look down upon him. Aunt Dicey scorns him for allowing the artist who is visiting with the Hallets to draw a picture of him in his shabby working clothes and call it "one dem low-down 'Cajuns." When Sylveste saves the artist's son from drowning and is offered breakfast with the Hallets, Aunt Dicey's son serves him "with visible reluctance and ill-disguised contempt."[9]

Yet Sylveste has something of the true gentleman in his dignity and lack of affectation. He sits down to table in "perfect simplicity," and he refuses to be called a hero: "I ent goin' to 'low dat, me," he says in his Cajun English. There is slight irony involved when he is allowed to pose in his best clothes and to choose the title of the picture. But Mrs. Chopin rarely ridicules her characters, and she makes us feel that the Cajun, for all his poverty and touchiness, deserves the title he chooses: "Dis is one picture of Mista Evariste Anatole Bonamour, a gent'man of de Bayou Têche."[10]

There is hardly a Kate Chopin story without a Negro. Often she depicts him with what a critic as late as 1924 saw as the characteristic traits of the colored man: his "irrepressible spirits, his complete absorption in the present moment, his whimsicality, his irresponsibility, his intense superstition, his freedom from resentment." Superstition, for example, is illustrated in Aunt Siney of "Polydore," who insists that a painful leg should be "wrop . . . up in bacon fat, de oniest way to draw out de misery," and in Tante Cat'rinette of the story of that name, who believes that the morning star communicates her dead master's order to her to care for his daughter.[11]

Fidelity to his former owner is another trait attributed to the freedman. Thomas Nelson Page and others even depicted him as yearning for the good antebellum days. Kate Chopin never went that far, but she did write a number of tales about Negro loyalty. "The Bênitous' Slave" and "For Marse Chouchoute" are examples. (That devotion also could go the other way is seen, for instance, in "Odalie Misses Mass.") Chouchoute is a happy-go-lucky Creole who forgets his duty to take the Cloutierville mail to the train, and the story tells how a Negro boy devoted to him is fatally wounded while attempting to perform the duty for him. Even in his last moments, the boy thinks of his idol: "who – gwine – watch – Marse – Chouchoute?" [12]

With Kate Chopin's background, it was probably inevitable that she should write about the faithful Negro. But while she occasionally falls into the sentimental or melodramatic when idealizing him, she often manages to break the regular pattern of the southern stereotypes. Aglaé Boisduré in "Nég Créol," for example, the last survivor of the family which once owned Nég, has nothing of the traditional glamor of southern womanhood, but is a haggard old lady who gives him nothing but complaints in return for his devotion. He is true to type in that he secretly keeps her alive and openly boasts about her distinguished family. But there is a nice turn at the end. When she is given a pauper's funeral, he pretends not to know her; by insisting that she belonged not to the prominent branch of the Boisdurés, but to a less illustrious part of the clan, he hopes to save her family honor and his own pride in it. There is an equally fine twist in "A Dresden Lady in Dixie." A piece of china is missing at the planter's, and to shield a Cajun girl, the old Negro Pa-Jeff invents a story of how he had taken it, telling so often how "Satan an' de Sperrit" had warred within him that he ends up believing the tale himself. [13]

That some of Kate Chopin's Negroes are stereotypes is hardly surprising. What is remarkable, meanwhile, is that she accepted the colored people as persons worthy of serious study, and that she in her writings treats them as people and with little condescension. She obviously could not see the whole Negro. For instance, she shows little resentment in him against the whites. (When Joçint in *At Fault* sets fire to a sawmill – her one example of evil in the non-whites – it is an act of vengeance against the modern machines rather than their owners.) Her picture of the Negro is thus somewhat limited. But it is truthful as far as it goes, and she often succeeds in making him into a full, convincing human being. She endows him with a basic vitality which includes not only such traditional qualities as irresponsibility and a blind fidelity, but also a sound skepticism and a sense of reality, qualities then more attributed to, say, the French, than to the Negroes.

Aunt Minty of "A Rude Awakening," for example, is kind as in the stereotype – she has come to look after Sylveste's sick child, bringing a chicken she has stolen from the Duplans; but in addition, she is cunning. She cleverly hedges questions about the origin of the chicken, and she tells Sylveste to his face what she thinks of his laziness, attributing her indictment to his daughter. Pierson of *At Fault* is true to life when he sneaks away as Grégoire Santien forces a store-owner to serve drinks to black and white at the same counter; he knows that if Negroes take part in this integration, the shopkeeper will "make it hot fu' 'em art'ards." La Folle of "Beyond the Bayou" might easily have been a stereotype with her devotion to the offspring of her former master, but the picture of her becomes an interesting psychological study when we see how circumstances relieve her of her life-long phobia of crossing the bayou to the world beyond.[14]

If we compare the fictional world of *Bayou Folk* and *A Night in Acadie* with that found in other important contemporary collections of Louisiana stories, we find certain differences in subject matter. In *Old Creole Days* (1879), Cable is dealing with the period before and after the Louisiana Purchase, concentrating on the Creoles and the quadroons of New Orleans. In *Tales of Time and Place* (1892) and *Balcony Stories* (1893), Grace King turns largely to old Creole women of New Orleans reminiscing about events of the war and Reconstruction periods. In *A Golden Wedding and Other Tales* (1893) and *Carlotta's Intended and Other Tales* (1894), Ruth McEnery Stuart deals in part with New Orleans, but mostly with rural Louisiana, and her typical story is about the courtship of contemporary plantation Negroes. Kate Chopin's range, meanwhile, is quite wide compared to these authors; she covers many parts of the state, and she deals fully with both the Negro, the Cajun, and the Creole.

These four writers were all classified as local colorists. Two characteristics usually attributed to this school do not apply to Kate Chopin: She was not interested in a dying civilization, and she had no wish to rescue the past. Sarah Orne Jewett, for example, was concerned about the disintegration of the values which she located in *The Country of the Pointed Firs,* the human qualities which could still be seen in its old inhabitants, but which were disappearing as modern ideas came in and the young people left for the cities. Her rural culture is declining, and her characters are survivors. Cable, on his part, used his short stories and *The Grandissimes* to dramatize the conflict between the French and the Yankee civilizations, showing the Creoles' resistance to change and their inevitable retreat in front of the growing pressure from *les Américains.* Mrs. Stuart also devoted a number of her New Orleans stories to the conflict between its different national groups, realizing, as she said, that its "heterogeneous population . . . made [the] most vivid appeal." [15]

Mrs. Chopin's Natchitoches, meanwhile, is a homogeneous cultural entity which is still nearly untouched by Yankee influence. The problem of a dying civilization is therefore not to be found here. As already noted, Kate Chopin's juxtapositions of Americans and French-descendants are rare, even in her New Orleans tales, and only in "A Matter of Prejudice" does she center on the conflict between the two cultures. It is the story of an old Creole widow of the Vieux Carré who has refused to see her son after he married a Yankee and settled in the American district, but whose prejudices against everything not French break down somewhat when she meets the son's child. Instead of fighting the new, this old *Française* now decides to learn English.

Kate Chopin was devoted to her Louisiana, and there is undoubtedly a *recherche du temps perdu* in her work, as Cyrille Arnavon has suggested. But unlike Cable and Grace King, for example, she had not spent her youth in that state, which may be one reason why she was not interested in its history as they were. Cable saw Louisiana's past as "a rich and profitable mine" of literary ores which it would be a pity to let go to waste, and therefore he proudly set out to rescue it. He developed into a veritable historian of the state, digging into old records and publishing *Strange True Stories of Louisiana.* Miss King, likewise, brought out a *History of Louisiana.* Lafcadio Hearn, on his part, used an 1856 Gulf Coast occurrence as the basis for *Chita: A Memory of Last Island* (1889), his most significant contribution to Louisiana fiction. Kate Chopin, on the other hand, had no desire to rescue the past or to use factual material. Only five of her stories seem to be non-contemporary. Of these, one is set in old Kaskaskia (later part of Illinois), and two each in antebellum and wartime Louisiana.[16]

Mrs. Chopin no doubt commanded a wealth of historical material, and her newspaper friends urged her to take advantage of the vogue of historical fiction in the nineties. She participated in a number of prize contests with her writings, hoping to win fame and money; and had she been interested in history, she might have made good use of what she had at her disposal. But we know that, for example, a "proposal to undertake a fictional account of the Spanish regime" in her territory "did not progress beyond the starting point." Only in "The Maid of Saint Phillippe," the Kaskaskia story, did she turn to an historic event, and the result was disastrous.[17]

For once she had here decided to "take pains," as she humorously describes it in an essay, and plot a tale set in the eighteenth century, even though she said she knew little about that era and had only what she calls "a feeble imagination." Determined to avoid inaccuracy, she read up on history. "For the first time in my life I took notes, – copious notes, – and carried them bulging in my jacket pocket, until I felt as if I were wearing Zola's coat." She lavished the same care on the writing of the story, she tells us, picking the words with an eye to color and artistic effect. When her notebook indicates that the actual composition of the tale was done in one day, it strongly suggests that she exaggerated the work which went into it, something which already her tone makes us suspect. What is certain is that the story shows a lack of artistic verve which is not characteristic of Kate Chopin, and we may well believe that the writing of it left the author "very, very weary."[18]

Historical fiction was thus clearly not her forte. She seems to have sensed this already when she wrote *At Fault*. We find, at least, that though she probably believed the traditional relationship between Robert McAlpin and Simon Legree to be of interest to readers, she makes little use of it in this novel which she set on the former McAlpin (here called McFarlane) plantation. Her art was not retrospective, and she was no antiquarian. What counted to her was the moment. Leaving the use of the past to such writers as Cable and Thomas Nelson Page and the reminiscent old women to Sarah Orne Jewett and Grace King, she concentrated on people living in the present, and particularly on the young.[19]

There are other respects, however, in which Mrs. Chopin does belong among the local colorists. Like them, she often had the plot of the small, pathetic event and the character of silent heroism, and

she generally used the media typical of these writers, that is, the brief
tale and the sketch, where their stress on setting and local customs
could more successfully dominate than in the longer forms of fiction.
But unlike a number of these authors, she never emphasized background and manners for their own sake. True, she praised Joel
Chandler Harris for his outstanding "power to depict character in its
outward manifestations." She loved his oldtime Georgia people with
their "plain and simple lives" and their quaint characteristics, just as
she loved the idiosyncrasies of the Louisianians as she knew them;
but in her own work, she never stressed the picturesque and exotic
or tried to create the illusion of a different world.[20]

Though the local color of Kate Chopin's Louisiana stories is unmistakable, they could be set almost anywhere. Her interest was universal human character rather than the local *per se,* and it is significant that she refused to be considered a local colorist and resented being
compared as such to Cable and Grace King.[21] That her vision went
far beyond the regional or topical can be clearly seen in her very first
piece of critical writing.

2. *Kate Chopin's Literary Criticism*

When the *Atlantic's* reviewer in 1894 saw Mrs. Chopin as something more than a local colorist and sensed in her latent powers, he
was more perspicacious than he knew. She did indeed have not only
the ambition, but also the faculty to go beyond regionalism, and it
is ironic that it was the success of the "dialect stories" of *Bayou Folk*
which encouraged her to start unfolding her powers in earnest.

One of the first results was a diary entry in June, 1894, written
after she had attended a conference in Indiana of the Western Association of Writers, an organization formed to "encourage . . . the
development of a true and healthy American literature." Only James
Whitcomb Riley and a few others of this largely Hoosier group
deserved to be called writers, one member has observed. (With his
sunny idealism, Riley was then one of the most popular poets in
America.)[22] Kate Chopin described them as earnest lovers of book-
learning and enthusiastic writers of idyllic, sentimental songs which
showed a "singular ignorance of, or disregard for, the value of the
highest art forms." Conventionality and provincialism sheltered them
from the world's new ideas, she said, and she added:[23]

[In their] garden of Eden . . . the disturbing fruit of the tree of knowledge still hangs unplucked. The cry of the dying century has not reached this body of workers, or else it has not been comprehended. There is no doubt in their souls, no unrest: apparently an abiding faith in God as he manifests himself through the sectional church. . . .

There is a very, very big world lying not wholly in northern Indiana, nor does it lie at the antipodes, either. It is human existence in its subtle, complex, true meaning, stripped of the veil with which ethical and conventional standards have draped it. When the Western Association of Writers . . . shall have developed into students of true life and true art, who knows but they may produce a genius such as America has not yet known.

This statement, which practically predicts the emergence of Theodore Dreiser, was highly resented by the members when it was published in the *Critic,* and Rankin dismisses it as "unfortunate." Its importance to the student of Kate Chopin cannot be overestimated, however, as it gives the quintessence of her views of life and literature.[24]

Basically, her attitudes had been formed already by Mme. Charleville, who had taught her to accept life fearlessly, to look beyond the mask of morality and try to understand rather than to judge. Her study of science ("Emancipation" suggests that she was familiar with Darwin as early as 1869) had confirmed her in her belief of the relativity of morals. Finally, Maupassant had demonstrated an approach to the short story which, both technically and morally, was unbound by tradition and authority.

When the thirty-eight-year-old Mrs. Chopin turned to writing in earnest in 1889, she was a very mature person. The attitudes which she formulated in the *Critic* in 1894 and elaborated in her diary and in further essays, were no doubt practically identical with those she had held as a beginning author. Certainly, the ideas reflected in her fiction are remarkably consistent throughout.

The major point in Kate Chopin's *Critic* article is one which she had already spelled out in *At Fault.* Here she lets one of the characters declare that "it's impossible to ever come to a true knowledge of life as it is – which should be every one's aim – without studying certain fundamental truths" of "Natural History." That this is the author speaking is clear from two observations she made, one objecting to "the hysterical, morbid, and false pictures of life which certain English women have brought into vogue," and another asserting that "a well-directed course of scientific study might help to make clearer [the] vision" of these unnamed women authors, or at least "bring them a little closer to Nature."[25] She had herself dared to eat from the tree of knowledge and to see the human being as a higher animal. In a world governed by "natural selection," nature was amoral, playing with man; moral purpose was "an article of exclusive human manufacture," as Thomas Huxley expressed it.[26]

The new view of man was probably less of a shock to Kate Chopin than it was to many of her contemporaries. However, when she accepted him as he appeared in the works of Darwin, Huxley, and Spencer, she did not quite escape the agony of a generation robbed of its former truths and certainties. She was shaken in her belief in God, and she apparently stopped wearing the cross which we see in photographs of her from 1869 and 1875. Yet she did not become an atheist. Her line from 1890: "O Love, O God, O Night come back to me!" was followed in 1898 by this couplet: "I wanted God. In heaven and earth I sought,/And lo! I found him in my inmost thought."[27] She also continued to believe in eternal life. But she now questioned the right of the clergy and of the sectarian Church to speak on behalf of God, and her answer to the "Madame Précieuse," who had found her writings to be without a religious impulse, suggests that she did not necessarily share Huxley's idea that a religious feeling was essential as a basis of conduct.[28]

She seems to have taken a middle position between the optimists and the pessimists among the Darwinians. She accepted neither Spencer's belief in progress and an advancing scale of altruism, nor Huxley's idea that evolution might involve retrogression; to her, man was basically the same now as when first encountered in history. Nor did she share the pessimism of the socio-economic and biological determinists who saw man as a helpless entity, more or less unable to assert a will of his own. Her poem "Because" indicates that she ascribed to the human being at least a modicum of free will and ethical responsibility:[29]

> Because they must, the birds sing.
> The earth turns new in Spring
> Because it must – 'Tis only man
> That does because he can

> And knowing good from ill,
> Chooses because he will –

With her deep interest in the human species, Kate Chopin followed very closely the newest developments in science and in fiction. Her library is long since lost, and she and her friends left few records as to what specific modern authors she had read. Even when we draw upon all that has come down to us bearing on her reading, only two authors can be added to those mentioned elsewhere in this book: Maeterlinck and Whitman. (She never commented on them, but Rankin was told in St. Louis that she liked the Belgian, and we know from Sue V. Moore that she always kept the American's writings at hand.) Thus we cannot prove that she had read, say, Flaubert and Tolstoy. All indications are, however, that she was very well acquainted with the classics and that she familiarized herself with all important new books as they appeared.[30]

If we turn to science, for example, it would seem that she read the works of such a psychologist as the Frenchman Gustave Le Bon the moment they were published. She kept up with a wide range of periodicals. Once she mentioned as particularly worth knowing those coming from the land "where 'the modern' holds sway" (obviously France), and she felt "a little blown and dizzy from the unaccustomed pace, but, on the whole, invigorated," she said, by these advanced magazines.[31]

At the same time, however, she did not see modernism as a guarantee of true art. The author "undervalues the importance of the past in art and exaggerates the significance of the present," she wrote in a review of Garland's *Crumbling Idols.* The young iconoclast had said that the old literary masters meant little to him and declared that "to the veritist, ... the past is dead." What he wanted was "actualities" and local color. He admired Ibsen because he was "a reformer" and particularly praised *An Enemy of the People* because it dealt with a "sociological" theme rather than love. Kate Chopin commented:[32]

Human impulses do not change and can not so long as men and women continue to stand in the relation to one another which they have occupied since our knowledge of their existence began. It is why Aeschylus is true, and Shakespeare is true to-day, and why Ibsen will not be true in some remote to-morrow, however forcible and representative he may be for the hour, because he takes for his themes social problems which by their very nature are mutable. And, notwithstanding Mr. Garland's opinion to the contrary, social problems, social environments, local color and the rest of it are not *of themselves* motives to insure the survival of a writer who employs them.

Exemplifying what she missed in the book, Mrs. Chopin turned to some of man's most immutable drives: "The author of *Crumbling Idols* would even lightly dismiss from the artist's consideration such primitive passions as love, hate, etc.," she wrote. "He declares that in real life people do not talk love. How does he know? I feel very sorry for Mr. Garland. ... He somehow gives the impression of a man who has not yet 'lived'." She also disagreed with his opinion that Chicago had reached the status of a literary center and regretted his abuse of the eastern publishers; it was they, she said, who had brought to light "whatever there [had] been produced of force and originality in the West and South since the war." Nevertheless she recommended Garland's book, calling him a sincere, vigorous, and representative western man of letters.[33]

The next Kate Chopin review was of Zola's *Lourdes*. She opened by saying that she had a certain belief in the sincerity of the Frenchman's work, but added: "I am yet not at all times ready to admit its truth, which is only equivalent to saying that our points of view differ, that truth rests upon a shifting basis and is apt to be kaleidoscopic." She praised Zola's style, but called the book ineffective and a "mistake" as its story was "more than two-thirds of the time swamped beneath a mass of prosaic data, offensive and nauseous description and rampant sentimentality." And she added: "Not for an instant ... do we lose sight of the author and his note-book and of the disagreeable fact that his design is to instruct us." She termed it "unpardonable" for Zola to make it so clear that a character who reveals certain clerical abuses is the author speaking.[34]

She added that she failed to see why the Church had banned the novel: "It is a book which I think a good Catholic would greatly enjoy reading, the only and easy condition being to set aside Mons. Zola's point of view and color his facts with one's own." Whatever suggestion there might be here of Mrs. Chopin's supporting orthodoxy is refuted in her next remark where she declared that she could not understand why the author should aspire to a seat in the Academy instead of being proud to stay out of it.[35]

While Kate Chopin praised Zola as "the great French realist" and called him "colossal in his bigness," she also complained that he took life "too clumsily and seriously." This was the fault she found even with Ibsen and Hardy.[36] In a review of *Jude the Obscure,* she objected to its total lack of humor and the everpresent gloom. Hardy's pessimism was displeasing to her, and also the social problems and the "derision and disaster [connected with the] . . . deadly war waged between flesh and spirit," which it was Hardy's professed aim to describe in *Jude.* Leaving this aside, she turned to what irked her most: "The characters are so plainly constructed with the intention of illustrating the purposes of the author, that they do not for a moment convey any impression of reality. . . . The book is detestably bad; it is unpardonably dull; and immoral, chiefly because it is not true."[37]

But at the same time, the fact that *Jude* had been withdrawn from circulation at the St. Louis libraries was inexplicable to Mrs. Chopin as there was nothing "seductive" in it. She was against censorship in general, and she observed that, in the case of children, it meant "robbing youth of its privilege to gather wisdom as the bee gathers honey." But young and old should be spared propaganda, she felt, in life as well as in literature. Speaking of Mrs. Humphry Ward, she said that unless an author was a genius like Dickens, it was inexcusable for him to be a reformer. As for herself, she declared that she "would not be guilty of advising any one to do anything."[38]

This open-mindedness was evident also in Kate Chopin the reader, who tried, as she expressed it, to set aside all prejudice, to distrust her own point of view, and to project herself into the atmosphere of the subject. (She showed the same openness when reading a manuscript thrust upon her: "I never pick up such a MS but with the hope that I am about to fall upon a hidden talent," she noted.) She regretted that critics so seldom made such an effort, and that they, for example, heaped senseless abuse on the disagreeable characters in Mary E. Wilkins Freeman's *Pembroke* instead of trying to understand the spirit of the work.[39]

How highly Mrs. Chopin valued an unbiased openness is seen also in what she wrote on Ruth McEnery Stuart. After praising her novelette "Carlotta's Intended" in which she found the character and dialect of its protagonists "singularly true to nature," and Mrs. Stuart's "lovable" stories in general with their demonstration of the author's fund of humor, her "wholesome, human note," and her sympathy and insight, she added: "I fancy there are no sharp edges to this woman's soul, no unsheathed prejudices dwelling therein wherewith to inflict wound . . . upon her fellow-man or woman. Mrs. Stuart, in fact, is a delightful womanly woman."[40]

One of the qualities she praised in this author turns up also in a diary entry on C. L. Deyo. She seems to pity him because he reached out to nature not directly, but only through Plato, and to declare "spontaneous insight, however circumscribed," to be of greater value than his purely intellectual outlook. As for herself, nature spoke directly to her. After reading the first instalment of James Lane Allen's *A Kentucky Cardinal,* she noted: "What a refreshing idealistic bit it is, coming to us with the budding leaves and the bird-notes that fill the air." The story is about Adam Moss, a nature-lover who observes: "In May I am of the earth earthy. ... Nature uses beauty now not to uplift, but to entice," that is, to ensure procreation.[41]

What struck Kate Chopin as idealistic in Allen's novel was probably its description of a man living in close contact with the timeless, ever-renewing urges in nature. She resented literary bans on the sensuous, and the reason why Whitman was a favorite of hers was very likely that he was occupied with Eros and that he had helped to extend the country's literary tolerance. It is significant that when William Schuyler in 1894 reported that she leaned decidedly to the French school and read Daudet, and particularly Maupassant, with pleasure, he added that she saw American writers as handicapped because "limitations imposed upon their art by their environment hamper a full and spontaneous expression."[42]

The picture we get of Kate Chopin from these essays, diary entries, and sundry remarks is that of an unusually well-read and very intelligent critic whose moderation and balance cannot hide her sharply defined profile.

In her view, true art presupposes an understanding of true life, which again cannot be attained unless we accept that man and nature form a continuum. A dog can better represent life than can a nun, because man is forever ruled by the same elementary forces which have always urged him on. To Mrs. Chopin, it is only a sense of these basic, eternal drives rather than of sectional problems and local characteristics that can give literature lasting value, and authors should be allowed to write freely on them.

3. Acceptance of the Whole of Man

What Kate Chopin wanted was nothing less than to describe post-Darwinian man with the openness of the modern French writers. She could not compete with them in experience. For example, it would have been hard for her as a woman to study the city slums closely with their depravity and fierce battles for survival. Nevertheless, she had seen a good deal of life, and what she saw she faced unflinchingly. For instance, though she was "wholly unable to comprehend, much less explain [Juanita's strange] attraction to men" – Juanita was an odd-looking female of Mrs. Chopin's neighborhood, whose appeal the author said Zola might have understood – she nevertheless proceeded to write about her.[43]

She accepted the whole of man and made no attempt to gloss over his less attractive sides. But she was still the same lover of "brightness and gaiety and life and sunshine" that she had been in 1869, and though she was well aware of evil, she was unwilling, and indeed constitutionally unable, to take the gloomy view of life which characterized the naturalists. She did not want to concentrate on the base and the sick, as Zola often did. She was closer to Daudet, the self-styled "marchand de bonheur," who looked at least as much for goodness and happiness as for misery.[44]

While Kate Chopin joined the naturalists in treating human foibles amorally, she wanted nothing of their experimental method of giving documented case-histories which attempted to demonstrate scientific laws and to arrive at conclusions, sometimes in the hope of improving man and the world. Though she had nothing against, for example, Goethe's Charlotte cutting bread, she could not, as Zola did, fill notebooks with prosaic data on a slice of life and turn it into a novel. A friend spoke of Mrs. Chopin's "sense that preaching is not the province of fiction," and she felt true art to be incompatible with a thesis.[45]

When Kate Chopin accepted Spencer's political laissez-faire, the reason was not that she shared his belief in progress, but, on the contrary, that she saw man and society as forever ruled by the gospel of selfishness which makes basic improvement impossible. She had seen the modest effects of the *Post-Dispatch's* crusades against corruption, and her remarks about herself show that she did not much believe in personal improvement either. To her it was somewhat presumptuous to proclaim, as Charlotte Eliot did before the Wednesday Club, that "wrongs demand redress" and that with "high ideals" one could "achieve the right."[46]

Mrs. Chopin felt very strongly on this point. She was highly irritated with the facile idealism displayed in so much contemporary fiction. She may even have objected to such serious works as Henry James' *The Portrait of a Lady* and Howells' *A Modern Instance* with their weight on the ennobling aspect of fulfilling marital responsibilities. She may also have disliked *L'Assomoir*, Zola's book on alcoholism, with its professed "morale en action." Her irritation with moral reformers was so strong that she had to get it out of her system before she could turn to what really interested her. The result was *At Fault*, one of the first American novels to deal with divorce.[47]

Thérèse Lafirme, the Creole widow who runs the former McAlpin plantation, loves and is loved by David Hosmer, a St. Louis businessman, who operates a sawmill on her property.[48] When she learns that he is divorced, she shrinks from a union that would have roused a storm of indignation in her Catholic community. He tells her that he married his Fanny after the briefest courtship and afterwards came to realize that they had nothing in common; that he left her upon finding out that she drank; and that he doubled the alimony she had asked for when she sued for divorce. But Thérèse regards it as a cowardly and egotistic act of David's to leave Fanny without moral support and fail to face the consequences of his actions. She tells him that they must both renounce their happiness so that he can "do what is right," which is to redeem his ex-wife. For the sake of his love for Thérèse, he does her bidding, which includes not only remarrying the divorcee, but also bringing her with him to live on the plantation.[49]

When David takes Fanny for the second time to their Unitarian minister, his friend Homeyer rails at "the submission of a human destiny to the exacting and ignorant rule of . . . moral conventionalities." It would be better, he says, to "let the individual man hold on to his personality." As Thérèse sees how both she and David suffer and how Fanny falls back into drinking, she begins to question her right to interfere with other people's lives and to doubt whether "Fanny and her own prejudices" were worth the sacrifices which she and Hosmer had made, when "the good things of life . . . are always at hand."[50]

The central drama is enacted against the background of several other relationships. One which is given much space is the old-fashioned romance between Grégoire Santien, Thérèse's nephew, and Melicent, David's sister. In spite of this love-story, the book is basically anti-romantic. Grégoire may be a sentimental figure in his almost abject adoration of Melicent, but he is also shown as the brutal murderer of the man responsible for the burning down of the sawmill. The Creole is proud of his deed, and no action is taken against him. The characterizations of Fanny's St. Louis friends are also anti-romantic. Little love is lost between the professional time-killer Belle Worthington and her bookish husband. Mr. and Mrs. Dawson seem better matched, until he detects her carrying on with another man whom he then shoots. There is little idealization of plantation life in the novel, and Aunt Belindy, Thérèse's Negro cook, represents reality when she cannot understand that Lucilla Worthington's intention to become a nun and not live in this world precludes her having a beau: "whar you gwine live ef you don' live in de worl'?" [51]

Aunt Belindy here speaks for the author, and David does the same at the end of the book. After Fanny's accidental drowning, the lovers formulate their new wisdom: "I have seen myself at fault in following what seemed the only right," Thérèse tells her future husband. "I feel as if there were no way to turn for the truth. Old supports appear to be giving way beneath me. They were so secure before." And David answers: "The truth in its entirety isn't given to man to know – such knowledge, no doubt, would be beyond human endurance. But we make a step towards it, when we learn that there is rottenness and evil in the world, masquerading as right and morality – when we learn to know the living spirit from the dead letter." [52]

While Kate Chopin's apprentice novel is undistinguished in its technique and lacks the depth and the seriousness of the works by Zola, James, and Howells, it is remarkable in that it refrains from all moralizing. Unlike *L'Assomoir*, it does not linger pointedly on the evils of alcoholism, but only hints at its effects, suggesting that circumstances may defeat even the best of intentions to keep a person from a relapse. Unlike *The Portrait of a Lady, At Fault* does not suggest that the protagonist gains in moral stature by fulfilling his duties toward his spouse. Though a certain ethical will power is seen in David's behavior toward Fanny, it cannot prevent a "demon of hate" from flaring up in him, an indication that their remarriage is stillborn. [53]

Unlike *A Modern Instance,* the book does not set forth the arguments against divorce. The "prejudices of [Thérèse's] Catholic education" are withered down, and no defense of marriage as an unbreakable union is given. This makes *At Fault* the first American novel to treat divorce amorally. (In France, meanwhile, the subject only entered fiction a year later, when Daudet published an attack on divorce in his *Rose et Ninette*.) What the author is saying is that we should accept man as he is; that the interference of moral busybodies is useless, and that they have no right to impose upon others a construct of ideals which may be no more than a mask for immorality.[54]

With this question off her mind, Kate Chopin could turn to certain other matters which, likewise, she wanted to get rid of before moving on to what was more important to her. This was the group of Southern issues which greatly occupied the public at the time: the integration and education of Negroes; slavery and miscegenation, and the ante-bellum glory of Dixie. As St. Louis' "littlest rebel," the wife of a White Leaguer, and the daughter-in-law of a harsh slave-owner, she could not help being affected by these problems. It is significant, however, that though she was in possession of so much material on these subjects, she only dealt with them in a few, early stories.

Kate Chopin was not interested in society and issues, but in the individual and character, and whatever views she held on Southern problems she usually hid behind a serene objectivity. Alexander De-Menil asserted that she spoke of the Creoles as "her own people," and if we can believe Felix Chopin, who was proud of his Creole blood, his mother "regretted that [Cable's] artistic ability was superior to his sense of justice": She did not believe he was "true to the Creole life he wrote about," we are told. But whereas Cable fired Grace King into answering what she termed his "libels," he caused no such reaction in Mrs. Chopin. While Miss King became something of an apologist for her people in trying to counteract what she saw as Cable's biased reformer's zeal, Kate Chopin occupied the more neutral ground between them. In accepting the whole of man, she realized that truth is manifold and not monopolized by anyone. She did not feel called upon to take sides or point a moral. She never defended the Creole slave-owners, for example; nor did she attack them, even though she apparently disapproved of slavery.[55]

"La Belle Zoraïde," one of her two stories about ante-bellum Louisiana, is more a plea for woman's right to choose her husband than a direct condemnation of slavery. The café-au-lait colored Zoraïde is envied for her elegant manners and graceful figure. She sees Mézor dancing in Congo Square, his ebony body naked to the waist, and falls in love with him. But her Creole mistress, at whose side she had been brought up, intends her for M'sieur Ambroise, a mulatto with cruel eyes and whiskers like a white man's. Zoraïde wants nothing of this racial pride on her behalf: "Am I white?" she pleads, but in vain, and when she gives birth to Mézor's child, she is falsely told it is dead. As a result she becomes demented; she plays with a doll, and is unable to recognize her baby when her mistress finally tries to give it back to her.[56]

"Désirée's Baby," Mrs. Chopin's other ante-bellum story, is her sole treatment of miscegenation. In this her best-known tale, there is a suggestion of Cable's indignation over the fate of those of mixed blood, but in its taut compression and restrained intensity it is more like a story by Maupassant, and the surprise ending, though somewhat contrived, has a bitter, piercing quality that could not have been surpassed by the master himself. Désirée, who had been a foundling, gives birth to a baby who soon shows Negroid traits, and when Armand, her Creole husband, blames her, she disappears with the child into the river. When burning everything that reminds him of her, he finds an old letter to his father from his mother which exposes his misplaced Creole pride with tragic finality: "I thank the good God ... [that] Armand will never know that his mother ... belongs to the race that is cursed with the brand of slavery."[57]

Even to the plantation legend, the most popular Southern theme at that time, Kate Chopin devoted only one story, "Ma'ame Pélagie." She first called it "In the Shadow of the Ruin," and there is no doubt that she sides not with Madame, who relives in memory the mythical days of grandeur, dreaming of rebuilding the Côte Joyeuse family mansion burned down during the Civil War, but with Pauline, Madame's younger sister, to whom this chimera of glory means nothing. But she deals impartially with them, making the reader admire the older woman who gives up her fixation only with a bleeding heart, building a smaller, modern house over the old ruins so that the younger sister can spring into bloom, finally allowed to live in the here and now rather than the past.

When we turn to Kate Chopin's treatment of desegregation, we find that she deals a little more at length, but less seriously, with this problem than with the three southern issues of the preceding stories.

The enforced integration of a saloon in *At Fault* was one of the first such incidents in American literature, but it loses in significance in that Grégoire is drunk when he stages the scene, gun in hand. Nor can we attach much importance to the attempt at school-integration in the tale "In and Out of Old Natchitoches." Alphonse Laballière may not be drunk when he takes his mulatto tenant's boy to the schoolhouse, but he is enraged by the slander that he is "mighty fon' o' mulatta." Rather than open the school to non-whites, the insulted mistress closes it. The mulatto family then moves to "L'Isle des Mulâtres," and the story turns to the romance between Alphonse and Mademoiselle.[58]

There is no doubt that Mrs. Chopin here treats desegregation with less seriousness than an Albion Tourgée or a Cable. In the latter's documentary story "The Haunted House," for example, he describes the White League's eviction of colored students from an integrated New Orleans school in 1875, tying it in with cruelties once committed against slaves in the same building. Cable here clearly sides with the evicted Negroes. Had Grace King written about the incident, she would probably have stood up for the League; this is what she does in her *History of Louisiana* when she gives the names of the White Leaguers who fell in the Battle of Liberty Place, urging that they "should never be forgotten."[59]

While Kate Chopin kept her impartiality in so far as she never spoke about the League, she seems to come rather close to belittling integration in the two examples of it just mentioned. (Her work does not touch upon her views on the segregated education of Negroes.) A third treatment of the subject is more serious in that it at least excludes everything that detracts from the central problem. This is "A Little Free-Mulatto," a sketch she wrote in 1892. (By that time, the discussion about integration had died down, while the question of whether to educate the Negroes remained under debate.) The title refers to Aurélia, whose father, M'sié Jean-Ba, is so light-skinned and so elegantly dressed that he could easily pass for white. Ruled by his "unyielding pride" he forbids her to play with others than mulattoes. But there are only Negroes and whites nearby; and without playmates, the girl is pining away, until Jean-Ba thinks about the mulatto-colony in Natchitoches: "The happiest little Free-Mulatto in all Louisiana is Aurélia, since her father has moved to 'L'Isle des Mulâtres'."[60]

This sketch would seem to say that racial pride is universal. At the same time, when we hear that "the white children ... would often willingly have had [Aurélia] join their games," it would also suggest that whites can be more tolerant than mulattoes. Yet it is hard not to suspect a white segregationist undertone in the story, especially when we are told – apparently more in the words of the author than of the protagonists – that "L'Isle des Mulâtres" is a paradise to Aurélia and her parents where they can "breathe an atmosphere which is native to them." [61]

It would have been surprising if Kate Chopin had been for integration, if for no other reason because she doubted that it would ever really work. It is also unlikely that the fact that she depicted the Negro with less condescension than most of her contemporaries meant more than that she accepted him in what was called "his place as an inferior." But her attitudes in these matters were well hidden. Whatever they were, however, it represented an achievement that she saw colored people as individuals and that she often managed to enter into them and portray them realistically. The Negroes had been well treated in the O'Flaherty home, and she was evidently unhampered by any feeling of guilt or ambiguity in connection with them. She was used to looking for individual rather than racial characteristics. Furthermore, the Cane River Negroes had many of the qualities she admired. [62]

Kate Chopin undoubtedly had her own set of standards, and they were rather at variance with those of the Gilded Age. One reason she loved children and her Natchitoches people was their directness and lack of sophistication and their unconcern with status and wealth. The Creoles and the Cajuns, and even more the Negroes and the vagabonds, were unambitious and unsmitten by Yankee speed and financial and social push, and they could therefore be more genuine and spontaneous, more natural and wholesome, and live for a hedonist enjoyment of the present, all of which were true values to Mrs. Chopin. We know from her diary how philistines exasperated her, and she was so irritated with the pretentious moralism of people whose goal was wealth and social acceptance that she had to relieve her mind by devoting one tale to the exposure of the sham.

The result was "Miss McEnders" (1892), the story which, as we have said, had to wait five years before anyone would publish it. It deals with a young woman "almost too white-souled for a creature of flesh and blood," who is a member of a committee of ladies formed to investigate the moral conditions of St. Louis factory girls. Reflecting Charlotte Eliot and the Wednesday Club, she has a "burning desire to do good – to elevate the human race." When she finds out that Mlle. Salambre, who is sewing her trousseau, has an illegitimate child, she tells her that there is a right way and a wrong way to live. The woman retorts that she may be at fault, but that she is at least no hypocrite. "Life is not all *couleur de rose,*" she observes, and suggests that the wealth of Miss McEnders' father may have been dishonestly acquired and that the bride-to-be's fiancé may be a roué. As the young lady finds out, it is common knowledge that her father's money was made in the Whisky Ring. Not waiting to be told the truth also about her fiancé, she then throws the white flowers he has sent her into the sooty fireplace.[63]

In an interesting study of Kate Chopin, Merle Mae T. Jordan first makes the point that the author praises those who dare to defy conventions, and then insists that her writings represent a strong social engagement and a condemnation of the false standards of her time. But to term her work social criticism is to strain the evidence. It would have been natural for her to lash out against dishonest financiers, for example, as one such operator had robbed her mother of "the greatest part of her family estate." But she tried to be impersonal as an observer and not to judge. Her objectivity is seen in a diary entry after a talk with C. L. Deyo: "There is good reason for his wrath against the 'plutocrats,' the robbers of the public – but there seems too much personal feeling in his invectives." An even more important reason for her refusal to hurt or condemn people was her conviction that criticism was meaningless as man would never change.[64]

"Miss McEnders" is Mrs. Chopin's one story about the corrupt businessman, and none of her tales is sharper in tone. Nevertheless, its characterizations are discreet and its irony softened by humor. Not even here does she in the least way preach or advocate any change. The chief point to be noted about her one story which perhaps answers to the term of social criticism is that it is not directed against the offenders, but against the idealists who think they have a right and a mission to reform others.

While Kate Chopin thus never really joined the critics of the social values of the Gilded Age, she was one of the first to seriously object to its literary precepts. As summarized by Arlin Turner, R. W. Gilder's attitude, for example, was that "a story should be pleasant, pre-

ferably a love story, and should avoid all touches of horror and all
hints of indecency, indelicacy, or immorality." Mrs. Chopin has three
cases of murder in her writings, but she softens the horror by showing
that they are not committed in cold blood. According to Gilder,
drunkenness was at the most to be suggested; yet in *At Fault,* she
insisted on not only saying explicitly that Fanny was "drinking" – one
reviewer of the novel thought the word so indelicate that he spoke
instead of the "habit of taking stimulants" – but also on making Fanny's alcoholism a central theme in the book.[65]

Where the author really offended, however, was in the matter of
sexual relations. In "Azélie," she describes how Polyte is attracted to
the heroine, "a being so wholly devoid of moral sense" that he feels
his love for her to be "a degradation." The young man of "A Vocation and a Voice" is shown more openly as a victim of the imperative
demands of Eros. He sees the young Suzima naked at the river, and
"her image . . . ate into his brain and into his flesh with the fixedness
and intensity of white-hot iron." Soon he becomes her lover. In time,
he seeks refuge in a monastery, but though he builds a stone wall
around it, she is so much "the embodiment of desire and the fulfillment of life" to him that he runs to her again when he later happens
to hear her voice.[66]

Kate Chopin was of course not the only one who objected to the
moral priggishness which ruled in American letters. Hjalmar Hjorth
Boyesen denounced the "Iron Madonna" – the young female reader
– who strangled all attempts at true realism. Echoing him, William
Schuyler complained in 1897 that while America accepted European
authors – they wrote about foreigners, "and of course foreigners are
different from us" – the American woman tabooed any local work
that was "permeated by a full-blooded virility and actuality." [67]

There was probably no woman in the United States of the 1890's
who was less of an "Iron Madonna" than Kate Chopin, who more
strongly wanted a free literary expression. After having in a manner
formulated her opinions on idealism, moralism, and certain Southern
problems, she turned to what she really wanted to write about: the
impulses which are found in men and women all over the globe,
especially love and sexuality. Her particular ambition was to describe
woman, to give a true picture of the fundamentals of her existence,
and to apply to it a more powerful realism than that introduced by
Mme. de Staël and George Sand.

V

A More Powerful
Female Realism

1. *Female Types, Old and New*

To many women of Kate Chopin's time, Mme. de Staël was not so much the brilliant center of a salon as the passionate woman who in her life and writings had courageously defied the conventions, who had exerted her independence and her ambition and often had been made to suffer for it. When she did not succeed in her attempts to combine the pursuit of fame with a happy domesticity, she blamed the men who "cannot forgive genuine superiority in a woman," as she expressed it, speaking of the fate of the female writer: "*Is she not an unusual woman?* Say no more." (That her own admirers often felt she treated them as slaves was immaterial to her.)[1] The poet Corinne's relationship with Oswald, her lover, is the author's strongest fictional illustration of the extraordinary woman's dilemma. A man may believe that he can live with her even if she refuses to sacrifice her gifts and fame, but the pressure of society, of the idea of the female's conventional place, is so strong that he gives her up.

Mme. de Staël was a pioneer in her frank treatment of the conflict between passion and "duty" in a gifted woman. But she was also in many ways a moralist. Believing in the perfectibility of man, she insisted that "virtue must be animated to struggle effectively against the passions"; she objected to Euripides, for example, who portrayed love as "a disease," and she felt that easy Protestant divorce struck at the sacredness of marriage.[2]

America had a native Mme. de Staël in Margaret Fuller, who shocked her countrymen by declaring in *Woman in the Nineteenth Century* that, just as the Negro ought to be freed from bondage, woman should be relieved of "well-meant restrictions" so that she could become independent of man. Even with this liberty, so many women will choose "nest-making," she maintained, that there is "no need to clip the wings of any bird that wants to soar and sing . . .

[rather than being] constrained to employments for which *some* are unfit." America was no place for this brilliant radical, and it has been suggested that she deliberately refused to be saved when shipwrecked on her return from Europe in 1850.[3]

George Sand, who had been Margaret Fuller's ideal, was then anathema to the Americans, even though she had left the passionate feminism of her first books and was now dealing with less explosive subjects. The French had not forgotten her notorious liaisons, but their admiration for intellectual genius – even in a woman – enabled them to accept and admire her. This was unthinkable in the United States, where she was still suspect when she died in 1876. Many critical Americans forgot that her later writings had mirrored a belief in God, in progress and good, and in what she declared had been the two most genuine passions of her life: motherhood and friendship. Becoming increasingly moralistic, she more and more spoke up for matrimony. Love should be an absolute union, and an ill-matched wife should not fall to temptation, she said once, but try instead to make her marriage work.[4]

To most people, it would have been hard to believe that George Sand now privately confessed that "if I had to start my life over again, I should choose to remain chaste." True, in *Lélia* she makes the protagonist – a woman of mysterious fascination – withdraw from life and become a nun; in *Valentine,* the unfaithful wife is punished, and in *Indiana* she seeks death by drowning. Still, in these early works, even in the watered-down second edition of *Lélia* (most likely the one Kate Chopin knew), she raised many questions that were generally considered sacrilegious.[5]

Full of idealized, self-justifying, and overly romantic treatments of so much from the young author's own life, these novels proclaim women's right to assert themselves, to live and love without regard to conventions and moral rules. To her, "physical love . . . [was] the most sacred fact in all creation" if it was coupled with a spiritual attachment, while being a sin – even within marriage – if it was not. (She resembled Mme. de Staël in being reticent about describing this physical love.) Ideal conditions could only be reached with a freedom to divorce and with such forms of equality as the single standard, and she flayed the law which exposed adulterous wives while letting guilty husbands go free. Even today these early works have a note of truth in their treatment of feminine passions and frustrations. As André

Maurois has pointed out, what made the author unacceptable was not so much that she had sinned against the moral rules as that she did not repent it, that she had "the serenity, the clear conscience, of the rebel," and above all, the fact that her iconoclastic books were written by a woman.[6]

If Mrs. Chopin ever spoke about this pioneer or confirmed that she had read her, it has not been recorded; nevertheless, her daughter Lelia was convinced that she had been named after George Sand's heroine. What can be proved is that Kate O'Flaherty was deeply interested in the occupation of a writer and fascinated by women who dared to defy conventions and strike out on their own.[7]

True, she seems to have entered marriage as a dutiful homemaker who did not "chatter about [her] rights," and she was obviously impressed by such a book as *The Woman's Kingdom,* in which the heroine is eager to marry "the ruler of her life ... [who is] coming to assume his rights, to assert his sovereignty," and ready to serve him with unlimited self-sacrifice. At the same time there was a deep impulse in Mrs. Chopin to follow her inclination, to come to her own conclusions, and to see more of human existence than most housewives did in their "useless degrading life," as Victoria Woodhull had termed it. Surely, none could symbolize better than George Sand the qualities Kate Chopin admired, many of which she herself possessed in embryo, including the ability to discuss practically any matter, without shame or guilt or self-consciousness.[8]

In the case of Maupassant, we recall, his importance to Mrs. Chopin is recorded. When he spoke so secretly to her it was undoubtedly because he discussed with such frankness the hidden life of women, or the contemporary "submerged sexual population," as Frank O'Connor has described his subject par excellence. When Kate Chopin called Mary E. Wilkins Freeman a genius and termed her *Pembroke* "the most profound, the most powerful piece of fiction of its kind that has ever come from the American press," it was again very likely because she depicted repressed passion and frustrated women.[9]

This novel and the two collections of stories which preceded it represent Mrs. Freeman's best work. As her heroines appear in these volumes, their central problem is to find a workable compromise between two forces: their craving for independence and self-respect, and the pressure exerted on them by their still Calvinistic environment that they submit to the men. Louisa Ellis of "A New England Nun" feels the duty to go through with her intended marriage, but is very happy when she can remain a spinster. More typically, the author's heroines are married women who make a brief attempt at asserting their own will. In general, her work is an exploration of what Edward Foster has called the "emotional atrophy" of many of her younger females and a plea for the expression of feeling.[10]

Mrs. Freeman's first collection, *A Humble Romance and Other Stories*, appeared in 1887, early enough to have been one of the many impulses which turned Kate Chopin to writing. Her great-grandmother's tales, her observations of other people, her reading, her marriage, and perhaps also her experiences as she "made her own acquaintance," had by 1888 given her a wide knowledge of the feminine psyche and a pronounced and very personal view of woman's existence, and she had a compelling urge to write openly about its various aspects.

Kate Chopin was never a feminist in the dictionary sense of the term, that is, she never joined or supported any of the organizations through which women fought to get "political, economic, and social rights equal to those of men." Not only did she shy away from societies and issues in general, but she probably regarded the New World feminists as unrealistic when they so closely allied themselves with efforts to elevate men to their own supposedly very high level of purity; she undoubtedly concurred with the early George Sand, who felt that woman largely had the same drives as man and therefore also should have his "rights."[11]

Though American literary permissiveness was slowly being somewhat extended in matters connected with the senses – we might point to the fact that R. W. Gilder published Whitman and that Reedy's *Mirror* gave space to sex-scientists like Krafft-Ebing and Havelock Ellis – the feminists turned their back on a novel like Sarah Grand's *The Heavenly Twins* because the author dared to combine her plea for a single standard with a discreet mention of male promiscuity and its results. As usual, Kate Chopin was a detached observer, a skeptic who could not share any easy optimism. When a friend praised Mrs. Grand's book, in which there is much talk about women's rights, but no suggestion that females as well as men have sexual urges, she exclaimed in her diary: "She thinks 'the Heavenly Twin' a book calculated to do incalculable good in the world: by helping young girls to a fuller comprehension of truth in the marriage relation! Truth is certainly concealed in a well for most of us."[12]

Just as Mrs. Chopin saw that the problems confronting her sex were too complicated to admit of easy solutions, she was also well acquainted with the manifold tendencies in the women themselves. It seems more than an accident that her three earliest extant stories are each in turn devoted to one of what we might call the three main types of women: the "feminine," the "emancipated," and the "modern" (to use the terminology of Simone de Beauvoir's *The Second Sex*), and that the tension between the two leading components of this triad was to reverberate through her whole *oeuvre*.[13]

"Euphrasie," Kate Chopin's first tale from 1888, is the story of a feminine or traditional heroine, that is, a woman of the kind who accepts the patriarchal view of her role very pointedly expressed, for example, in the marriage sermon of Father Beaulieu of Cloutierville: "Madame, be submissive to your husband. . . . You no longer belong to yourself."[14]

In a society where man makes the rules, woman is often kept in a state of tutelage and regarded as property or as a servant. Her "lack of self assertion" is equated with "the perfection of womanliness," as Mrs. Chopin later expressed it in a story. The female's capital is her body and her innocence, and she should be attractive and playful enough for the man to want her, while showing a reticence and resistance which can gratify his sense of conquest, or "the man-instinct of possession," as the author termed it in another tale. What man wishes, writes Simone de Beauvoir, "is that this struggle remain a game for him, while for woman it involves . . . [a recognition of] him as her destiny." In the man's world, woman should accept a special standard for the "more expansive" sex, and for herself, she should eagerly welcome the "sanctity of motherhood." As Mme. de Staël's Corinne is told: Whatever extraordinary gifts she may have, her duty and "her proper destiny is to devote herself to her husband and to the raising of her children."[15]

Euphrasie is a dutiful daughter, and also a loyal fiancée as she tries to hide even from herself that she has suddenly fallen in love with someone else than the man she is engaged to. In the tradition of the feminine woman, she accepts the role of the passive, self-obliterating object as she makes no attempt to influence her fate, and she is willing to break her heart and proceed with the marriage, even though she considers it immoral to kiss her fiancé when she does not love him. (It is interesting to note that the author, in her very first story, on this

point echoes George Sand; she does not openly offend by saying in so
many words that Euphrasie should have kissed the other man when it
becomes evident that they are mutually attracted, but that is what she
implies.) As behooves a feminine woman, she lets the men decide her
destiny: When her fiancé learns the truth by accident, he sets her free,
thus – in Euphrasie's words – saving her from the sin a marriage to
him would have meant to her.

As has been noted before, Kate Chopin put this story aside for a
few years and destroyed the next two she wrote. The original draft of
"Euphrasie" is lost, and we do not know why she titled the tale after
the girl's fiancé when she later revised and shortened it. Nor do we
know anything about the two other stories, except that the first was
set on Grand Isle, and that the second, "A Poor Girl," was offensive
to editorial eyes, perhaps because the author already here was too
open about untraditional urges in women.[16]

The next of Kate Chopin's tales which has come down to us is
"Wiser than a God." It is the story of Paula Von Stoltz, a young
woman who works hard to become a concert pianist. She loves the
rich George Brainard, but when he asks her to follow a calling that
asks "only for the labor of loving," she replies that marriage does not
enter into the "purpose of [her] life." George insists that he does not
ask her to give up anything; she tells him, however, that music to her
is "something dearer than life, than riches, even than love." This is
too contrary to George's idea of woman's role; calling Paula mad, he
lectures her and declares that even if the one who loved him had
taken the vows as a nun, she would owe it to herself, to him, and to
God to be his wife. But Fräulein Von Stoltz leaves to become an
internationally renowned pianist, and her later constant companion
is a composer who is wise enough not to make any emotional demands
on her.[17]

Paula largely answers to Simone de Beauvoir's definition of the
emancipated woman, that is, a female who "wants to be active, a
taker, and refuses the passivity man means to impose on her"; who
insists on the active transcendence of a subject, the *pour soi,* rather
than the passive immanence of an object, the *en soi*; and who attempts to achieve an existentialist authenticity through making a
conscious choice, giving her own laws, realizing her essence, and making herself her own destiny.[18]

The pride indicated in Paula's family name does not manifest itself in a haughty attitude toward her admirer; she is soft-spoken compared to the impetuous, youthful George who insists that she is throwing him into "a gulf . . . of everlasting misery." But she speaks up when she realizes they are in two different worlds, that he represents the patriarchal view of woman, and she the view of Margaret Fuller that women so inclined should be allowed to leave aside motherhood and domesticity and instead use their wings to soar toward the transcendence of a nonbiological career. "Wiser than a God" has something of Mme. de Staël's *Corinne* in that George for a moment believes he can accept a wife who lives not solely for him and his children; unlike the French heroine, however, Paula tells her suitor that life is less important to her than the unhampered exertion of what she considers her authentic calling and her true self.[19]

The self-sacrifice represented by Corinne's suicide to set Oswald free is unthinkable in the Kate Chopin heroines who are awakened to unusual gifts or impulses in themselves and to self-assertion. "Euphrasie" proves that it is not female submission as such which the author leaves out in her writings, but only the concessions to sentimentality and conventionality, the violations of the logic in the various types of heroines. The author combines in these two tales a detachment and objectivity with a tender understanding and respect for both the feminine and the emancipated young lady.

In the third story we have from Mrs. Chopin, "A Point at Issue," she turns to modern woman, that is, the female who insists on being a subject and man's equal, but who cooperates with the male rather than fighting him, without any of the antagonism often attributed to her emancipationist sister. Such modern women were not uncommon at the time, and when they married, some decided not to take their husband's name, that sign of ownership, but to keep their own. In 1895, for example, the St. Louis *Post-Dispatch* printed the statements which such a woman and her husband had made when they entered their "advanced matrimony." She not only kept her maiden name, but also declared that she and her suitor entered marriage with the understanding that both should preserve their individuality and that he should not "let this marriage interfere with the life work she had chosen."[20]

Unlike Paula of the previous story, Eleanor Gail of "A Point at Issue" does wed her suitor, Charles Faraday; they decide, however:

... to be governed by no precedential methods. Marriage was to be a form, that while fixing legally their relation to each other, was in no wise to touch the individuality of either; that was to be preserved intact. Each was to remain a free integral of humanity, responsible to no dominating exactions of so-called marriage laws. And the element that was to make possible such a union was trust in each other's love, honor, courtesy, tempered by the reserving clause of readiness to meet the consequences of reciprocal liberty.[21]

The Latin proverb which Kate Chopin gave as a motto for the previous story: "To love and be wise is scarcely granted even to a god," should more appropriately have been put at the head of "A Point at Issue." While Euphrasie disregards the conflict between love and reason because she has been indoctrinated with the idea of leaving the responsibility for her life to a man, and Paula avoids it by devoting herself to art and making her own decisions, Eleanor is the one really to be put to the test, as she, like her husband, believes that she can both love and be wise as they share a life in "Plymdale" as equals.

The two progressive lovers seem well fitted for their venture. Eleanor, who combines her "graceful womanly charms" with a lack of self-consciousness, has chosen to "diverge from the beaten walks of female Plymdaledom ... [and taste] the sweets of a spiritual emancipation." This strange person is, like her mathematician husband, "possessed of a clear intellect: sharp in its reasoning, strong and unprejudiced in its outlook. She was that *rara avis*, a logical woman." The two are ready to take broad views of life and humanity as they live in the harmony of a united purpose and "a free masonry of intellect." Being more learned, Charles leads the way when they, for example, study science, but with her "oftentimes in her eagerness taking the lead." [22]

Faraday agrees with his wife that she shall spend a year or two alone in Paris learning French. Once he tells her in a letter how a girl had momentarily charmed him, feeling no qualms in doing so as he saw it as unimportant, and, besides, "Was not Eleanor's large comprehensiveness far above the littleness of ordinary women?" While he thinks no more of the matter, Eleanor cannot escape old-fashioned jealousy; nor can Charles when he joins her in Paris for the summer and one day sees her with another man, who later turns out to be a painter doing her portrait. For a moment he wants to kill the "villain," but reason takes over, even before he learns that his jealousy was unfounded.[23]

As a result of these incidents, both retreat one step from their advanced stand. Eleanor rejoins her husband in America, and, being unable to forget how jealousy made her suffer like a "distressed goddess," she has gained insight into her own nature and knows that, as she tells Charles, "there are certain things which a woman can't philosophize about." He has learned nothing from *his* agony, however, while Eleanor's affliction causes him to slip into the traditional attitude of the male when he patronizingly concludes: "I love her none the less for it, but my Nellie is only a woman, after all." And the author adds: "With a man's usual inconsistency, he had quite forgotten the episode of the portrait."[24]

In her first two stories, Kate Chopin had betrayed a possible involvement with marriage only when she in "Wiser than a God," with what looks like mild irony, speaks of "the serious offices of wifehood and matrimony" which constitute all of life to the woman Brainard eventually marries. When there is a somewhat more pronounced suggestion of an engagement in the third tale, it is again on the issue of woman and matrimony. The author by no means makes it clear that she speaks only for Eleanor when she writes: "Marriage, which marks too often the closing period of a woman's intellectual existence, was to be in her case the open portal through which she might seek the embellishments that her strong, graceful mentality deserved." It is interesting to note the surprising juxtaposition of marriage and death with which the story opens when it informs us that the wedding announcement of the Faradays was printed side by side with a "somber-clad" advertisement for "marble and granite monuments."[25]

The impression we are left with by this tale is that Kate Chopin sympathizes with Eleanor even more than with Euphrasie and Paula and that she wishes the Faradays success in their venture to live as perfect equals. She appears to favor female emancipation, not the "quasi-emancipation" she authorially attributes to women showing their protest by wearing strange clothes, but the true, inner kind of growth and independence. She also seems to favor the couple's lack of preconceptions as they attempt to make "innovations into matrimony" by introducing a marital liberty. But Mrs. Chopin saw the complexities of this point at issue: "Reason did good work," she observes in connection with Eleanor's fight with jealousy, "but against it were the too great odds of a woman's heart, backed by the soft prejudices of a far-reaching heredity." Among the inherited factors imposing themselves upon even a modern woman and a modern man are fundamental impulses, such as jealousy, and notions, such as that of male supremacy.[26]

The idea of man's superiority is emphasized as Charles falls back into the age-old concept that his wife is "only a woman." It is perhaps a little surprising to find inconsistency attributed to him, a quality which traditionally typifies the so-called changeable women; however, it serves to stress his male overevaluation of himself: As a female, Eleanor is not expected to know much; therefore she can allow herself to feel that "she knew nothing," and at the same time be open for learning. Charles, on the other hand, is a man, thus a superior being, and as such he does not need to be taught anything.[27]

With her three first stories, Kate Chopin had stated her major theme: woman's spiritual emancipation – or her "being set free from servitude, bondage, or restraint," as the term has been defined – in connection with her men and her career. The sensuous is not touched upon in these tales, except in the case of Faraday. His "stronger man-nature" may refer to expressions of eroticism, and we are told, apropos of the matter dealt with in his letter, that "it is idle to suppose that even the most exemplary men go through life with their eyes closed to woman's beauty and their senses steeled against its charm." The modest success of *At Fault* gave the author a certain encouragement and self-confidence, and seemingly as a result of this, she began, as she entered the second stage of her career, to deal with woman's emancipation also in the field of the senses.[28]

2. *The Developing Heroines*

In dealing with basic human drives, Kate Chopin did not have the naturalists' emphasis on heredity. "Mrs. Mobry's Reason" is her only treatment of this subject, and her interest here is not so much in the hereditary madness as in the awakening love which brings it out. This theme of activated passion inspired many of her tales. In "A Harbinger," Diantha's eyes lose their baby look when Bruno gives her a kiss, and she is ready to be "gathered [as a] wild flower." In "La Belle

Zoraïde," the heroine catches fire the moment she beholds "the stately movements of [Mézor's] splendid body swaying and quivering through the figures of the dance." [29]

Mildred Orme of "A Shameful Affair" is Mrs. Chopin's first heroine who is awakened to both a spiritual and a sensuous emancipation. She spends a summer on a Missouri farm, where a young man first annoys her with his indifference and then stirs her with the boldness of his glance. While he remains inactive, one day she follows him when he is out fishing. She borrows his pole, and a fish bites; he tries to help her, and in the confusion, he gives the girl her first kiss. Then, embarrassed, he hurriedly leaves the scene.

Kate Chopin had probably read certain American writers who more than others had shocked their prudish compatriots with their literary kisses. In 1883, Ella Wheeler Wilcox' *Poems of Passion* spoke of lovers who "shudder and groan" in the "convulsive rapture of a kiss"; though many were offended by this book, it insured the author's popularity. Five years later, Laura Daintrey was considered daring when she described in *Eros* a kiss so hot that the lovers' "lips [were quivering] with desire." In 1895, Gertrude Atherton, then already a well-known author, was to shock her readers with *Patience Sparhawk and Her Times;* in this novel, the heroine realizes that she let her suitor kiss her not because she loves him, but because "the electrical forces of the universe . . . conquered her." Though she wants to kiss him again, she reminds herself that she has "seen nothing of sexual sin that did not make [her] abhor it," and she ends her soliloquy by putting the blame on "the brute! the brute" who had led her astray. [30]

"A Shameful Affair" differs from the two first books in that it does not dwell sensuously on the kiss itself, and from the last in that Mildred does not blame the man. She realizes that her eyes had "gleamed for an instant unconscious things into his own," and she is not "wildly indignant" as traditional feminine modesty should prompt her to be. She also decides that "she would avoid nothing. She would go and come as always." When Mrs. Chopin went on to say that the heroine was nevertheless ashamed of the "hideous truth" that the kiss had been the most delicious thing she had ever known, it was perhaps because the author felt her protagonist had already sinned enough against the legend of female purity. [31]

Later, the man calls himself a "consummate hound" and asks whether Mildred can forgive him some day, thus giving her a chance to play the conventional role of woman as the innocent party who makes no advances in sexual relations. But her answer shows that she is not satisfied with being only a passive object. In a striking illustration of the type of the emancipated woman, she claims instead the role, or at least the responsibility, of being an active subject when she replies: "some day – perhaps; when I shall have forgiven myself." The man is horrified when he realizes what a violation of the current rules for female attitudes, for womanly reticence this answer represents: "He stood motionless, watching her ... as she walked slowly away from him. He was wondering what she meant. Then a sudden, quick wave came beating into his brown throat and staining it crimson, when he guessed what it might be." [32]

This story was written in 1891. Other facets of emancipation are dealt with in further tales from the same year. One of these, "The Going Away of Liza," is a maudlin, unsuccessful piece of writing, yet of a certain interest as the heroine is the author's first to leave her husband. (In calling him Abraham, Mrs. Chopin evokes the prototype of the patriarch.) Liza's reason is that she considers him commonplace and unable to give her the joys of existence which she craves. She goes to the city, but after months of "sin or suffering," she returns to the safety of their home on the farm. [33]

Other Kate Chopin heroines are more successful in their attempts to defy conventions and decide over their own lives. Marianne of "The Maid of Saint Phillippe" refuses to become a traditional housewife and joins the Cherokees for a hunter's life instead. Eva Artless of "An Embarrassing Situation," the author's one-act comedy, also takes her life in her own hands. She is a modern Eve, "brought up on unconventional and startling lines," and by suddenly visiting the man she admires, she puts him in a situation which can only be saved by that offer of marriage she is hoping for. Melicent of *At Fault* and Clarisse of "At the 'Cadian Ball," meanwhile, are examples of women who manipulate their men by the less elaborate engineering of simply blowing hot and cold. [34]

In this, Mrs. Chopin's second phase, we also find examples of traditional women who fill their serving or submissive role with loyalty and unselfish devotion. Mentine of "A Visit to Avoyelles," for instance, is happy to toil faithfully for the husband who misuses her, although it makes her lose her beauty even faster than the hard-working Cajun women do in general. The heroine of "Madame Célestin's

Divorce," on the other hand, is a Catholic prepared to brave the scandal it would create if she left her husband.

As Kate Chopin was warming up, she was getting closer to an open, amoral treatment of woman's sexual self-assertion. That the Creole female may be tempted to trespass beyond her traditional chastity or fidelity is seen in Mme. Delisle of "A Lady of Bayou St. John," who only at the last moment gives up her intention to desert her husband for a lover. In "A Respectable Woman," a story written just before *Bayou Folk* was to appear, the question of infidelity is left open. Mr. Baroda is visited by Gouvernail, a New Orleans newspaper man. Mrs. Baroda is first openly irritated at his presence, but later secretly attracted to him: "she wanted to draw close to him . . . as she might have done if she had not been a respectable woman." To escape temptation, she leaves, and on her return she tells her husband, in words wonderfully ambiguous to the reader: "I have overcome everything! you will see. This time I shall be very nice to him." [35]

The success of *Bayou Folk* launched Kate Chopin on the third phase of her career, and in "The Story of an Hour" she gave her most startling picture of female self-assertion. She does not say what Mrs. Mallard would do with her life now that she believed she could live for herself rather than for her husband. In "Lilacs," her next story, however, it is clear that Mme. Farival has lovers. As a French artiste living in Paris, she is in a way outside the realm of American literary censors; but even so, she is "punished" in that the convent, where she had gone to school, no longer permits her to come for her yearly retreat. That Nathalie of "The Kiss," who is fully American, also loses in that the lover she had planned to keep after marrying a rich nonentity refuses to acquiesce, is no more than could be expected in the America of 1894. What is new, however, is the author's amoral, detached attitude toward infidelity, and the wonderful light touch with which she ends such a story: "Well, she had Brantain and his million left. A person can't have everything in this world; and it was a little unreasonable of her to expect it." [36]

Also in this period of Kate Chopin's career do we find an interplay between her self-assertive and self-forgetting heroines. Mamzelle Fleurette of "A Sentimental Soul," for example, defies her confessor and instead heeds only her own conscience, and Dorothea of "The Unexpected" abandons her rich fiancé when he becomes ill, refusing to serve as his nurse. The widow Mrs. Sommers of "A Pair of Silk Stock-

ings," on the other hand, is used to thinking only of her children, and
Azémia of the story "Ti Frère" marries her stupid suitor because she
realizes he needs "a friendly hand to lead him." In "Regret," meanwhile, we meet a self-centered woman who learns to think of others.[37]

Just as Mrs. Chopin was occupied with the duality of the egotistic
and the altruistic, she also devoted a few stories to the double attraction of the sensuous and the religious, a common literary theme at the
time. We find it in "Two Portraits," for example, where the author
shows how Alberta, a young girl, may later develop into either a nun,
who has the "glow of a holy passion" in her eyes as she devotes herself to God, or a wanton, whose body is made for love and who lives
accordingly.[38] The next time she presented such a juxtaposition – in
"A Vocation and a Voice" – there was no longer any doubt that the
protagonist chose the flesh rather than the spirit. "A Mental Suggestion," meanwhile, describes passion fighting a different kind of struggle. Mrs. Chopin had a certain interest in what she called projected
mental energy, and in this story she deals with the powers of hypnosis
as they are first used to induce love, and then – in vain – to
quench it.[39]

If Kate Chopin was only half serious in this latter treatment of the
power of love, she is deeply involved in "Athénaïse," a story dealing
with the fundamentals of woman's existence, that is, the influence on
her life of husband and children, marriage and liberty.

Athénaïse is an example of the not uncommon phenomenon, the
immature girl who marries merely because it is customary and only
to find that she would rather be a Miss again. Not that she hates
Cazeau, her husband, but she just "can't stan' to live with a man."
Feeling marriage to be a galling yoke and a trap set for unsuspecting
girls, she flees to her parents. In their opinion, however, there is nothing like marriage to develop and form a woman's character, particularly when she is guided by "a master hand, a strong will that com-
pels obedience." Cazeau realizes that the marriage had been a blun-
der, but since he believes it to be their duty to make the best of it,
he fetches her home. On the way, they pass "a great solitary oak-tree,
with its seemingly immutable outlines, that had been a landmark for
ages." It was here, Cazeau suddenly recalls, that as a small boy he
had seen his father allow Black Gabe to rest, the runaway slave he
had just recaptured and was taking back to thralldom.[40]

In revolt against her husband and against a society which does not accept "a constitutional disinclination for marriage" as a reason for dissolving it, Athénaïse runs away again. Cazeau knows he can once more force her to come back and "compel her cold and unwilling submission to his love and passionate transports." But he refuses to undergo again "the humiliating sensation of baseness that had overtaken him in passing the old oak-tree" and tells her to return only if it is her own will to do so.[41]

Meanwhile, Athénaïse is living incognita in a New Orleans pension. Here she becomes friendly with Gouvernail, the newspaper editor we have met before. The author tells us that he is part of a "congenial set of men and women, – des esprits forts, all of them, whose lives were irreproachable, yet whose opinions would startle even the traditional 'sapeur,' for whom 'nothing is sacred'." Then she adds with light irony: "But for all his 'advanced' opinions, Gouvernail was a liberal-minded fellow; a man or woman lost nothing of his respect by being married." The editor falls in love with Athénaïse: "He hoped some day to hold her with a lover's arm. That she was married made no particle of difference to Gouvernail." But at the same time he respects her for not being "the woman to be loved against her will," feeling – with George Sand – that "so long as she did not want him, he had no right to her, – no more than her husband had."[42]

After a few weeks in the city, Athénaïse becomes ecstatic when she understands that she is pregnant. As she whispers her husband's name, the thought of him causes the "first purely sensuous tremor of her life" to sweep over her. Finally knowing her mind, which has come to her "as the song to the bird," she hurries home to nest-making and wifehood: "As [Cazeau] clasped her in his arms, he felt the yielding of her whole body against him. He felt her lips for the first time respond to the passion of his own." And the story ends on a note which suggests that the heroine has learned to think of others, or at least of children: "Listen, Cazeau! How Juliette's baby is crying! Pauvre ti chou, I wonder w'at is the matter with it?"[43]

It is easy to join Reedy of the Mirror when he sees Athénaïse as becoming "a wife in very deed and truth." But in spite of the happy end, the story contains a deep protest against woman's condition (while not forgetting its sensuous joys). Athénaïse's early "sense of hopelessness, [her] instinctive realization of the futility of rebellion against a social and sacred institution," is supported by the story's subtle symbolism.[44]

Kate Chopin's names are sometimes emblematic. (An example is that of the chivalrous hero of a sketch she called "Dr. Chevalier's Lie.") Here, Cazeau's name would seem to stand for the *casa* or chateau in which woman lives her hemmed-in existence, and his stern manner, his jangling spur, and his snarling dogs to represent the authority which forces her to submission. Athénaïse, whose name perhaps refers to Athena, the patroness of spinning and weaving, is indirectly compared to a slave. (The word "emancipation," of course – the title of Kate O'Flaherty's early fable – is used to describe the releasing from bondage not only of women, but also of slaves.) Gabe then stands for the Archangel Gabriel, the herald of pregnancy, and the oak-tree for marriage and motherhood, woman's eternal destiny which makes her the tree of life rather than the free bird envisaged by Margaret Fuller.[45]

"Athénaïse" is one of Kate Chopin's most important efforts. Not even in "The Story of an Hour" had she treated the female condition with such seriousness as here. She had opened her career by presenting the three main types of women, but we note that Eleanor of "A Point at Issue" was followed by no other clear-cut representative of her category, possibly because the author doubted that man could accept woman as his equal. Instead, Mrs. Chopin concentrated on the feminine and the emancipated females, and the fact that she often created these two opposites in pairs, exemplifying – in the course of a few weeks – first the one and then the other, would suggest that she was keeping up a running dialogue with herself on woman's lot.[46]

In one of these pairs ("Madame Célestin's Divorce" and "An Idle Fellow"), the author first deals with a Catholic attempting to go against the Church, and then with a person searching for God.[47]

I am very tired. I have been studying in books the languages of the living and those we call dead. ... Now my brain is weary and I want rest.

I shall sit here on the door-step beside my friend Paul. He is an idle fellow with folded hands. He laughs when I upbraid him, and bids me, with a motion, hold my peace. He is listening to a thrush's song that comes from the blur of yonder apple-tree. He tells me the thrush is singing a complaint. She wants her mate that was with her last blossom-time and builded a nest with her. She will have no other mate. ...

Paul is a strange fellow. ... He knows the reasons that turn [people] to and fro and cause them to go and come. I think I shall walk a space through the world with my friend Paul. He is very wise, he knows the language of God which I have not learned.

Besides being a possible reference to Kate Chopin's own situation, "An Idle Fellow" is a central document in her demonstration of woman's various roles. With her meaningful use of names, the figure with folded hands is very likely Paul of the Bible who bids woman hold her peace. "Let your women keep silence," as he said, and also: "Wives, submit yourselves unto your own husbands." He is, to be sure, an unconventional Paul who drinks "deep the scent of the clover-field and the thick perfume from the rose-hedge," but this sexual symbolism is warranted when we recall that Paul, when he said it was Eve, not Adam, who "was in the transgression," added that "she shall be saved in childbearing." [48]

Against the docile acceptance of these Biblical teachings as seen in the speaker of "An Idle Fellow," Mrs. Chopin poses the views of the emancipated female. Of the many such women in the author's work, the clearest antithesis to Paul is Paula of "Wiser than a God." Refusing wifehood and motherhood in order to live for her non-biological career, she is a proud, defiant answer to the patriarch who condemns woman to be merely an object.

Kate Chopin's first extant tale was written in 1889. The story vividly expresses Paula's views, but artistically it is poor. As we shall see, however, the author quickly progressed beyond the apprentice stage. By the time she wrote "An Idle Fellow" in 1893, she was already an accomplished writer, and when she portrayed Athénaïse two years later, the *Century* was just publishing a story by her ("Regret") which shows unquestionable artistic mastery.

VI
Spontaneous Artistry

1. *Literary Apprenticeship*

The typical length of Kate Chopin's stories is about 3,000 words. (Only five are longer than 5,000, while not a few are shorter than 1,000.) In her notebooks she recorded the exact dates of composition for most of her tales. It appears that more than half of them were written in one day. This suggests that she wrote quickly and easily, and all our evidence bears this out.

For example, Felix Chopin recalled how "the short story burst from her: I have seen her go weeks and weeks without an idea, then suddenly grab her pencil and old lapboard (which was her work bench), and in a couple of hours her story was complete and off to the publisher." And William Schuyler put it this way (apparently quoting Mrs. Chopin): "When the theme of a story occurs to her, she writes it out immediately, often at one sitting, then, after a little, copies it out carefully, seldom making corrections. She never retouches after that." In most instances where it can be checked, her stories were indeed "printed practically without an alteration or correction of the first draught," as the author expressed it.[1]

Kate Chopin wanted her writing to be a spontaneous thing. In a letter which otherwise shows her desire for publicity, she told Waitman Barbe, an editor who thought of giving an article to her in his *Southern Magazine:* "I never discuss a story or sketch with any one before writing it." And Sue V. Moore reported after an interview with her: "She takes no notes and has never consciously observed people, places or things with a view to their use as literary material."[2] We know that certain Cloutierville people felt Mrs. Chopin had used them in her books.[3] Even so, there is no reason to doubt her sincerity when she explained why material forced upon her – stories told her by her friends or characters they introduced her to – was never "of the slightest service" to her:[4]

Story-writing – at least with me – is the spontaneous expression of impressions gathered goodness knows where. . . .

There are stories that seem to write themselves, and others which positively refuse to be written – which no amount of coaxing can bring to anything. I do not believe any writer has ever made a 'portrait' in fiction. A trick, a mannerism, a physical trait or mental characteristic go a very short way towards portraying the complete individual in real life who suggests the individual in the writer's imagination. The 'material' of a writer is to the last degree uncertain, and I fear not marketable. . . . I am completely at the mercy of unconscious selection. To such an extent is this true, that what is called the polishing up process has always proved disastrous to my work, and I avoid it, preferring the integrity of crudities to artificialities.[5]

The author thus refused to force herself in her work. In the account of her experience with "The Maid of Saint Phillippe," she touched upon a guiding principle behind her insistence on letting the stories write themselves "without any perceptible effort on [her] part," as she put it:[6]

I am more than ever convinced that a writer should be content to use his own faculty, whether it be a faculty for taking pains or a faculty for reaching his effects by the most careless methods. Every writer, I fancy, has his group of readers who understand, who are in sympathy with his thoughts or impressions or whatever he gives them. And he who is content to reach his own group, without ambition to be heard beyond it, attains, in my opinion, somewhat to the dignity of a philosopher.[7]

The group Mrs. Chopin wanted to reach with "Wiser Than a God" was clearly the one interested in female self-assertion. This tale contains her most outspoken demonstration of the self-sufficient woman. It is the only story she provided with a motto and her one example of what can be considered quite overt feminism, and the picture of the girl who becomes a famous pianist suffers from the strong emphasis.

When George Brainard wants Paula to marry him rather than become an artist, she is allowed to slip into the declamatory: "I must keep myself fitted to my calling. Rest would mean deterioration." The diction is, in fact, often poor; it ranges from the formal ("you have spoken the signal that must part us") via the stale ("the cruel blow that fate had dealt her") to the colloquial ("very swell people").[8]

Sometimes Kate Chopin enters authorially. "How little did her auditors appreciate in the performance the results of a life study," she observes, and she tells us rather than demonstrates that the listeners' reactions were "inane compliments." Usually, however, she keeps herself out, letting the story tell itself, and showing character mainly through action. The tale is well-constructed; the opening leads straight to the problem, which is logically developed. There is nothing inorganic, everything serving to illustrate the theme of career versus marriage.[9]

But while the author already here demonstrates a certain sense of form, she is unsure about distance. Her humor is now and then strained, as when she observes about George's sister, who believes she can sing, that "True genius is not to be held in abeyance." For the most part, however, her tone is objective. As for characterization, she tries to make Paula three-dimensional; though the heroine loves George, she wishes "he had not been so proficient with the banjo," and though she refuses the professor who persists in courting her, the last paragraph suggests that his dogged patience may win in the end. But on the whole, the figures are mere abstractions of the theme rather than living individuals.[10]

This is also the chief defect in the main characters of *At Fault*. Though Kate Chopin objected to a thesis in a novel, she clearly invented Thérèse, David, and Fanny to illustrate her own views on issues like alcoholism and intervention in other people's lives. No other explanation can be given for such improbable constructions as Hosmer's and Fanny's remarriage and their stay at the plantation. That the latter falls back into drinking is believable, but her drowning is another machination, arranged to enable the two survivors to marry after all and express the moral of the tale. Fanny is realistic when she warns David that "it would be the same thing over again," while he is implausible with his insistence that he "will not be the same" this time.[11]

In exposing the narrow marriage rules and the exaggerated belief in ethical will power, the author tries to be not too direct. An example of this is her use of the Reverend Alban Butler's well-known book on the lives of the saints. She lets Mr. Worthington, one of her spokesmen, read its description of the intemperance of St. Monica:

a woman whose habits it appears had been so closely guarded in her childhood by a pious nurse, that even the quenching of her natural thirst was permitted only within certain well defined bounds. This mentor used to say "you are now for drinking water, but when you come to be mistress of the cellar, water will be despised, but the habit of drinking will stick by you." Highly interesting, Mr. Worthington thought, as he ... seated himself the better to learn the fortunes of the good St. Monica who, curiously enough, notwithstanding those early incentives to temperance, "insensibly contracted an inclination to wine," ... a "dangerous intemperance" which it finally pleased Heaven to cure .... [12]

While Mrs. Chopin's quotations from Butler's book represent an indirect approach to Fanny's cravings, her own phrases, such as "curiously enough," betray her attitude toward the "asceticism [and the] ... superhuman possibilities" which she lets Worthington read about in the next paragraph. When she earlier had let him expound on how religions follow a course of "progress and inevitable death," it is as if she is still so close to her own discovery of this fact that she has to spell it out. [13]

On the last pages of *At Fault,* the author again tries to infuse aesthetic distance into her more or less direct statements. Thérèse looks at David, noting "the dull scar on his forehead, coming out like a red letter when his eyes looked into her own." The cicatrice is the result of his attempt to save Fanny in the river, and it will tell "its story of pain through the rest of his life." Looking away, Thérèse asks him whether he thinks "it's right we should find our happiness out of that past of pain and sin and trouble." Kate Chopin here appears to use the scar as an objective correlative: When it is a red letter to Thérèse, it inevitably evokes the implications of Hawthorne's scarlet "A." As if reading her thoughts, David asks her to look at him, and he seems to ask her to accept the cicatrice, not as a symbol of sin, but of the natural forces of life, when, with a new use of Thérèse's term for the scar, he insists that we should "know the living spirit from the dead letter." [14]

While Mrs. Chopin is moderately successful in these attempts at subtlety, the novel as a whole shows that she was not ready for the longer forms of fiction. The framework is acceptable, but it is filled with inorganic matter. The visit to McFarlane's grave, for instance, does not advance the main conflict. There is also a lack of focus due to the many subplots and secondary figures. The author has not been able to fuse her local color with her theme.

Nor are the romantic and the realistic elements of the work happily united. For example, they clash in the description of Joçint preparing to set fire to the sawmill. In a juxtaposition of two pictures of trees, we are told, first, of the murmuring pines "telling their mystic secrets to the night," and then of the young man strangling his dog with a piece of rope, leaving him "hanging to the limb of a tree." This movement from a pathetic fallacy to an attempted realism is reversed when the author lets the shooting of Joçint be followed by melodrama and sentimentality as his father comes to claim his body and falls dead himself. The language, meanwhile, is at times either too stilted or too colloquial, and the tone is inconsistent; such an address to the reader as "My friend, your trouble I know weighs," clashes with the author's general attempt to keep herself out of the work.[15]

At Fault is not without artistic merits, however. The setting is convincing, and there are vivid scenes. Though we get no real sense of Thérèse's development from reformer to laissez-faire philosopher, she has a certain authenticity in her role as chatelaine. Several of the subsidiary characters are true to life, particularly the down-to-earth Aunt Belindy, who expresses the essence of the book when she observes that "Grégor gwine be Grégor tell he die," and the rough Texan who spits tobacco juice when he tells Thérèse of Grégoire's death and then rides away, "his elbows sawing the air."[16]

The comparatively long time Kate Chopin spent on the writing of *At Fault* (and on "Young Dr. Gosse") shows that she was taking pains, but the novel's merits could not help it from being a failure. If it is true that her crucial meeting with the work of Maupassant took place already in 1888 or 1889 (she could be careless with dates), she had not yet been able to apply the lesson he had taught her. She knew that she needed to improve her style. As Alexander DeMenil put it, she was "fully conscious of her limitations as to literary art." She probably also realized that it was too ambitious to start with novels, and she may have thought of Miss Jewett and Mrs. Freeman, who both went through an apprenticeship as a writer of shorter tales for children.[17]

The short story was at that time gaining recognition as a serious art form, and it was discussed as such by Brander Matthews and others. We cannot prove that Mrs. Chopin was familiar with Matthews' literary theories, but there is no doubt that she studied Maupassant and Miss Jewett intensively. In his preface to *Pierre et Jean,* the Frenchman had told her that in order to present life rather than fiction, the writer must not "machiner une aventure" nor use complicated language. As he demonstrated in his own work, a story is most effective when it tries to offer truth rather than sentimentality, when it strives for simplicity, clarity, and moderation rather than the extravagance of the old-fashioned stage-trappings. He had shown her how to use the telling detail and how to give the story with the utmost economy.[18]

She found a similar direct and simple technique in the two New England authors she admired. In *A Country Doctor,* Miss Jewett had exemplified how a woman's difficult choice between career and marriage could be presented with not too much preaching. Her work in general demonstrated a simplicity of form; a supple handling of point of view, of involvement and distance; an emphasis on characterization, and an ability to lift the trivial into art. "I have no objection to a commonplace theme if it be handled artistically, . . . [with] freshness, spontaneity, or originality of perception," Kate Chopin noted in her diary, contrasting her neighbor's story with the art of Miss Jewett. Mrs. Freeman, on her side, could show her how to portray frustrated women with a mixture of frank realism and artistic control, of direct statements and subtle symbols.

After her first two novels, Mrs. Chopin settled down as a writer of shorter tales, most of which were intended for the *Youth's Companion.* Many of them were written in one sitting, and they show that she was learning to use the simplicity and directness she admired in Maupassant. She now relied less and less on the kind of improbable coincidence which we find in an 1889 story, in which a marriage depends on the very unlikely meeting in a faraway place of two lovers who have been forbidden to see each other.[19] Her early children's stories sometimes touch upon the sentimental or the pathetic, but they also show her lambent humor and her growing control of her material. "A Matter of Prejudice," for instance, manages, in the course of a few pages, to characterize perfectly the dictatorial Mme. Carambeau and her entourage. This story also illustrates Kate Chopin's mastery of the ironic twist when she lets Madame, at the end, declare herself to be free of prejudices but her son to be full of them. In short, the author seemed to have passed the apprenticeship stage.

2. *Short Story Mastery*

Kate Chopin did not disdain the miniature forms of fiction. She saw a significance in even the smallest events, and her emphasis was generally on character rather than plot, on atmosphere rather than action. Such a very brief sketch as "Ripe Figs," for example, shows her ability to evoke, in a few paragraphs, the mood of a little girl's impatience as she measures the slow march of time by the advance of the seasons. With its delicate touch and its suggestive imagery of flowers, fruits, and sunshine, this sketch comes close to being a poem in prose.

One reason why Daudet spoke to Mrs. Chopin was his seductive style infused with the meridional warmth, the sunny, sensuous atmosphere of his Midi. She had herself responded to the luxurious southern fragrance of Louisiana and to the erotic ambiance of her Gauls. Once she fused these elements in a way which is reminiscent of the Frenchman: "He held the rose by its long, hardy stem, and swept it lightly and caressingly across her forehead, along her cheek, and over her pretty mouth and chin, as a lover might have done with his lips." [20]

In "Désirée's Baby" (1892), Kate Chopin's first outstanding story, she creates atmosphere with the hand of an expert. The impending doom and death of two of the Aubignys are very subtly suggested when the shadow of the trees surrounding their home is likened to a pall, a term which gives a new meaning to the "cover" already indicated in the name of the house, L'Abri. Almost imperceptibly the author builds up toward the revelation that the baby is Negroid: "Yes, the child has grown, has changed," Désirée's foster mother observes as she looks up at the Negro nurse; there are unexpected visits of neighbors who want to look at the baby, and Aubigny's manner changes. [21]

There is a wealth of irony in the story. The quadroon whose traits finally make Désirée see the truth is called La Blanche; Aubigny is aware that he is darker than his wife; yet the revelation – after he had driven her to her death – that it was he who was Negroid, comes as a complete shock to him, as it does to the reader. The ending undeniably has intense dramatic value, but its artifice mars what is otherwise an excellent piece of writing.

With "Madame Célestin's Divorce" (1893), Kate Chopin reached a new peak in her artistry. Everything is infallibly right in this story about a contemplated divorce caused by M. Célestin's desertion of his

wife. Coaxed by the staid lawyer Paxton, who is more in love with
her than he knows and made young by it, Madame braves the opposition of her mother, her confessor, and finally the bishop. We follow
the development of her relationship with Paxton as they occasionally
talk with each other over the fence, she gathering up "the train of
her calico wrapper in one hand, and balancing the broom gracefully
in the other," and he holding to a couple of shaky pickets. But one
day comes Madame's truly final remark: "You see, Judge, Célestin
came home las' night. An' he's promise me on his word an' honor
he's going tu turn ova a new leaf." [22]

What Mrs. Chopin achieves here is a surprise ending which is
entirely justified in spite of its reversal of all that precedes it. Madame's abrupt change of heart makes her a full, complex, convincing
being, as we realize that there is no contradiction in her manner, that
the change was inherent in her from the beginning. She is the kind of
woman who lets herself be persuaded by men, first by the eager judge
that she deserves his pity and praise, his help and attention, and then
by her husband that she loves him and believes in him after all. This
revealing glimpse of feminine psychology is given with detachment by
the invisible author, with unobtrusive humor which springs from
character rather than plot, and with subtle, yet radiant charm. Nothing is superfluous and nothing is forced in this brief story, which
constitutes a landmark in Kate Chopin's artistic development.

It was in 1894, we recall, that she spoke in her diary of her "growth
into a writer of stories." This was a year in which she wrote a number
of remarkable tales, such as "The Story of an Hour," "Lilacs," "Regret," and "Ozème's Holiday." The last three belong among Kate
Chopin's best dozen tales, particularly because of their excellence in
character delineation.

"Ozème often wondered why there was not a special dispensation
of providence to do away with the necessity for work. There seemed
to him so much created for man's enjoyment in this world, and so
little time and opportunity to profit by it." With these words, the
author leads us straight into the theme already suggested in the title
of "Ozème's Holiday." We are told that he likes to sit and do nothing,
to be with companions, and to go fishing. He is not lazy, however; the
whole year he works faithfully at Laballière's plantation. But he does
not hesitate to take his yearly vacation in mid-season as it helps to
build the image he wants to present to the world of a person who sees

the enjoyment of leisure as a major thing in life, or as a man who is enough of a somebody to be able to do what he wants.[23]

To support this image, he wears expensive clothes: "When Ozème went 'broading,' he dressed – well, regardless of cost." This year he plans to visit the Fédeaus and many others, such as the Beltrans, who might be giving a ball, but not the St. Annes – "after St. Anne reproaching him last year with being a fainéant for broading at such a season!" Yet he feels at peace with himself when he borrows "Mr. Laballière's buckboard and Padue's old gray mare, and a harness from the negro Séverin" and sets out along the Joyous Coast for his eagerly awaited usual round of parties.[24]

As a Natchitoches critic has pointed out, to understand the full significance of Ozème's later actions, it is necessary to note his position in the Cane River community. By speaking of "Mr. Laballière" and "the negro Séverin," the author shows him as belonging somewhere in between these two on the social scale. Very likely he is a Cajun; he has blue eyes and light hair, and he is apparently the equal of Padue, about whom we know from another story that he is a Cajun. But the people of the Côte Joyeuse are united in their desire for merriment, and it seems quite natural that Ozème intends to visit both Creole planters, fellow Cajuns, and even free mulattoes during his week of pleasure.[25]

Two paragraphs are given to a description of the expected delights of his holiday, which are then offset by the whistles of the steam-gins, indicating that everybody is at work. When he buys a cigar at the store – a significant detail – he meets with his first setback: The Fédeaus have gone to town, and "it was at Fédeaus' that Ozème had intended to dine." This makes him think of Aunt Tildy, a Negro who did the cooking for a family with whom he once boarded, and he decides to make a little detour on his way to the Beltrans plantation and induce her to fry him a chicken.[26]

On reaching her little cabin, however, he finds that she has one arm in a sling and a grandson in bed with a fever. When he asks her who she thinks is going to pick her over-ripe cotton, she answers: "Ef de Lord don' pick it, I don' know who gwine pick it, Mista Ozème." The visitor's tone is rather haughty; he undoubtedly knows that she cannot afford hired help. The "Mista" illustrates the social difference between Aunt Tildy and the Cajun. Though she nursed him once when he was ill, she makes no suggestion that he might help her in her predicament. Even so, the outlook appears menacing to Ozème, "to his personal comfort and peace of mind." That is, he worries about his dinner, while he knows he will have to look at the sick boy.[27]

He gives him quinine; spends the night at the cabin; starts picking the cotton, and stays on for a second day. But while he gets increasingly involved with Aunt Tildy's problems, he becomes louder and louder in his protestations that this is no way for him to spend his holiday; at the same time, she becomes less deferential in her answers. There is an effective interplay between his biting tone and her references to God, as there is between his words and his actions.

When Ozème starts picking the cotton, Aunt Tildy exclaims: "I knowed de Lord war gwine sen' somebody to holp me out. . . . De Lord gwine shove you 'long de row, Mista Ozème." "Neva you min' w'at the Lord's goin' to do," he answers. But on the third day – it looks like rain, so he is still picking cotton – he invokes God himself: "if the Lord gets me safe out o' this ditch, 't ain't to-morro' I'll fall in anotha with my eyes open, I bet you." The author's gift of humor is illustrated in Aunt Tildy's reply:[28]

Keep along, Mista Ozème; don' grumble, don' stumble; de Lord's a'watchin' you. Look at yo' Aunt Tildy; she doin' mo' wid her one han' 'an you doin' wid yo' two, man. Keep right along, honey. Watch dat cotton how it fallin' in yo' Aunt Tildy's bag.

When he tells her to work harder herself or he will use the rawhide on her, it is again a reminder that he has no obligation to help a former slave. This racial and social prejudice is one of the reasons why he "felt quite shamefaced as he drove back to the plantation," his work completed. He is not going to own that he has helped a Negro, and as for his standing as a glorious holiday-maker, he tries to save it by announcing that this year he preferred camping to his yearly spree, because "it's 'mos' always the same thing on Cane riva."[29]

If Mrs. Chopin here demonstrates her deep insight into character, her light touch, and her economy of means, she reaches even higher in "Regret." In this story, she shows how on occasion she could take a Maupassantian theme and transform it into her own, surpassing the master in technique and in depth of vision, and making the tale into a truly moving experience.

Mamzelle Aurélie of this story is her counterpart to the Frenchman's "Reine Hortense" of the *conte* of that name.[30] Both are spin-

sters, living alone except for a maid, a dog, and some fowls; both have
something military in their appearance and manner, and neither of
them seems sorry about her unused womanly capacities – until it
appears that their maternal instincts have indeed been alive under the
surface. To be sure, there are differences between the two plots. The
heroine of "Regret" is asked to take care of her neighbor's children,
and their later departure reveals to her the emptiness they leave behind. What happens in "La Reine Hortense," however, is that the
spinster's relatives are called to her deathbed, where they are surprised
to hear the delirious woman speak to her imaginary husband and
children. Although we cannot know that Maupassant here furnished
Mrs. Chopin's point of departure, the tales are close enough for us
to compare the two authors' treatments of a similar theme.

Before Maupassant starts the action, he gives one-sixth of his story
to a presentation of Hortense. She reigns over her underlings, not
missing them when they have to be replaced, and showing tenderness
to no one, not even her relatives. Kate Chopin's opening is much
shorter and must be quoted in full:

Mamzelle Aurélie possessed a good strong figure, ruddy cheeks, hair that
was changing from brown to gray, and a determined eye. She wore a
man's hat about the farm, and an old blue army overcoat when it was
cold, and sometimes topboots.

Mamzelle Aurélie had never thought of marrying. She had never been
in love. At the age of twenty she had received a proposal, which she had
promptly declined, and at the age of fifty she had not yet lived to
regret it.

So she was quite alone in the world, except for her dog Ponto, and the
negroes who lived in her cabins and worked her crops, and the fowls, a
few cows, a couple of mules, her gun (with which she shot chicken-
hawks), and her religion.[31]

In this brief opening, the author gives us all we need to know about
the protagonist, and she does so discreetly. Where Maupassant informs us that Hortense is imperious and speaks like an officer, Mrs.
Chopin only suggests the same thing with Aurélie's "determined eye."
Where he tells us specifically that "la reine" is an old maid and
comments at some length on the fact that she never complains about
it, she confines herself to the observation that Mamzelle has never
loved and never regretted it. While he enumerates the men's tasks

which his heroine performs around the house, she only gives the touch of Aurélie's hawkshooting.

As the plot opens, the two stories part company. In four brief paragraphs, Mrs. Chopin shows the unwelcome appearance of Odile, the Cajun neighbor, and her children, who are characterized with a single expression: Ti Nomme was "dragged ... by an unwilling hand," and Marcéline and Marcélette "followed with irresolute steps." [32] The visitor has to go to her sick mother, and her instructions to the bewildered Mamzelle are recorded. The last sentence of this section is particularly effective, rendering Odile's final words and her departure with a mixture of humor and sympathy:

"Me, there, I'm half crazy between the chil'ren, an' Léon not home, an' maybe not even to fine po' maman alive encore!" – a harrowing possibility which drove Odile to take a final hasty and convulsive leave of her disconsolate family.[33]

The next two paragraphs present the group which Aurélie now looks at "with a critical eye," and the setting. As Robert B. Bush has noted in a suggestive discussion of the author, she here, with a few telling details, calls into play the various senses as she records the beating sunlight, the odor of pinks, and "the sound of negroes' laughter" coming across the field.[34] (In the case of "Regret," we have what appears to be the first version of the story, and we can thus see the changes she made. They are very few. One of them is found in the foregoing sentence where she with sure instinct replaced "voices" with the more suggestive "laughter.") [35]

As Mamzelle determines "upon a line of action which should be identical with a line of duty," we pass to the first stage of her adaptation to the new conditions. Again there is a touch of kind humor, of amusement paired with understanding, as the author represents the children's insistence on the attentions they are used to and the caretaker's groping attempts to provide them.[36]

In an intermediate section Aurélie tells Aunt Ruby, her cook, that she would "rather manage a dozen plantation' than fo' chil'ren," and exclaims: "Bonté! Don't talk to me about chil'ren!" The cook's ideas about childrearing turn out to be based on a set of superstitions, which at first seem out of place in the story. But Aunt Ruby is functional after all. When Mamzelle "was glad enough to learn a few little mother-tricks to serve the moment's need," it suggests that she was now, probably for the first time, emotionally ready to be interested in the cook's many children and ready to take her advice even though she retained her skepticism about the woman's intellect.[37]

This interlude prepares the reader for the change reflected in the next paragraph. Aurélie has learned that she cannot order the youngsters "one and all to bed as she would have shooed the chickens into the hen-house," and by now they have become individuals to her. She accepts Ti Nomme's sticky fingers and moist kisses and "little Elodie's hot, plump body pressed close against her" at night, and she becomes accustomed to their incessant noise.[38]

The author sums up this development in a brief, casual sentence: "At the end of two weeks Mamzelle Aurélie had grown quite used to these things, and she no longer complained." The children's attitude shows that she performs her task fairly well. But no clear suggestion is given that it is more than a duty to her, not even in the "flutter that was almost agitation" which Odile's sudden return throws her into, or in the fact that "she could still faintly hear the shrill, glad voices of the children" after they had left. It is only in the last few lines that the author admits to the surface what has very subtly been at work in the story and the protagonist for some time. Aurélie does not at once begin the task of righting the disorder left by the young people, but sits down at the table:[39]

She gave one slow glance through the room, into which the evening shadows were creeping and deepening around her solitary figure. She let her head fall down upon her bended arm, and began to cry. Oh, but she cried! Not softly, as women do. She cried like a man, with sobs that seemed to tear her very soul. She did not notice Ponto licking her hand.

In these final, unemphatic yet charged lines, the story ties up again with that of Maupassant, which in the meantime has followed a different course. Hortense's married relatives have come to her, and nearly half the *conte* is given to a description of these visitors who, together with her animals, clearly provide a counterpoint to her single, loveless life and to her death. Edward D. Sullivan, in his book on Maupassant's short stories, terms this "a very successful story" and speaks of "the feeling of pity" it evokes for the spinster who had missed so much in life.[40] The Frenchman's title would indeed suggest that it was the woman's fate he wanted to illustrate. "La Reine Hortense" was written when he was still at the height of his powers;

nevertheless, for reasons which are indicative of the general difference between the two authors, "Regret" is the superior story.

For one thing, there is the question of psychological validity. Maupassant makes a point of saying that Hortense is without softer feelings and not interested in company. There is not one detail to make likely the axiomatic co-existence of this cold external life with an inner role of a tender wife and mother. As for Aurélie, however, her gradual development from self-sufficiency to what looks like an involvement with others is convincingly portrayed. Her brief new reality, which is given with authenticity and no false notes, makes it entirely believable that she can realize with a shock what it is she has missed.

Furthermore, Kate Chopin's means are fewer and subtler and her effect greater. Maupassant detracts from the main story by giving too many details of the visitors' doings, and his symbolism is a little too heavy when he lets the dog play on Hortense's bed as she dies and when he has the hen sit next to her, "desperately calling her chicks." [41] In "Regret," Mrs. Chopin concentrates entirely on the subject of her title. As is usual with her, her point of view is that of the omniscient author who only sparingly enters the heroine's mind; she gives little analysis, relying instead on indirection and suggestion. Hardly a word is wasted in this story which leaves so much to our imagination. For example, we never hear Aurélie speak except in the one brief remark to Aunt Ruby, and the ending leaves the reader to guess what it is – in the past, present, or future – she regrets, thus heightening the resonance of the low-keyed, yet intense conclusion. The use of symbolism is discreet; as Robert B. Bush has pointed out, only the evening shadows – and we might add Ponto's licking of Aurélie's hand – suggest the solitude which will grow on her. [42]

That Kate Chopin relied more on the children in her illustration of unlived life than Maupassant did in his may be due in part to the fact that she loved and understood youngsters, whereas he had little sympathy for them. Furthermore, that she only suggested the heroine's masculine attributes and he strongly emphasized them may be a result of her feeling that woman should be allowed the role she wants, whereas he would restrict her to "two functions in life, love and motherhood." Maupassant was probably the strongest literary influence upon Kate Chopin's writings, in which we find a reflection of his themes as well as his techniques; yet with her independent spirit and her personal views, she stood entirely on her own. [43]

9 Kate Chopin

This first-rate story shows that Kate Chopin now had fully mastered the technique of her medium. She had learned to express her impressions and ideas – particularly about woman's existence – not overtly, as in "Wiser Than a God," but through indirection. She knew now how to express more by saying less, and she had perfected the art of using setting and dialect sparingly and only to support character. Her protagonists throb with authentic life, warmed by the emotion she transmits right through her restrained, simple prose. Her sympathy and understanding is matched by her sure grasp of form. Her style is swift and sure.

Mrs. Chopin was an instinctive teller of stories. There can be little doubt that her writings gained in freshness through her method of drawing more or less unconsciously upon her various gifts. She had a keen interest in musical form and a marked gift for composition; she felt the influence of the oral tradition of the Creole South, and she had inherited much of the Irish genius for story-telling. Even though she was "never 'working over' a story," as her daughter described it, her writing demonstrated an instinctive artistic sense which made use of the best of the Celtic and Gallic traditions. She had learned to apply her inborn French simplicity and clarity, logic and precision, and the Gallic sense of form, economy of means, and restraint, together with the pathos and humor, the warmth and gaiety of the Irish.[44]

She rarely forced herself as a writer. She did not have Maupassant's graphomania and seldom repeated herself. But though there is little hack work in her writings, and though she usually shows a natural ease and rarely strained for effect, she undeniably let many crudities slip through, particularly in the diction. When, in a brief tale, she uses the expression "went and stood" or "went and leaned" five times, it is hardly elegant; nothing is gained by employing the word "confab" instead of a less colloquial term, and no stress on integrity can excuse a construction like "Once within the convent Adrienne's soft brown eyes moistened with tenderness." But these flaws cannot alter the fact that she was very conscious of technique, both in matters of detail and of form. Her best tales are fully born, organic entities, firmly controlled, and entirely satisfying works of art which show that she knew exactly what she was doing.[45]

"Athénaïse" is a case in point. Here is art concealing art, in the gradual revelation of character and the logical progression of the plot.

This story of 14,000 words moves more slowly than the author's shorter tales so as to give a sense of the lapse of time which is needed for the psychological development. Yet it moves constantly, wasting no motion as it reaches toward its objective.

"Athénaïse" opens with the disappearance of the heroine as it is seen by her husband, Cazeau. He tells himself that he does not care, but the "gloom" of his dining room reflects his mood. At night, he hears the cries of a baby and the plaintive notes of an accordion. These sounds are repeated at the end of the story, but now his mood is different because his wife has come back. In between these two points we witness the change taking place in both of them. The severe-looking Cazeau comes to feel that he should not force his wife to return, a sign that he has learned a certain humility. Athénaïse is at first "nothing but a chile," but, as is subtly indicated in her increasing homesickness, she is unconsciously developing toward an acceptance of her husband and of a grown-up life. Her reactions to the news of her pregnancy – first a feeling of shock, then of ecstasy – are reported, whereas the pivotal revelation scene itself is presented only indirectly and with the utmost economy: "Sylvie was very wise, and Athénaïse was very ignorant." [46]

The three main characters – the third being Gouvernail, Athénaïse's admirer in the New Orleans pension – are presented with a mixture of sympathy and detachment. While the author respects and feels for them, she modifies – and enriches – the picture of them through small glimpses from unexpected angles. Cazeau is admirable in the seriousness with which he tries to see his wife's point of view, but earnestness can be exaggerated: The dances given by Athénaïse's parents, we are told, are "pleasures not to be . . . despised, unless by such serious souls as Cazeau." Gouvernail succeeds in making no sign that he is aching for Athénaïse, but he cannot help "assuming . . . an air of proprietorship" when they dine at a restaurant. Before returning to Cane River, the heroine buys "little presents for nearly everybody she knew." Into this picture of sudden kindness is introduced an illuminating realistic detail when she gives the maid of the pension both a silver dollar and "a pair of stockings with two tiny holes at the toes." [47]

As George Arms has observed of Kate Chopin, she is "unwilling to extract a final truth." Athénaïse's attack on the institution of marriage is offset by her return to Cazeau, and her parents' belief in male authority is balanced by Cazeau's loss of absolute faith in it. The author seems to give equal weight to the early and the late Athénaïse, and the story is governed by a many-sided view of the female condition. Its focus is on woman's role in the life cycle, and this emphasis is subtly supported by the imagery. In such stories as "Miss McEnders" and "Lilacs," Mrs. Chopin had already made effective use of flowers as symbols for her themes. In "Athénaïse," there is a constant mention of flowers and shrubs, of fields and trees. What makes Cazeau draw a parallel between Athénaïse and a slave is the sight of the oak-tree in the meadow and the smell of elderberry; when she runs away, she inhales the odor of the fields, and just before she learns of her pregnancy, she is homesick for the woods and "the scent of the ploughed earth." [48]

In all this, the chief image is that of the tree. The oak is the symbol of the life process, of the immutability of seasonal growth. While the author here draws upon the pre-Christian symbolic use of the tree, she refers to the Bible's use of it as the tree of knowledge when she tells us that Athénaïse is "embarrassed as Eve after losing her ignorance." In this outstanding work, Mrs. Chopin achieves a large degree of indirection in the presentation of her deepest views; skillfully fusing her theme with the life and the atmosphere of Louisiana, she subordinates the elements of the story to the unifying principle represented by the live-oak in the meadow. [49]

When Kate Chopin had achieved the necessary self-confidence to go even deeper into her particular subject than she had done in "Athénaïse," and also to move one step closer to a French literary openness, she chose a larger canvas for her story. In 1894, she had observed: "The novel does not seem to me now to be my natural form of expression. However, should the theme of a novel present itself I should of course try to use it. I do not consider one form of more value than the other." [50]

The theme of *The Awakening* – that of a married woman seeking self-fulfillment and sexual gratification outside her home – is of course an old one, and we do not know for certain what made her begin the novel, apparently in June, 1897. [51] Before she started it, however, she wrote "An Egyptian Cigarette," a story in which she let the – presumably female – speaker indulge in a passionate evocation of her lost lover. Smoking a hallucinatory cigarette, she is transported into a dream in which she seeks death and reunion with her god, as she calls him, who had departed to "where the monster stones are rising heavenward in a monument for the unborn ages." She drags herself through the desert and reaches the river at nightfall. Soon the water envelops her: "Oh! the sweet rapture of rest! There is music in the Temple. And here is fruit to taste. Bardja came with the music –." When the narrator wakes up, she decides that she wants no more of these visions which make her taste "the depths of human despair." [52]

With these words, Kate Chopin the writer left the sensuous, if not sexual, dreams about the lost companion and plunged into a novel on the very real problems of a woman who sets out on her own, a project which finally gave the author a chance to display a substantial part of her power awaiting opportunity.

VII
The Awakening

1. *Edna and the Female Condition*

Kate Chopin's third novel opens at the pension of Mme. Lebrun on
Grand Isle, where the twenty-nine-year-old Edna Pontellier is vaca-
tioning with her children, Raoul and Etienne. At weekends, the ambitious money-maker Léonce Pontellier leaves his brokerage business
in New Orleans to join them. Adèle Ratignolle is there, too, with her
youngsters. She is the supreme example of "the mother-woman," the
self-effacing species of nest-makers dominating the island. Edna is no
such female, however, and though she in a way is fond of her sons,
she vaguely feels motherhood to be "a responsibility which she had
blindly assumed and for which Fate had not fitted her." [1]

Edna is an outsider also in another respect. Born in Kentucky of
Presbyterian stock, she is the only "American" in this all-Creole,
Catholic group from the Vieux Carré, and although married to one
of these Creoles, she is not yet quite at home among them. Their total
lack of prudery is particularly incomprehensible to her, though she
easily reconciles it with the "lofty chastity which in the Creole woman
seems to be inborn." [2] She is thoroughly shocked, for example, when
Adèle gives a gentleman a description of one of her accouchements
and when a daring French novel is freely discussed at table. She is
also bewildered by the attentions devoted to her by Robert Lebrun,
the twenty-six-year-old son of the hostess, while to Léonce and the
others they are harmless courtesies in the Creole fashion.

As a motherless girl, influenced by a stern father and two uneffusive
sisters, Edna had never learned to show affection, and the three –
innocent – passions of her youth were hidden even from their objects.
Her marriage to the twelve years older Léonce was "purely an accident": he fell in love, and she liked him and was flattered by his
devotion. She thought that they had much in common, but, once
married, she found out that this was not so. In a way she grew fond

of her husband, however, "realizing with some unaccountable satisfaction that no trace of passion or excessive and fictitious warmth colored her affection, thereby threatening its dissolution."[3]

As the book opens, there is little contact between the spouses, Léonce spending most of his time in his clubs. Edna is therefore in a vulnerable position, and she is subtly influenced by the presence of Robert and by the general Grand Isle atmosphere. She is intoxicated when the effusive Adèle makes her open her heart; the new candor is like a breath of freedom, and she is suddenly beginning to make her own acquaintance.

One day, a pianist's music rouses her in a new manner. A few hours later, she discovers that she has suddenly learned to swim. She is elated, and when that evening she observes Robert's figure, she feels the first vague throbbings of desire, at the same time becoming aware of her own body and her dormant will. The next day she asks Robert to join her on a sailing trip. In the boat, she feels as if the chains of her anchor have snapped, leaving her free to take her own course. Robert understands that he loves her, and leaves for Mexico. Left alone, Edna finally realizes the nature of her feelings for him. She recalls how it used to disturb her that her three former passions had melted out of her existence, but she does not heed the lessons of the past: "The present alone was significant; was hers, to torture her as it was doing then with the biting conviction that she had lost that which she had held, that she had been denied that which her impassioned, newly awakened being demanded."[4]

On her return to New Orleans, Edna completely disregards her duties as a wife, suddenly discontinuing, for example, the reception day which she for six years has held each week to further her husband's business interests. She defies Léonce, who has a tendency to regard her as one of his "possessions," and decides never to take another step backward. When her sister marries, she declares a wedding to be "one of the most lamentable spectacles on earth."[5]

As she yields to every caprice, she takes up painting, which she has dabbled in before. She even imagines herself to be an artist, but Mlle. Reisz – the musician – tells her that "to succeed, the artist must possess the courageous soul, . . . the soul that dares and defies."[6] Meanwhile, Léonce believes her to be unbalanced, whereas in reality she is just becoming herself. The Pontelliers are visited by Edna's father, a former Confederate Colonel, who seems to wear the mantle of the harsh patriarch Dr. Chopin when he tells his son-in-law to use his authority with Edna. Dr. Mandelet, however, the wise old family physician, advises Léonce to leave her alone and not ask her to go with him to New York, where he is to speculate on Wall Street. When the children are carried off by old Mme. Pontellier and the house is empty, Edna feels a sense of restfulness such as she has never known.

While Edna keeps in indirect contact with Robert through reading his letters to Mlle. Reisz, she meets Alcée Arobin, a roué. He means nothing to her, but she grows accustomed to him. She decides to rent a small house with her own money: "Instinct had prompted her to put away her husband's bounty in casting off her allegiance. . . . When he returned, there would have to be an understanding . . . ; but whatever came, she had resolved never again to belong to another than herself." On learning from Mademoiselle that Robert is coming back and that he loves her, Edna confesses that she loves him, too. The musician tells her that it takes strength to defy the rules of society, and Edna feels that she must one day decide what character of woman she is: "By all the codes which I am acquainted with, I am a devilishly wicked specimen of the sex. But some way I can't convince myself that I am." [7]

When Alcée kisses her, she responds fully and yields to him. She feels Robert's reproach, and regrets that "it was not love which had held this cup of life to her lips," yet without repenting. [8] While Léonce saves appearances by announcing that the house will be remodeled in his absence, Edna gives a last dinner before moving out of it. She is a prey to conflicting emotions. She feels an acute longing for Robert; at the same time, the thought of him gives her a feeling of hopelessness. Her animalism is stirring impatiently within her, and she acts with no feeling of responsibility.

When Robert returns, he avoids her. When they meet by accident and Edna arouses him with a kiss, he finally admits that he loves her and that his return had been prompted by a wild dream that Léonce would set her free. She laughs at the idea that others should decide for her, and she tells her friend: "we shall love each other, my Robert. . . . Nothing else in the world is of any consequence." Her kisses and her seductive voice awaken his senses. At this very moment she is called away to Adèle, whom she has promised to help when she is to give birth. She leaves, disregarding Robert's protestations, while telling him to wait for her. [9]

At the Ratignolles', Edna regrets that she has come: "With an inward agony, with a flaming, outspoken revolt against the ways of Nature, she witnessed the scene of torture." Before she leaves, Adèle implores her to think of her own children. When Dr. Mandelet walks her home, she concedes that "One has to think of the children some time or other; the sooner the better." While she here reflects Euripides' Phaedra, who recognizes the duty to preserve the "honorable name" of her family, she at the same time protests that no one – "except children, perhaps" – have the right to force one into doing things. The Doctor senses that she is in trouble; he tells her not to blame herself, but to come to him, because *he* would understand her. Edna has decided to think of the children – later. As she sits on the porch before entering, her senses are again awakened, and she looks forward to the "possession of the beloved one." But inside, she finds only a note: "Good-by – because I love you." [10]

That night, Edna does all the thinking that is necessary. She realizes that her needs will lead her to a series of lovers. Not that she minds, or thinks of Léonce, "but Raoul and Etienne!" She wants no one near her except Robert, but she sees that the day will come when even he will mean nothing to her. She views her children as "antagonists who . . . sought to drag her into the soul's slavery for the rest of her days. But she knew a way to elude them." She goes to Grand Isle and swims to her death. [11]

2. *Woman Her Own Destiny*

Phanor Breazeale, Kate Chopin's brother-in-law, apparently believed that the author had taken the main theme for *The Awakening* from the life history of a woman well known to the Creole elite of New Orleans. While he may have been right – Edna's story is not entirely unusual – nothing has come down to us to verify the existence of this possible model. [12]

What can be demonstrated, however, is that there are similarities between the novel and Maupassant's "Réveil," a brief tale which describes how a woman is passionately aroused by one admirer only to live out her free-floating sensuality with another. The awakening and disillusionment indicated by the title are those of Jeanne Vasseur, a woman who loves her husband, but is sexually cold. While she is visiting Paris, her senses are awakened by a young man, but after she dreams that she gives herself to him, she makes him promise to respect her. On leaving the man one day, she is in a trance, ready to yield to him, and when another admirer, a roué, at that moment comes to see her, she is an easy prey as she imagines his caresses to be those of the youth. But she rouses from her trance, throws the lover out, and leaves Paris to join her husband. When seeing the young man later, "she suddenly perceived that she had never loved him, except in a dream from which [the roué] had brutally awakened her." [13]

While Kate Chopin's novel may owe the title and a central situation to this story, it also has something of *Madame Bovary*, in theme, incidents, and details. Both heroines become estranged from their husbands; neglect their children; have lovers; lose the sense of responsibility, and take their own lives. There are traits of Léon Dupuis in Robert Lebrun and of Rodolphe Boulanger in Alcée Arobin, and both books include such matters as a crucial party and a haunting song.

These and many other similarities might justify us in calling *The Awakening* an American *Madame Bovary*. Mrs. Chopin did not use the French classic as a model, however, but only as a point of departure, giving the story an entirely new emphasis. Flaubert paints the manners and the mediocrity of bourgeois life. A major part of Emma's motive power stems from her belief that the fortunate ones – the elite, the Parisians – lead charmed lives, and, to a large degree, she stands for both sexes in her self-dramatization and her frenetic attempts to escape her dull environment. Edna, meanwhile, is socially secure and satisfied with her upper middle class position, and she even has certain means of her own. This constitutes a basic difference between the two women, and, unconcerned with her protagonist's social and economic situation, Kate Chopin could focus very sharply on the truly fundamental problem of what it means to be a woman, particularly in a patriarchy. Edna's revolt against her conventional roles as a wife and mother and against her biological destiny is naturally more representative for the female than the male mind, and it is possible to see *The Awakening* as a woman's reply to a man's *Madame Bovary*.

The common starting point of the two heroines is that both have grown up on romanticism with its exalted ideas of transcendent love. Emma enters marriage believing that it will give her the "'bliss,' 'passion,' and 'rapture' ... that had seemed so beautiful to her in books," and as soon as the ball at the chateau has made her reality unbearable to her, she is ready to act out the roles she has inherited from romantic literature. When Edna meets Léonce, she is infatuated with a tragedian and dreams of the "acme of bliss" that a marriage with him would mean; she weds Pontellier, however, and imagines that she will take her place in the world of reality and forget her dreams forever, but finds years later that they can suddenly flare up again.[14]

In their attempts to realize their visions, the two women illustrate a second basic dissimilarity. In her fight for the fulfillment of her dreams, Emma persists in trying to conform to models, blaming others rather than herself when she is disappointed in her roles, and gaining little insight into her own nature; thus, Bovarysme, as Jules de Gaultier defined it, is the urge to imagine oneself to be different from what one is in reality. "Pontellierism," on the other hand, represents a wish for clarity and a willingness to understand one's inner and outer reality, besides a desire to dictate one's own role rather than to slip into patterns prescribed by tradition.

By necessity, the two books in many respects mirror the difference between the French and American customs and mores of the nineteenth century, for example in the traditional attitudes toward the family. When a man in the Latin countries sought love outside his marriage, as happened fairly often, financial and religious considerations combined to keep the family intact and to reject the idea of divorce as irresponsible self-indulgence. The wife's possible urge for freedom was crippled by Catholic strictures and by the dominant husband's control of even the dowry. The emancipationism of Mme. de Staël and George Sand had not in the least affected the masculine mythology of the submissive woman.

While French females were strictly chaperoned until they married, their Yankee Protestant counterparts were allowed an expansive, innocent playfulness. The American girl, as Howells established her, was an important person with her vivacious charm and her will power and independence. (In certain states she already had the right to vote.) When love came to her and her suitor, it was supposed to be strong and lasting, and marriage was based on mutual affection rather than on money arrangements. With the American Constitution's emphasis on personal happiness, and with what has been described as the Yankee insistence on seeing the highest romantic attachment as incompatible with an illicit, secret liaison, affairs generally resulted in a divorce and a subsequent proud display of idealistic love in a new marriage.[15]

A similar idealism was of course reflected in the Victorian American decorum, which banned many facts about human nature from speech and writing, partly to spare the young Iron Madonna, to whom the country's literature was mainly directed. (Mrs. Chopin, on her part, once observed that books "written by thoughtful men ... are not addressed to the youthful imagination .... If they are written by other than thoughtful people, there is apt to be no truth in them, and they cannot appeal to lovers of sincerity of any age.") Scorning idealism, the French and the Creoles accepted human nature in a relatively free manner which was bound to shock Mrs. Pontellier. Their literary openness made Howells complain of "certain nudities which the Latin peoples seem to find edifying." As we know, American authors loved to stage a European confrontation of the supposed New World innocence with a Latin sinfulness, or to contrast a blonde heroine at home with a dark-haired, dangerous, usually Gallic woman. *Scribner's* complained in 1891 about "the current ... attempt to Frenchify" American fiction; but as a rule, the native literary temptresses were still punished in one way or another.[16]

When Kate Chopin turned to an American heroine abroad – that is, abroad in the still largely French Louisiana – she made use of one progressive aspect of each of the two worlds: the Yankee female emancipationism in the spiritual field, and the Gallic openness about even woman's sensuous awakening. Breaking the usual pattern, she contrasts Edna not with a dark-haired, sinful temptress, but with an eminently respectable Latin wife and mother. The Creole and undoubtedly Catholic Adèle is a striking illustration of the patriarchal ideal of the submissive female who writes her history only through her family.[17]

While such confinement of the female made Margaret Fuller consider her to be "only an overgrown child," it was exalted by Catholics of both sexes in their deification of the Virgin Mary, the Goddess Mother. Mme. Ratignolle clearly reflects this cult; she is a "faultless Madonna" and a supreme example of the "mother-woman," a species defined – again with a Biblical ring – as the "women who idolized their children, worshiped their husbands, and esteemed it a holy

privilege to efface themselves as individuals and grow wings as min-
istering angels." She is thus a perfect foil for Mrs. Pontellier as she
becomes aware of her craving for independence and of her sensuous
nature.[18]

Edna's emancipation starts with her physical attraction to Robert.
Concurrently she begins "to realize her position in the universe as a
human being, and to recognize her relations as an individual to the
world within and about her." The author introduces a discreet feminist touch in the next sentence when she suggests that woman is
usually not granted much wisdom. This note is developed in connection with Edna's first swim. "A feeling of exultation overtook her, as
if some power of significant import had been given her to control
the working of her body and her soul. She grew daring and reckless . . . . She wanted to swim far out, where no woman had swum
before. . . . As she swam she seemed to be reaching out for the unlimited in which to lose herself." When she vaguely feels the first
suggestions of desire, her will blazes up, and her tacit submissiveness
to Léonce comes to an abrupt end. But conditions restrict her, and her
dreams only leave her dejected.[19]

What dominates her imagination during this period is not so much
a feminist revolt as the idea of a transcendent passion for Robert of
the kind suggested by romantic literature; and not seeking help from
any source, external or internal, to check it, she dreams about such
a love, lending herself to any impulse as if freed of all responsibility.
The novel echoes Romantic fiction when Robert stirs Edna's fancy
with his talk about Gulf spirits and his suggestion of their going to a
treasure island. She pities Adèle for her blind contentment which excludes her from ever tasting "life's delirium," and what she means by
this is suggested in a story which she invents: "They could hear the
long sweep of the pirogue through the glistening moonlit water . . . ;
they could see the faces of the lovers, pale, close together, rapt in
oblivious forgetfulness, drifting into the unknown." [20]

We have many elements here of the romantic syndrome of the
great, overpowering, irresponsible love which was the undoing of
Emma Bovary. Though Edna recognizes the symptoms of her pre-
marital infatuations and finally realizes that it is desire that is shaking
her, she is still very much the sentimental heroine of the Romantic
era, for example where she sobs over Robert's letter while Mlle. Reisz
plays Wagner for her. Even the mournful notes of her occasional des-

pondency seem to fit into this picture of a nineteenth century heroine. In reality, however, they form the accompaniment to her gradual emancipation as she revolts against housewifely duties and finally moves to a house of her own. As she is "becoming herself and daily casting aside that fictitious self which we assume like a garment with which to appear before the world," she throws her ring on the floor, seeing both Léonce and her children as foes.[21]

Meanwhile, her infatuation with Robert fills her with an incomprehensible longing as she imagines her love for him to be a grand, beautiful, and undivided passion. She is restless and excited and wants something to happen. Then Alcée shows her a cicatrice on his wrist, and she clutches it for a moment. He looks at her, and "the effrontery in his eyes repelled the old, vanishing self in her, yet drew all her awakening sensuousness." In spite of her few drops of French blood, Edna is a Yankee, and she is bewildered by the Creole erotic forwardness. But the author does not believe in a particularly American innocence. Nowhere does she ascribe this "French" sexual awakening to an offensive Gallic influence. She makes a point of showing Edna's sensuous urges as inherent; thus, the heroine feels desire long before she senses Robert's feelings for her. Like Mildred of "A Shameful Affair," Edna does not make a show of virtuous reticence: "He saw enough in her face to impel him to take her hand" and to kiss it.[22]

For a moment she feels as if passion had betrayed her into an act of infidelity, that is, toward Robert; but she goes on seeing Alcée, who increasingly appeals to her animalism. It is during another session of romantic music at Mlle. Reisz' that she learns of the exile's return. Invigorated and happy and looking forward to future bliss with him, she gives an entirely sentimental description of her loved one. That evening, when she is in a sort of trance, filled with ecstatic thoughts about Robert, Alcée kisses her. She does not repel him, but "clasped his head, holding his lips to hers. It was the first kiss of her life to which her nature had really responded."[23]

After this exposition, the author – in a single, crucial paragraph – explodes the romantic myth of the noble, undivided passion. Leaving behind all traits of the maudlin heroine of the dime-novels, Edna now realizes that the physical component of love can stand apart from the spiritual one, that sensuous attraction is impersonal and can be satisfied by a partner she does not love. Her awakening to the true nature of love has thus something of Maupassant's "Réveil." But unlike Mme. Vasseur, Edna is not shocked and does not return to a disappointed respectability. Instead of blaming the roué, she looks her own animalism in the eye. She realizes that life is a "monster made up of beauty and brutality," and she feels neither shame nor remorse. Her action of clasping Alcée's head symbolizes her double awakening, as an erotic being, and as an independent individual who craves to be an active subject rather than a passive object. For her, all return to past submission and all continuation of self-delusion is impossible.[24]

Woman's emancipation is a difficult and lonely process, however, and the author accompanies it with a tone of pessimism. As Edna gives the party before moving to a house of her own, she feels hopelessness as she spreads her arms like "the regal woman, the one who rules, who looks on, who stands alone." She has a sense of the unattainable, and she falls back a little into the role of an object as she becomes supple to Alcée's seductive entreaties. Yet she grows in independence. "Every step which she took toward relieving herself from obligations added to her strength and expansion as an individual. She began to look with her own eyes; to see and to apprehend the deeper undercurrents of life. No longer was she content to 'feed upon opinion' when her own soul had invited her." While not thwarting Léonce's efforts to save appearances, she herself does not care about them, nor about Adèle's warning that Alcée's company could ruin her name.[25]

Edna still has certain illusions about her love for Robert, and when she meets him on his return, she presses him for a sign that he loves her. But he leaves her unsatisfied, and she alternates between hope – "if he really loved her, [his reserve] could not hold against her own passion" – and despondency. All sense of reality leaves her, and she indifferently abandons herself to fate, awaiting the consequences with near-apathy. Meanwhile, she depends on the ever-present roué for physical satisfaction, and when she yields to him again, both despondency and hope leave her.[26]

Yet she cannot give up Robert, and while realizing that he might consider her "unwomanly," she takes the initiative toward him when they next meet, giving him the voluptuous kiss which sets him on fire. Refusing to be what she regards as the inessential adjunct to man, she has something of the emancipated woman who wants to play the man's role as a taker. It is not his role *per se* that she wants, however, but only those aspects of it which make the creation of one's own essence, as Jean-Paul Sartre terms it, easier for the male than it is for the female. "I would give up the unessential; I would give my money, I would give my life for my children; but I wouldn't give myself," Edna observes. "I don't know what you would call the essential, or what you mean by the unessential," Adèle answers; to her, woman's ultimate gift is her life, and she does not understand that as Edna's eyes are gradually opened, it is less important to her to live than to have a self, and that she now insists on an individual, authentic existence and wants a freedom to exert a conscious choice which can bring out her own essence.[27]

It is when Edna caresses Robert in an action "full of love and tenderness" that he tells her of his dream that Léonce would let her marry him. While Robert thus, a little surprisingly, for a time had thought of braving opinion with such an American idea as a new marriage (the Louisiana divorce rate was far below the national average), Edna does not take him up on it; it is another aspect of the problem which is important to her: "I am no longer one of Mr. Pontellier's possessions to dispose of or not," she answers. "I give myself where I choose. If he were to say, 'Here, Robert, take her and be happy; she is yours,' I should laugh at you both."[28]

What Edna demands is in part the right to be "a Free Lover," as Victoria Woodhull had termed it when she in 1871 had publicly declared: "I have an inalienable . . . right to love whom I may, to love as . . . I please!" But her demand goes beyond this to include the right to direct her own life in general. No wonder that Robert turns pale as he guesses that she is flouting not only the French notion of a secret affair and the American idea of a new marriage, but also his Creole idea of the men deciding woman's fate.[29]

As Kenneth Eble has pointed out in his excellent article on *The Awakening*, Edna "is not an Emma Bovary, deluded by ideas of 'romance'." Instead she is goaded on by sexual hunger much in the manner of Euripides' Phaedra and E. A. Robinson's heroine in "Eros Turannos." Yet she is not one of those who "with a god have striven," as Robinson puts it. When the Greek heroine falls into "the abyss" or "the great sea of love," she feels shame and tries to fight her passion. Likewise, Euripides may tell us that the tide of love is not withstandable and that "It is natural for men to err when they are blinded by the Gods," but his emphasis is on retribution for moral blindness. Edna is a different case. She feels no shame, and she knows by now that passions are transitory and transferable; therefore, she seems to foresee only an affair with Robert.[30]

The idea that she is somewhat exceptional in being smitten by the gods would also be quite foreign to her. She sees Eros as a universal, amoral drive, and in this she reflects George Sand's Lélia who observes that erotic "pleasure" was once the only bond between man and woman, that is, before "moral passion with its obstacles [and] sufferings" had yet been invented. Edna does not apply moral considerations to the fundamental force. Though she is aware that love is indiscriminate and evanescent, she cannot join Euripides who likens it with a flitting bee which brings destruction to the flowers, or Zola who makes it a disintegrating force, or Hardy who has Sue in *Jude the Obscure* trying to mortify the flesh. When Edna cannot convince herself that she is a profligate woman it is because she sees Eros as a deep urge which antedates and takes precedence over all morals.[31]

Edna's sexual emancipation is so completely interlocked with her spiritual breaking of bonds that she insists on both with equal force. Even so it is a remarkable feature of *The Awakening* that the protagonist thinks nothing of disregarding her traditional duties toward her husband and of challenging the sacred concept of matrimony which the heroines of Mmes. de Staël and Sand had been fighting. "Infamous tyranny of man over woman! Marriage, society, institutions, woe to you!" George Sand wrote in *Valentine*. It is as if Edna's creator considers these aspects of woman's emancipation too elementary for further comment and wants to move on to the really fundamental – and more taboo – factor which her predecessors had shied away from: the children.[32]

As Mrs. Pontellier develops, she accepts nothing that hinders her from exerting her own free will and making her own rules; she wants to be an absolute and create her own destiny, and unlike Ibsen's Nora, she is sure she is right rather than society. Edna had for many years been a tolerably good mother, and we cannot simply include her among those women who are "not born to be mothers," as Ibsen put it in his worknotes for *Hedda Gabler*. But now she sees her boys as opponents and refuses to live for them rather than for her self. When Edna parts from Robert to go to the childbirth, she still believes that she has a certain power to direct her own life. But Adèle's reminder of the mother's duty toward her children; her own reflections as she watches her friend's birth agonies, and Dr. Mandelet's comments as he walks her home after the ordeal, change her view of her possibilities for a self-directed, emancipated life. "Youth is given up to illusions," the Doctor observes. "It seems to be a provision of Nature; a decoy to secure mothers for the race. And Nature takes no account of moral consequences, of arbitrary conditions which we create, and which we feel obliged to maintain at any cost." [33]

Edna realizes that sex is not only separate from love, but also largely independent of our volition, being a fundamental force of nature which spurs us blindly on toward procreation. This is the function of the brutal juxtaposition of the love-scene and the childbirth: to suggest how pleasure and pain, conception and delivery are inextricably intertwined. She sees how sex and pregnancy represent nature's play with woman, and she concludes that a woman's links, or chains, to her children make her hopes for independence illusory. She realizes that patriarchal society is quick to condemn particularly a freedom-seeking woman who neglects her children since she – rather than her husband – is "intended by nature" to take care of them.

The note which Edna finds when she returns to her house is a further illustration of woman's situation in a man's world. Robert's words signify to her not only that he is afraid of braving conventions, but also that "he would never understand" her, or ever accept that kind of independence and equality without which she cannot exist. He is Kate Chopin's example of the ordinary man who cannot tolerate the unusual woman, and his reactions emphasize the reasoning which relentlessly leads Mrs. Pontellier to her final exertion of responsibility and of her will as she pays the price of freedom.[34]

3. *The Curse of Freedom*

Edna thus takes her life because she, on the one hand, insists on sexual and spiritual freedom, and, on the other, acknowledges a duty not to "trample upon the little lives." Her suicide was entirely valid for her time, when her ideas of self-assertion were bound to be condemned outright by the Victorian moral vigilantes. But social conditions were mutable to Kate Chopin, and she never lets her heroine attack them. As if she foresaw that the era would come when the advanced woman would be less branded and her children thus less stigmatized, she included also two aspects of the human condition which she must have seen as destined to plague even the modern Edna.[35]

The first of these is the inevitable loss of illusions, particularly the "singular delusion that love is eternal," as Mrs. Chopin expressed it in a story, and the idea that we can see the reality involved in our passions. "Romances serve but to feed the imagination of the young; they add nothing to the sum of truth," she said in another tale, and in a third: "It was the time when the realities of life clothe themselves in the garb of romance, when Nature's decoys are abroad; when the tempting bait is set." In response to Dr. Mandelet's even more outspoken statements, Mrs. Pontellier remarks: "Yes. ... To wake up and find – oh! well! perhaps it is better to wake up after all, even to suffer, rather than to remain a dupe to illusions all one's life." What pains Edna is her realization that the idea of the great passion with its lofty, personal attachment, its one-ness with the beloved is largely a fiction, a euphemistic disguise for a basically sexual attraction, an animalistic, impersonal drive. "To-day it is Arobin; to-morrow it will be some one else. It makes no difference to me," she thinks as she walks into the water, and in spite of the love she feels for Robert, she foresees that one day he, too, "would melt out of her existence, leaving her alone." [36]

It was perhaps no accident that of the eight Maupassant stories which Kate Chopin translated, one is called "Solitude" and another "Suicide," and that these two tell us that "We are the everlasting playthings of ... illusions" and that we are always alone, ironically more so when contact with the opposite sex momentarily makes us forget our solitude. Edna realizes the emptiness in sex-rotation, and she sees herself as driven by sovereign sexuality and selfishness, forces which make for loneliness. [37]

As appears from Mrs. Chopin's notebook, she originally titled her novel "A Solitary Soul." [38] When she did this she was no doubt referring in part to Edna's awakening to the loneliness of imperative sexuality, of illusory, evanescent love. But the term refers even more to another aspect of the human condition: the curse of freedom. Kate Chopin's view of life was to a large extent independent of such important currents of thought as idealism, socio-economic determinism, and even religion. The attitude she lets Mrs. Pontellier illustrate comes close to that of existentialism. She seems to say that Edna has a real existence only when she gives her own laws, when she through conscious choice becomes her own creation with an autonomous self. But while such a developmental freedom may strengthen the self, it is accompanied by a growing sense of isolation and aloneness, and also anguish. To realize existence as an authentic subject demands a painful choosing, and man is tempted to run away from it as he – in Sartre's term – feels "condemned to be free." [39]

If the process of existential individuation is taxing on a man and freedom a lonely and threatening thing to him, it is doubly so for a woman who attempts to emancipate herself from the state of immanence to which our patriarchal world has assigned her for milleniums. Feminism was well advanced in Kate Chopin's America, and she probably foresaw that woman would obtain the degree of equality with man that she has today. But she could also see that what women mostly demanded, and men only bit by bit granted, was a technical equality which did not alter the basic roles and attitudes of either sex.

She seems to have realized that in the patriarchy, man would not willingly relinquish the role of the conqueror, nor woman that of the conquered. To her, man's instinct of mastery, and the "constant rebuff" which a man feels if a woman lacks "the coquettish, the captivating, the feminine," as she expressed it in a story, were enduring realities. Adèle captivates men by being coquettish and naive and by acting the role of the weak, while Edna is incapable of using her friend's "feline or feminine wiles" or "kittenish display" to attract their notice. Kate Chopin could see how even George Sand's Indiana, for example, stresses that she is "only a weak woman," and she may have guessed that also her creator, in spite of all her militancy, somewhere deep down subscribed to the myth of the strong man and the weak woman. Had Mérimée loved me, Mme. Sand wrote in a letter after an expected affair with him had failed to get started, "he would have dominated me, and if I had found a man capable of dominating me, I should have been saved, for liberty is eating my life away, and killing me." [40]

The French pioneer here touches the fundamental problem confronting the female emancipationist. As long as girls play with dolls and boys with guns; as long as men dominate and women submit and the Madonna is the chief Christian ideal of a feminine being, society will show a quite compact resistance against woman leaving her traditional role as the weaker sex; consequently, the female feels a tremendous pressure to prove that she is a woman first and only secondly an individual.

The old role is of course in many ways convenient for the woman;

she is materially provided for, and also metaphysically – as Simone de Beauvoir has emphasized – in the sense that she does not need to justify her existence as a wife and mother and that she can largely leave the responsibility for her fate to the man.[41] But the moment she feels it more important to be an individual than to be a woman (or at least a mother-woman), as Edna does, she is in deep water: Unassisted, she has to create her own role and status and define her aims; she must fight society's opposition as well as her own feelings of insecurity and guilt, and – more than a man – she suffers under the liberty in which she must justify her existence. When a woman in the existential manner assumes sole responsibility for her life, which then depends on her own efforts, freedom becomes something of a negative condition and she herself indeed a solitary soul.

Kate Chopin was undoubtedly familiar with the existence of the matriarchies of old and of her own day, and thus aware that the patriarchy was no law of nature. Even so, she seems to see no happy end to woman's quest for freedom. Edna wants to decide over her own life, but this urge brings her despair rather than happiness. She appears to need all her strength to want freedom *from* rather than freedom *to,* and to be too weak both to break the chains and to justify her non-conformist existence through positive performance. The note of pessimism which runs through the book may be due in part to the romantic syndrome which Edna mirrors in her passion, her anguish, and her occasional passivity and desire for nothingness. The ultimate reason for the heroine's feeling of hopelessness, however, is her urge for spiritual emancipation which is so strong that there is no turning back for her: "She did not look back now, but went on and on." [42]

Edna is defeated in the sense that she cannot meaningfully relate herself to the people around her and in some way integrate her demands with those of society, a society, to be sure, which is responsible for the fact that emancipation is her goal rather than her birthright. Not attempting to come to terms with her selfish drives, she is unable to reach that harmony, that feeling of creative cooperation and companionship with the people around her at which Athénaïse apparently arrives. Yet she is not defeated like Emma Bovary: Her death is not so much a result of outer forces crowding her in as a triumphant assertion of her inner liberty.

Mrs. Chopin's heroine does not try to "escape from freedom," to

use Erich Fromm's term. Rather, her suicide is the crowning glory of
her development from the bewilderment which accompanied her early
emancipation to the clarity with which she understands her own
nature and the possibilities of her life as she decides to end it. Edna's
victory lies in her awakening to an independence that includes an act
of renunciation. The novel is something of a landmark in nineteenth-
century American literature in that it reaches out beyond woman's
obtaining equality in law and love to the existentialist demand for
dictating one's own destiny, and even beyond that to the horror of
freedom, the immutable affliction for both the women and men who
venture that far. What is most important, however, is that the book is
a great artistic achievement.

4. The Work of Art

A few months before she started on *The Awakening,* Kate Chopin
reviewed Joel Chandler Harris' *Sister Jane.* "There is everything
weak, unjointed, melodramatic about the plot," she observed. "He
has not the constructive faculty that goes to the making of even the
mediocre novel; while he lacks the 'vision' which gives us the great
novel." Mrs. Chopin here suggests her own development, from the
weak plot and lack of focus in *At Fault* to the constructive faculty and
the vision she demonstrates in her *chef d'œuvre.* To these qualities we
may – with Kenneth Eble – add the novel's excellence in its characterizations and in its use of symbols to unify the structure. *The Awakening* shows that the author had learned, now also in a longer work,
to eliminate irrelevancies and to make everything contribute to a
single, strong effect.[43]

The framework of the novel is simple. The opening scene presents
Edna and two of her men and suggests the awakening that has just
begun in her, which we then follow chronologically to its climax half
a year later; once, only, are we offered an extended cutback to her
past. Like many a short story writer turning novelist, Kate Chopin
may have conceived of the chapters as independent entities. But the
book is not episodic; the author's constant focus on the heroine makes
for an unbroken continuity between the successive scenes.[44] All chapters are given to her inner growth. The other figures and the setting
are worked out only to the degree they can support or contrast her
development.

A little more than half the book is set in New Orleans. But, as Cyrille Arnavon has observed, the city makes itself less felt than Grand Isle, and the reason is that the latter is more important as a sounding-board for Edna's growth. Even though Mrs. Chopin devotes only little space to the setting, she gives an unmistakable sense of place. With a few, quick strokes she manages to evoke powerfully the whole scene, to create an ever-present Southern atmosphere. We see the Lebrun pension and the bent oaks, the sandy path and the Gulf caressing the beach. We feel the luscious charm of the summer. We sense the "tangle of the sea smell and of weeds and damp, new-plowed earth, mingled with the heavy perfume of a field of white blossoms . . . ." But above all, there is the sea itself:[45]

The voice of the sea is seductive; never ceasing, whispering, clamoring, murmuring, inviting the soul to wander for a spell in abysses of solitude; to lose itself in mazes of inward contemplation.
The voice of the sea speaks to the soul. The touch of the sea is sensuous, enfolding the body in its soft, close embrace.

Observing that Kate Chopin's use of the sea as a seducer of the body and the soul has much of Whitman, Robert B. Bush has pointed to how these paragraphs echo phrases in "Song of Myself": "I loafe and invite my soul," and "You sea, I resign myself to you also – I guess what you mean/ . . . Dash me with amorous wet . . . ." Kenneth Eble, on his part, has noted how the refrain beginning "The voice of the sea . . ." is repeated in the novel, with subtle variations.[46]

In general we may say that the Gulf serves as the seductive and invigorating force behind Edna's drifting into a sensual awakening and her learning to strike out toward authenticity. As in "Song of Myself," these aspects of self-awareness are inextricably fused: "Is this then a touch? quivering me into a new identity . . . ."[47] Mrs. Chopin's ocean suggests a number of the primordial qualities which later commentators on this archetypal element have emphasized in it: It is our beginning and our end (Freud); it is a free place, but therefore also a lonely place of alienation (W. H. Auden); and it is an element which inspires to spiritual endeavor (Gaston Bachelard). Encompassing these and other associations with the water, Kate Chopin's Gulf forms the great controlling metaphor of *The Awakening*.[48]

It would seem that it is particularly Edna's exposure to the sea and to Robert during the daily swimming lesson that stirs her passions. In our first glimpse of her, the advanced intimacy with him is brought out by a little incident in the water, and we are returned to this element in the picture of the music arousing her like the waves swaying and beating upon her. When she learns to swim and imagines she can control her body and her soul, she spends more and more time in the water; and after Robert's departure, this is the only activity which pleases and invigorates her. Through frequent brief references to the Gulf, or to the seductive odor and the breeze coming from it, or to its murmur which is like a "loving but imperative entreaty," the sea is kept constantly before us. Back in town, Edna recalls the water and the hot wind and is swept by desire, and she makes the Gulf the stage of the love-fantasy she invents.[49]

The sea and the beach are also involved in two further pictures she evokes. Gazing out over the Gulf, she recalls how she as a little girl had walked through a Kentucky meadow "that seemed as big as the ocean." She was "beating the tall grass as one strikes out in the water," she tells Adèle. "My sun-bonnet obstructed the view. I could see only the stretch of green before me, and I felt as if I must walk on forever, without coming to the end of it." Two men are also part of the recollection: her father, whose gloomy Sunday service she had just run away from, and the cavalry officer who at that time, as the first, had made her "passionately enamored." The second picture is evoked in her by a piece of music which she calls "Solitude." In it, a man is standing naked on the seashore in an attitude of "hopeless resignation as he [looks] toward a distant bird winging its flight away from him."[50]

While we may see no immediate significance in the latter picture, we may more easily note the author's symbolic use of the sun, the ultimate life-force, and its correlates, a family of images which here undoubtedly stands for Eros. Robert had "lived in the sunlight" of a young lady, we are told, and later been so inflamed by Adèle that the sea sizzled when he took his daily plunge. Edna dreams of being alone with him in the sun, to watch the wriggling gold snakes and the slimy lizards writhe in and out of the fort near Grand Isle, a picture with clear sexual overtones. The fire is going in Mlle. Reisz' stove when she acts as a go-between, and when Edna reads that Robert is to come back, it is "red-hot." That night, after splashing through the streets, Edna sits in front of her own fire and tells Alcée that the sun will return; a moment later, the roué's kiss lights the "flaming torch that kindled desire." [51]

The dynamic eroticism suggested by the elements of water and fire is reflected even in the least developed characters. We find it in two young lovers who lean against each other, exchanging sighs and vows as they tread upon blue ether. We find it also in M. Farival, an old man who gives his attentions in vain to a jaded-looking lady in black; and the fact that she combines her devotion to God with a spying upon the lovers suggests that even she is not above earthly passions. Given only a single trait, these figures are less living persons than silent actors in a pantomime on love.

When another set of characters is a little more developed, it is again with emphasis on erotic passions. They are Victor, Robert's brother, and Mariequita, a sly Spanish girl. Victor tells Edna of his amorous exploits, while insisting that they must be incomprehensible to a woman. He considers Mariequita his property. She has sand and slime between her toes. This is a rare detail in the book, an earthy, realistic note which underlines that she is a girl of the people who knows the facts of life. Her openness about immorality is contrasted by the deviousness of Mrs. Highcamp, an apparently tainted woman who uses her daughter "as a pretext for cultivating the society of young men of fashion" while keeping the forms with her husband. Alcée, with his "dreadful reputation," fits well in her circle. [52]

This emphasis on the passion which peoples the earth is entirely natural in a novel which covers two gestations and births. *The Awakening* is a finely wrought system of tensions and interrelations set up between Edna's slow birth as a sexual and authentic being, and the counterpointed pregnancy and confinement of Adèle.

There is also the interaction between the heroine and her men and a constant interplay between Edna's passion and her attitude to her boys. We find the latter already in an early incident in which her still only lightly suggested attraction to Robert is offset by Léonce's reproach that she neglects her children. When she later is able to show greater tenderness toward them on occasion, it is apparently both a result of her emotional thaw and an expiation for her affairs. In his discussion of this point, George Arms stresses the element of penance. Yet Edna's growing ability to show affection is also significant. After the total unfolding of her sensuality, she spends a week with her boys at old Mme. Pontellier's, and now she is able to give them "all of herself." [53]

The children themselves are somewhat anonymous. We see the sturdy fellows of four and five who run to their mother not for comfort, but to ask for bonbons. But we never hear them speak directly, and we are given no details similar to Edna's description of the shape of Robert's nose. It seems as if the author wants to show that while the boys may be living realities to the heroine, they are so more in their capacity of demands put upon her than as living individuals who directly influence the awakening that is the subject of the book. She may part from them with a wrench, but after a few hours their voices no longer echo in her soul, and she is "again alone." [54]

As Edna's counterpart, Adèle is presented more at length. We are shown her total devotion to her family, and the domestic harmony in her home. But there are shades in this picture of a mother-woman who has a baby every two years and is always talking about her "condition": Though she is the embodiment of unselfishness in her care for the children, she also uses them as an excuse to draw attention to herself. She complains of faintness though the color never leaves her, and she insists that she only keeps up her music on account of her youngsters while her use of it in her soirées musicales helps give her social standing. [55]

In general, however, she is "the embodiment of every womanly grace and charm," the perfect representative of the Bible's idea of the female. Through a subtle use of Biblical allusions, the author sets up a duality between Adèle and Edna. The former is compared to a Madonna, and she speaks of her duty in terms of the Bible. Edna, meanwhile, is shown as not belonging to the realm of Christianity. As a child, she ran away from the Presbyterian service. Now, as she begins to make her own acquaintance, her knowledge is described as "perhaps more wisdom than the Holy Ghost is usually pleased to vouchsafe to any woman." Finally, church oppresses her with its "stifling atmosphere." [56]

Edna's half-hearted attempt at becoming an artist is one of her means to escape from this oppression. Mlle. Reisz, the musician, is therefore another natural foil to her. She is far from the Bible's idea of woman. She objects to babies, and she is rude and self-assertive, with "a disposition to trample upon the rights of others." But this disagreeable and unpopular person is at least an individual, and this fact – together with her music – attracts Edna as she struggles with her own individuation. As with Adèle, there are facets to Mademoiselle's leading trait. Though she is a career woman with independent opinions, she is full of the female's traditional hero-worship of the man. If she should love, she declares, it would have to be some *"grand esprit."* [57]

It is of course Edna's three men who serve as the real catalysts for her double awakening. Robert's role is suggested very early. He takes her swimming. He puts a hat on her head or carries a sunshade over her. These simple actions can be fully accounted for on the realistic level; yet they are also symbolic. He has unleashed the waves that continue to beat upon her; at the same time, he is – in Adèle's words – a *bon garçon* and a gentleman who prevents the sun from withering Edna's good name. When he accompanies her from the beach after her first momentous swim, he invents a fairy tale about a spirit from the Gulf which has haunted the shores "for ages," looking for prey. This invention is on one level a nineteenth-century cliché fully consistent with Edna's romantic infatuation. (Its note of Romanticism is sustained through legends and stories in later chapters.) But a further function is involved even here. When Robert suggests that the Gulf spirit may cast a spell over Edna which might unfit her for living with an "unworthy earthling," he foreshadows the effect on her of what the Gulf stands for. [58]

Also the first encounter between Edna and Léonce is presented in a picture which draws on the sun and suggests both the situation and the later development. "You are burnt beyond recognition," he observes, looking at her "as one looks at a valuable piece of personal property which has suffered some damage." Sensing that his house to him is a showplace for his belongings, and feeling herself as one of them, Edna flings a vase on the floor. While he thinks of appearances and speaks of moving with the procession, she is independent of and "different from the crowd," and while his expansion and integrity refer to the material world, she concentrates on the spiritual. Thus the clash between them is inevitable. [59]

The scene after Léonce's departure for Wall Street is typical of the author's suggestive use of images. With "a big, genuine sigh of relief," Edna inspects the house as if for the first time, digging around the plants, picking dry leaves, and plucking a bunch of "bright flowers." In contrast to a previous scene where she had "absently picked a few sprays of jessamine," she is thus now shown as consciously involved with a part of nature. And then:[60]

That night Edna dined alone. The candelabra, with a few candles in the center of the table, gave all the light she needed. Outside the circle of light in which she sat, the large dining-room looked solemn and shadowy. ... The wine tasted good.

Previously, "every light" had been ablaze on the evening she first felt desire for Robert, and none when she later dined with Léonce. The candles continue the fire emblem, and the shadows help sustain the pessimistic tone of the book. The wine is also significant: She had refused to drink with Léonce, while she gladly drank wine in Robert's company. After dinner, Edna "read Emerson until she grew sleepy." She may concur with the transcendentalists in their disregard for external authority, but she is not yet ready to wake up to the full light, or perhaps not interested in communion with their kind of divinity. Instead, she symbolically unites herself with the Gulf by taking "a refreshing bath." [61]

In Alcée, the author has created an accomplished seducer. The way in which she presents him is illustrative of her technique. His reputation is first hinted at when we hear that he played a role in "that story of the consul's wife." Later, Edna meets him at the race-course. That night, the Doctor observes that she is no longer repressed and listless, but "palpitant with the forces of life," and he mutters: "I hope it isn't Arobin." The reader is now ready to meet him. We are not told that he is a shrewd connoisseur or given his interior mono-logue about the heroine, or presented with such an exclamation as that "I'll have her!" as we are in the case of Flaubert's Rodolphe. All Kate Chopin tells us is that "There was a perpetual smile in his eyes"; that "His manner was quiet, and at times a little insolent," and that Edna "had seemed to him unapproachable until that day." The author then uses the fever of racing which stirs their blood as an indicator of what is intoxicating them. Alcée shares her excitement as they go again and again to the races, and the horse is made his metaphor when his continuous unfolding of Edna's sensuality is men-tioned in one breath with his horses, which are "full of mettle, and even a little unmanageable." [62]

There are two editorial chapters in the book, both brief comments on Edna's state of awareness. The first, which follows her yielding to Robert's urge that they go for a swim, suggests that her desire is not yet to be allowed into her consciousness. In the second, which comes after her yielding to Alcée, she has achieved understanding and accepts the sexual urge open-eyed and without shame. Her farewell party a few days later is a sensuous feast with subtle overtones of a ritual for Eros.

The table has something "extremely gorgeous," with the silk cover, the fragrant roses, and the glittering crystal. *Mets, entre-mets,* and wines are served. Soft music and a heavy odor of jessamine complete the picture. While this has a note of Lucullan Rome, we are soon taken further East. A "mystic cord" of joy unites the guests. Mrs. Highcamp weaves a garland of roses and lays it on Victor's black curls, thus transforming him into "a vision of Oriental beauty." This makes the usually composed Alcée exclaim: *"Sapristi!"* [63]

The author's use of colors suggests that she here stages a rite for the primordial forces of the sun and the blood. We find many pairs of colors indicative of the two: The roses are yellow and red; there is champagne and a garnet cocktail; Edna's gown is golden and flesh-colored, and Victor's eyes are fiery and his cheek the color of grapes. One of the guests makes it clear that the divinity which inspires the party is Eros when he quotes: "There was a graven image of Desire/ Painted with red blood on a ground of gold." [64]

While this heathen rite for the life-forces is being enacted, the concomitant themes of birth and death are also kept before us. The monotonous splash of a fountain heard from the garden is a symbol of everlasting birth; Adèle is *"bien souffrante,"* and Edna is close to her spiritual confinement. She feels an acute longing for Robert. But at the same time she has a sense of the unattainable, and the hopelessness and the "chill breath" which sweep over her seem like premonitions of her death. As if to suggest that her end will in part be caused by her insistence on sexual freedom, such votaries of Eros as Alcée and Mrs. Highcamp are clad in death's color. [65]

Adèle's "hour of trial" gives the author a further opportunity to fuse Eros, birth, and death. The confinement scene is set between a real and an imagined embrace, and its core is a double birth which leads to death. When Adèle's agony starts, Edna's throes begin in the form of a vague dread as she thinks of her own births. In this recollection, Mrs. Chopin again unites the sensuous with the beginning and the end of existence, adding a touch of the sadness of eternity, and suggesting the theme of a waking up to a responsibility: "She recalled faintly an ecstasy of pain, . . . and an awakening to find a little new life to which she had given being, added to the great unnumbered multitude of souls that come and go." The focal birth scene is dealt with in a single sentence. It echoes Euripides' term in *Hippolytus* of "the torturing misery . . . of childbirth," but adds Edna's revolt against the ways of nature. Adèle's words complete her birth: She has determined what character of a woman she is, and her unwillingness to give up her new-won essence can only lead to the determination which drives "into her soul like a death wound." [66]

The title of the book is singularly appropriate. The dualities of sleep (or drowsiness)-awakening and bewilderment-understanding are introduced early and thereafter frequently approached from shifting angles. Edna's intermittent anguish and the voices which speak to her "without promise" also prepare us for the denouement. The original title fits well, too: There will always be physical partners for the heroine, but none to understand or accept her spiritually. Thus as she develops from bewilderment to clarity and from egocentricity to a kind of responsible renunciation, she also moves from quasi-attachment to solitude. [67]

She is not tragic in the sense that she struggles with fate and loses. Up till the birth scene, she abandons herself to it, but thereafter she takes fate in her own hands, making herself the supreme master over her destiny. But this element of modern existentialism is fused with a Greek tragic sense of the cosmically inevitable as the author, at the very end, gives her heroine a meaning and a dimension which surpass the personal and contemporary.

In the last chapter we return to Grand Isle, where Victor tells Mariequita about Edna's party. When he calls the female guests enticing houris and compares the hostess with Venus rising from the foam, Mariequita becomes jealous and threatens to run away with a married man. Victor cheers her, however, by promising to kill his competitor. This scene forms an interlude of comic relief before Edna's arrival and her last swim. At the same time, its allusions to classic myths suggest that the author wants to raise her into a symbol of womankind. A beginning is made when she walks down to the beach, the sun beating down upon her:

The water of the Gulf stretched out before her, gleaming with the million lights of the sun. The voice of the sea is seductive, never ceasing, whispering, clamoring, murmuring, inviting the soul to wander in abysses of solitude. All along the white beach, up and down, there was no living thing in sight. A bird with a broken wing was beating the air above, reeling, fluttering, circling disabled down, down to the water.[68]

In this rhythmic, compelling prose-poem, the book returns to the kind of bird-imagery it has used before. On the very first page we meet a parrot and a mockingbird; both of them are caged imitators, the one repeating its master's words, the other echoing the voice of other species. The mother-women flutter about with extended angel-wings to protect their brood. When Edna moves to a "pigeon house" it suggests that this is to be a place of cooing love. But being neither an imitator nor a protector of others, Edna wants to combine sex with independence. The only ornithological image which springs from her mind is one evoked by the piece of music which she called "Solitude": that of the bird flying away from the naked, resigned man on the beach.[69]

In the words of Robert B. Bush, this figure apparently stands for man "without the clothing of respectability"; to this we may add that he also seems to represent that striving for spiritual freedom and independence which is traditionally represented by a flying bird. Such a quest inevitably makes for solitude. Mademoiselle had told the heroine: "The bird that would soar above the level plain of tradition and prejudice must have strong wings." While Edna had not understood her then, she is now identified with the man (and the bird) when she takes off her clothes: "for the first time in her life she stood naked in the open air, at the mercy of the sun, the breeze that beat upon her, and the waves that invited her." This is awful and delicious to her, and she feels like "some new-born creature, opening its eyes in a familiar world that it had never known."[70]

Edna's action of casting off her garments symbolizes a lifting of the veil with which conventional ethics have draped the true meaning of existence. She is new-born in the sense that she comprehends and accepts life's basic urges in all their nakedness. At the same time she also wants the spiritual freedom which is sought mostly by men; but, while the man may believe that the bird of male freedom *can* fly, she has learned that the woman's wings are broken when she attempts such a flight.

Nothing can hinder Edna from being intimately joined with the universe, however. With the wavelets curling like serpents about her ankles, she walks into the water, and the refrain is heard for the last time: "The touch of the sea is sensuous, enfolding the body in its soft, close embrace." She is here a Venus returning to the foam, continuing the earlier sensuous feasts of the novel as she closes the circle it has described.[71]

Out there, she recalls "the blue-grass meadow that she had traversed when a little child, believing that it had no beginning and no end." She thinks of Léonce and the boys who were never to "possess her, body and soul." She evokes the picture of the Doctor who might have grasped what Robert would never comprehend. And then:[72]

She looked into the distance, and the old terror flamed up for an instant, then sank again. Edna heard her father's voice and her sister Margaret's. She heard the barking of an old dog that was chained to the sycamore tree. The spurs of the cavalry officer clanged as he walked across the porch. There was the hum of bees, and the musky odor of pinks filled the air.

Edna thus recalls the officer who had awakened her incipient passions at the time when she walked through the Kentucky grass, her bonnet limiting her view. The author's last lines turn that scene into a parable on the female condition, the condition which Edna had tried to transcend, only to become a solitary soul. The meadow is a picture of how nature makes woman wear blinders to continue the species.[73] As Edna grows exhausted, she thinks of the clanging spurs, the emblem of male dominance used also in "Athénaïse," and of the bees humming among the pinks, a generative symbol found in *Hippolytus*. Nature and man dictate the life of woman, and Eros, like the ocean, has no beginning and no end. The Gulf she enters is not only the whirlpool of sexuality into which Phaedra falls, but also the abyss, the unbridgeable gap between the male and the female condition which will exist as long as men and women remain in their present position to each other.

The Awakening can be seen as a eulogy on sex and a muted elegy on the female condition. From its appearance, it has been read as a novel on a woman's gradual arousal to passion. But the book is not just another love story, albeit daring for its time and place, and – in

Edmund Wilson's words – "beautifully written." We miss its richness
and deeper meaning if we overlook the vision which is evoked at the
end, a vision which is reflected in the novel's focus, tone, and point
of view.[74]

Nearly everything in the book has a bearing on Edna, and most of
it is seen through her eyes. Not wanting to dwell on "moeurs de
province," as Flaubert had done, the author develops a matter like
the difference between Yankees and Creoles only in so far as it relates
to the heroine. Thus, such a reference to the melting-pot as Alcée's
remark that "one is really forced . . . these days to assume the virtue
of an occupation if he has it not," is functional in that it shows his
availability as a seducer. In focusing her omniscience on Mrs. Pontellier, Kate Chopin presents glimpses of the heroine's mind which
most often tell us no more than she at any time can know or suspect
herself. (The use of the word "desire" in Chapter X seems a mistake;
Edna is still only dimly aware of it, while we can sense it anyhow.)
Only in a few instances does the author give such general comments
as the one on women and the Holy Ghost.[75]

When dealing with the chief character, Mrs. Chopin maintains a
consistent aesthetic distance, keeping clear of the extremes of irony or
judgment and sympathy or compassion. Not once does she suggest that
Edna represents "corruption," as Flaubert observes about Emma, or
that her unhappiness is due to her "vice," as Byron implied when
speaking of Corinne. When Mrs. Pontellier is "led on and deceived
by fresh promises which her youth held out to her," it is a muted
comment on universal human nature rather than an ironic note on
Edna. Her final swim is given enough space to make it into a solitary
soul's reunion with nature. Nevertheless, it has a classical brevity
compared to Emma's last suffering, and never does the author elicit
pity or invite a close identification in the way Flaubert is said to do
when he speaks of the heroine's "poor hands" or lets Dr. Larivière
shed a tear. Thus, when Kate Chopin – like the Frenchman – uses the
heroine's last impressions to raise her into the stature of a symbol,
she escapes the somewhat abrupt change in distance which some
critics find in *Madame Bovary*.[76]

While the author displays humor and light irony in her pictures
of the other characters, she approaches the main protagonist with a
basic seriousness.[77] The vision which Edna embodies is so important
that nothing is allowed to disturb it, and, as in "Athénaïse," Kate

Chopin's sympathy is instead expressed by means of the symbols. As the images are given fresh meaning through repetition and development, they point to the process going on, while leading up to the view of the world which is embedded in the final lines.

There is a touch of impressionistic technique in *The Awakening's* use of glimpses of the Gulf to suggest Edna's spiritual climate. The novel also makes occasional use of poetic elements, such as repetition and verse rhythms and the play on images and ambiguous words. ("Arouse" at the end of Chapter XXXVIII is an example.) Cyrille Arnavon finds the style a little too poetic and mannered. The poetic traits would seem appropriate, however, in a work which we may well call Kate Chopin's *Leaves of Grass*. And while it is true that there are samples of period language in the novel, the words are often functional as pointers to Edna's early romanticism. No new ground is broken in the novel's diction; but the author gives the impression of expressing exactly what she wants to say. Her style is easy, graceful, and pellucid, with a directness and honesty which make it a perfect vehicle for the unsparing emotional truth.[78]

This is not to say that there are no flaws in *The Awakening*. The symbolism is too obvious when Robert, at his first, abortive reunion with Edna, leans on the piano-keys and brings forth "a crash of discordant sound." [79] Their subsequent dialogue is perhaps more stilted than the situation calls for. Such an incident as Victor's ice-cream-making could well have been left out. But otherwise there is hardly anything inessential in the novel. Everything contributes to the effect: setting, characters, and symbols; atmosphere and tone; parallels and contrasts. Such a seeming contrivance as having Edna called away when she is to possess Robert is a highly conscious means to an end. The book shows a rigorous selectivity in description and dialogue, and a concentration which makes everything play together in a functional unison. The work is simple and clear in conception. Its structure is complex, yet completely coherent, making full use of the realistic and symbolic elements, and bringing all strands together at the end. Its texture is rich, with a wealth of images, a warm Southern color, and a resonant tone, in which the pessimistic note is offset by a basic vitality reflecting man's authentic, immutable heart-beat.

The Awakening may echo both Flaubert and Darwin. Yet it is entirely independent, and fundamentally not dated. Edna's sexual awakening is as valid and full of reality today as it was when *Hippol-*

ytus was written, and her basic existentialist quest is as modern now as it probably will be in a still patriarchal tomorrow. But the mature author does not force her views upon us. Edna's story is given with a detachment which joins with the general artistic excellence to make it into a convincing and deeply moving experience and a balanced and highly accomplished work of art.

VIII
A Daring Writer Banned

1. *"The Storm"*

When Kate Chopin submitted *The Awakening* to Way & Williams on January 21, 1898, it represented about half a year's intensive work. A total gap in her notebooks during this period suggests how completely she concentrated on the novel. The moment it was finished, however, she resumed such activities as giving readings and offering her stories to editors. The fact that she asked R. W. Gilder for names of literary agents indicates how strongly she desired to be published, and when Way & Williams, in the early summer of 1898, accepted both *The Awakening* and "A Vocation and a Voice," her third collection of stories, this success undoubtedly marked a new peak in her career.[1] Again she was encouraged to a further unfolding of her power in describing life unbound by conventional ethics. Now, with three books in print and two more about to be published – one of them the boldest treatment so far in American literature of the sensuous, independent woman – she must have felt that she could do almost anything.

On July 18, 1898, Mrs. Chopin wrote "The Storm," a brief story which shows her completely detached attitude toward generally accepted moral ideas. Quite aware of how daring she had been in this tale, she never tried to publish it, and even as late as 1932, Rankin chose to pass it over in silence.[2] As its subtitle indicates, it is "A Sequence to 'The 'Cadian Ball'," the story in which the planter Alcée Laballière is on the point of running away with Calixta, the Spanish vixen, when Clarisse claims him for herself.

The sequel is divided into five sections. The first presents Bobinôt, Calixta's humble husband, deciding with his little son to wait out the oncoming storm at the store. The second, which makes up the bulk of the tale, is set at Calixta's home, where Alcée – who has not seen her alone since her marriage – seeks shelter. When lightning strikes outside, she staggers backwards – into his arms. This physical contact arouses their old desire for each other, and he kisses her. When he had known her before, he had respected her, but "Now – well, now – her lips seemed in a manner free to be tasted, as well as her round, white throat and her whiter breasts." The story then moves to the bedroom, a part of the house rarely mentioned by American authors of the time, and turns directly to a part of life which they hardly ever even hinted at: [3]

They did not heed the crashing torrents, and the roar of the elements made her laugh as she lay in his arms. . . .

When he touched her breasts they gave themselves up in quivering ecstasy, inviting his lips. Her mouth was a fountain of delight. And when he possessed her, they seemed to swoon together at the very borderland of life's mystery.

He stayed cushioned upon her, breathless, dazed, enervated, with his heart beating like a hammer upon her. With one hand she clasped his head, her lips lightly touching his forehead. The other hand stroked with a soothing rhythm his muscular shoulders.

The growl of the thunder was distant and passing away. The rain beat softly upon the shingles, inviting them to drowsiness and sleep. But they dared not yield.

The rain was over; and the sun was turning the glistening world into a palace of gems. Calixta, on the gallery, watched Alcée ride away. He turned and smiled at her with a beaming face, and she lifted her pretty chin in the air and laughed aloud.[4]

In section three, Bobinôt and little Bibi return home. After an attempt to tidy themselves, they enter cautiously, "prepared for the worst – the meeting with an over-scrupulous housewife." But Calixta kisses them effusively, happy with their safe return and grateful for the shrimps which Bobinôt has brought her. "We'll have a feas' to night!" she exclaims, and at dinner, "they laughed much and so loud that anyone might have heard them as far as Laballière's."[5]

The last two sections deal with the "loving letter" Alcée writes Clarisse that night, in which he tells her that he misses her but is willing to bear the separation a month longer. She, on her part, is delighted to remain with the babies at Biloxi, where she enjoys the first free breath since her marriage, which seems to restore "the pleasant liberty of her maiden days"; though she is devoted to her husband, she is glad to forego "their intimate conjugal life" for a while. And the story ends: "So the storm passed and every one was happy." [6]

Maupassant was one of the most daring sex-writers of his time. Nevertheless, he respected decorum enough to restrict his descriptions of the actual love-making. On occasion he would belittle the sensual by making it comic; the "accouplement violent et maladroit" in *Bel-Ami* is an example. At other times he would at the critical moment turn away from the human action and represent it only indirectly; in "Une Partie de Campagne," for instance, the ecstatic song of a bird stands for the defloration of the young heroine. [7]

Sex is never comic in Kate Chopin's writings. In "The Storm" it is so elated and "happy," so full of joy that we are reminded of the *Song of Solomon,* which it parallels also in its use of the lily and the pomegranate. The story leaves aside all suspense of plot; while Clarisse in "At the 'Cadian Ball" plays with Alcée before she catches him, Calixta shows here no "guile or trickery." The author concentrates instead on the delights of *sexe pur.* There is nothing to hide in this naked pleasure, she seems to say as she discards the bird and the idealized representation of Maupassant's *conte.* Surpassing that "courage . . . of our perceptions" which Henry James had observed in the Frenchman, Mrs. Chopin turned to the matter at hand without circumlocutions. Particularly the love-making scene is an example of her courage to treat the forbidden and of her stylistic daring in describing it with the unreserved directness and supreme authenticity of truth. [8]

Sex in this story is a force as strong, inevitable, and natural as the Louisiana storm which ignites it. Given the opportunity, imperative Eros will, for better or for worse, take a hand in the shaping of our lives. This lends a serious undertone to the tale even though it is lightly told. Kate Chopin neither ridicules nor condemns Alcée and his two women. She is a detached observer who nowhere raises a moral finger, not even where Alcée tries to make his wife stay away so that the affair he seems to plan can have free play. We might even say that the author suggests that the effects of his visit are beneficial to all: Bobinôt and Bibi gain as Calixta becomes more amiable; Clarisse feels a greater sense of freedom, and the two lovers are for the first time fully sexually awakened. But the conclusion that "every one was happy" is of course ambiguous. Mrs. Chopin may refuse to sit in judgment on morals, but she covers only one day and one storm and does not exclude the possibility of later misery. The emphasis is on the momentary joy of the amoral cosmic force, but the story's all-pervasive use of primordial symbolism strengthens the undertone of the serious, timeless aspect of Eros.

"The Storm" is about the tension between the male and the female, the assertive and the receptive principles. The immobile land is threatened by the active river; the fields are exposed to rain and wind, as they are to the lightning which strikes through the inter-mediary of the tall trees. There is a constant play on the actions of opening or closing: Calixta unfastens "her white sacque at the throat" as she begins to shut the house; after riding in at the gate, Alcée tries to stay outside on the gallery, but is forced in by the storm; the rain threatens "to break an entrance and deluge them"; the her-oine tries to keep the water out, and she is also afraid that the levee will give way. When we first see her, she is sewing – a popular meta-phor of sexual intercourse. In connection with Alcée we are presented with such male symbols as the horse and the plow; another perfectly natural, yet very suggestive detail is the fact that the one piece of garment which he helps save from the rain is the trousers of the man whose privileges he shortly usurps. As for Calixta, her mouth is "a fountain of delight" and her flesh "a creamy lily" that is influenced by the sun.[9]

The story's diction is mostly fresh and honest; for example, Calixta is allowed to show "sensuous desire." But occasionally we find an ex-cessive, old-fashioned, or stale phrase, such as "creamy lily," "well nigh," or "lips . . . to be tasted." Alcée's rather formal remark: "Let us hope, Calixta, that Bobinôt's got sense enough to come in out of a cyclone," may be functional, however, as an expression of how he tries to contain himself; and if we find a romantic ring in "swoon," we must add that D. H. Lawrence used the term, too, in connection with the same fundamental drives which, as Mrs. Chopin expresses it here, "contribute . . . to the undying life of the world."[10]

Though the story in one sense is Calixta's (she is nearly all the time in the foreground), it seems, with its Whitmanesque pervasive erotic atmosphere, dedicated to nature's undying urge rather than to any person. All details are suggestive of this central impulse. There is complete correspondence between theme, on the one hand, and set-ting, plot, and character, on the other. The elements of this piece are inextricably fused as the tale moves relentlessly forward, in one sustained, effortless sweep, toward the inescapable outcome of the cyclone. With a minimum of characterization this highly effective story gives a convincing picture of the figures – at once representative and individual – who are influenced by the storm. The tone greatly contributes to the artistic impact: detached and unsentimental, yet warm, and serenely free.

Artistically, "The Storm" is a first-rate story. It is important also for its daring. The frankness about sex of such books as *Madame Bovary* and *Nana* was of course slowly having an impact even on American fiction. But with this tale, Kate Chopin not only outdistanced her compatriots, but also went a step beyond the Frenchmen. That her description of physical union is more open than theirs is a relatively minor point in this connection; what is important is its "happy," "healthy" quality.

Flaubert, who once owned that he had been obsessed by the word "adultery," makes Emma Bovary's amatory exploits into a frantic flight from dreariness; Zola sees those of Nana as the vile expressions of a degenerating heroine. Kate Chopin was not interested in the immoral in itself, but in life as it comes, in what she saw as natural – or certainly inevitable – expressions of universal Eros, inside or outside of marriage. She focuses here on sexuality as such, and to her, it is neither frantic nor base, but as "healthy" and beautiful as life itself. That "happy sex" should somehow be "indecent" – the answer Mary McCarthy gave when asked why she had described sex as "unhappy" in *The Group* – would be a completely foreign idea to the author of this story.[11] In "The Storm," there is exuberance and a cosmic joy and mystery as Alcée and Calixta become one with another and with elemental nature. With its organic quality, its erotic elation, and its frankness, the story almost makes its author an early D. H. Lawrence.

André Malraux has observed of Lawrence that he thought it more important to be a man than to be an individual. For Kate Chopin, the individuality of her heroines was more important than their femaleness. But to be a woman writer in her time meant almost the same as Virginia Woolf has said it did for Charlotte Brontë, that is, to be unable to avoid the "jerks" of a female "at war with her lot." When the author of *Jane Eyre* complains that "women . . . suffer from too rigid a restraint," it represents an indignation which prevents her from getting "her genius expressed whole and entire," Mrs. Woolf goes on. "It is fatal for any one who writes to think of their sex. . . .

One must be woman-manly or man-womanly." It is particularly fatal for a female "in any way to speak consciously as a woman. . . . Anything written with that conscious bias is doomed to death. . . . There must be freedom and there must be peace." [12]

There is of course a fundamental female protest in *The Awakening*. But though what could be called her feminist stories are so greatly important in Kate Chopin's *œuvre,* they are rather few in number, and the rest of her writings show a detachment on the relationship between the sexes. The man-woman relationship of "The Storm" – the most intimate possible – is a crucial touchstone for objectivity, and Kate Chopin, who now had, on the one hand, the protest of *The Awakening* off her mind, and, on the other, literary success within her reach, here gives the impression of having achieved true freedom and real peace.

She is not consciously speaking as a woman, but as an individual. Even her previous writings had been free from misandry and from suggestions of either sex being superior to the other. In the present story, there is no trace of the covert bitterness of "Athénaïse," nor any complaint like Edna's that women learn so little of life. There is no antagonism or competition between Alcée and Calixta, no wilful domination in his manner or subservience in hers, even though he is higher up in society than she. In short, Mrs. Chopin appears to have achieved that thing – comparatively rare even today: to become a woman author who could write on the two sexes with a large degree of detachment and objectivity.

2. *Poetic Interlude*

Except for "The Storm" and two other stories, Kate Chopin wrote no prose while she eagerly waited for *The Awakening* to appear. The reason may well have been that she somehow felt that the reaction to her novel would decide what subject matter she would deal with next and how far she would go in her realism. Instead, she turned to verse, and she wrote comparatively many poems during this interlude. Occasionally they reflect the carefree attitude to sexual urges demonstrated in "The Storm." One poem entitled "By the Meadow Gate," for example, deals with a girl asleep and dreaming "in the long, cool grass" while "The birds call: 'Awake'!" Meanwhile, a youth with "A glow in his soul and a flame in his eyes/Follows a voice that is never still," and "The voice and the dream are near – so near." But the young man does not listen to the voice, and "The dream of the maiden will never come true." [13]

In this period, too, we find poems referring to a lost lover who seems to be in the spheres, but when Mrs. Chopin makes the speaker of one of them called "An Ecstasy of Madness" want to fly atop the hill and dance around the Maypole, the appeal may equally well be to a living person as to the distant star: [14]

> There's an ecstasy of madness
> Where the March Hares dwell;
> A delirium of gladness
> Too wild to tell.
>
> The Moon has gone a-maying
> And the Sun's so far!
> O! what's the use of staying
> With a blinking star!
>
> Let us join hands this instant
> And fly a-top the hill,
> And whether near or distant,
> We'll ne'er stop still
>
> Or we find the Moon that's Maying
> And the Sun so far,
> That left us here a-praying
> To a blinking star.

Meanwhile, Way & Williams were going out of business, and in November, 1898, *A Night in Acadie, The Awakening,* and "A Vocation and a Voice" were all transferred to Herbert S. Stone & Co., the successors to Stone & Kimball.[15] The novel was quickly accepted, and there is nothing to indicate that the avant-garde publishers suggested any changes in its contents. In February, 1899, when Kate Chopin in all likelihood was just reading proofs of *The Awakening,* she wrote a poem which presents in abbreviated form a fate which brings to mind that of Edna.

The Haunted Chamber

Of course 'twas an excellent story to tell
Of a fair, frail, passionate woman who fell.
It may have been false, it may have been true.
That was nothing to me – it was less to you.
But with bottle between us, and clouds of smoke
From your last cigar, 'twas more of a joke
Than a matter of sin or a matter of shame
That a woman had fallen, and nothing to blame,
So far as you or I could discover,
But her beauty, her blood and an ardent lover.
But when you were gone and the lights were low
And the breeze came in with the moon's pale glow,
The fair, faint voice of a woman, I heard,
'Twas but a wail, and it spoke no word.
It rose from the depths of some infinite gloom
And its tremulous anguish filled the room.
Yet the woman was dead and could not deny,
But women forever will whine and cry.
So now I must listen the whole night through
To the torment with which I had nothing to do –
But women forever will whine and cry
And men forever must listen – and sigh –

The fact that Kate Chopin tried to place a number of her nearly fifty poems would suggest that she attached a certain importance also to her efforts in this medium; nevertheless, most of her poetry is undistinguished, when it is not downright awkward or trite. Though she admired Whitman, she seems to have been satisfied to use in her own verse only conventional diction and meter. Even in the one instance where she appears to have attempted free verse – in an unrhymed, four-line fragment – the stress pattern is fairly metrical.[16] Some of her poems are songs, with refrain-like short lines. ("You and I" – p. 55 – and a few others were set to music by William Schuyler.) Typifying its period, Mrs. Chopin's poetry comprises both quatrains accompanying gifts and the inevitable imitations of the Rubaiyat. Particularly in her early verse, she uses archaic words like "list" and "hath"; her imagery is traditional, including birds and flowers, the moon and the stars, and her use of them has little freshness or originality.

Kate Chopin once noted on the manuscript of a poem: "This is not dedicated to you or to anybody." This suggests that she was aware that her many "I"-poems could be read as being self-revelatory. When she deals with her two main poetic themes – the awakening urges of spring and the longing for the lost companion – she can be very personal. She often shows true feeling, but in many instances she is defeated by stale language or by a certain monotony of form. Her earliest fairly good effort – "In Dreams throughout the Night" – is also the first in which not all lines are rhymed.[17] As she gained in self-confidence, she was on occasion able to fuse all elements into a successful whole, particularly in "If Some Day" (p. 71) and "The Haunted Chamber," her two best poems.

The first of these offers a pleasing irregularity. It consists of a stanza of nine lines followed by one of five; the rhyme scheme is *xaaxbbxcc* and *xaabb;* and every third line is short, breaking the overall pentameter pattern. It is full of fresh, precise expressions of sensory phenomena which make a convincing evocation of a vibrant, Whitmanesque sensuousness.

"The Haunted Chamber," meanwhile, consists of rhymed couplets. The mostly four-beat lines are often logaoedic, and this supports the casual, conversational tone which is struck immediately in the opening line. The poem is structured around the pivotal conjunction "But" in the middle, which marks the shift from the light, almost frivolous tone in the first part, to the serious, pitying note in the second half. The "excellent story" turns into an anguished "wail." There is a significant difference when the heavily stressed phrase "a fair, frail, passionate woman" is echoed later in the poem; the important adjective "frail" – a stock feminine attribute – turns into "faint."

This is a significant word. The poem focuses upon a woman's inarticulate anguish. Her affliction is viewed with a meaningful ambiguity which is reflected in appropriate diction. There is an effective tension between the "anguish" and "torment," on the one hand, and the slightly contemptuous indifference expressed in the repeated "women forever will whine and cry," on the other. The banal phrasing of the last couplet with its clichés about males and females suggests that the speaker resorts to facile stereotypes in an effort to negate all concern and pity for the suffering woman.

We have no proof that "The Haunted Chamber" represents the writer attempting to remove herself from an unconscious involvement

with Edna Pontellier. In general, little in Kate Chopin's fiction can
be said to represent her own life. However, the whole tone of this
poem would suggest that it is entirely genuine and that the author –
on the unconscious level – identified herself deeply both with Edna's
struggle and with her torment. What is quite clear is that Mrs.
Pontellier forms the logical extension of the author's more and more
self-assertive heroines and that she and Mme. Ratignolle constitute
the extreme example of Mrs. Chopin's juxtapositions of the emancipated and the feminine woman.

The most likely explanation for Kate Chopin's various writings on
woman's position is that she had indeed loved her husband deeply and
had fully accepted him, as all reports indicate, but at the same time
had had secret emancipationist urges (William Schuyler's observation
from 1894 that she might have developed earlier as a writer had her
environment been different very probably originated from herself),
and felt so hemmed in by marriage that she kept a continuous internal
discussion already then.[18] Such a supposition would explain in part
why she in her work frequently opposes a woman who stays home and
one who strikes out, and why she advocates no "best way" to live for
a female, evidently understanding and sympathizing with all her different heroines. It also helps to explain why she welcomes both sexuality and men and shows no sexual antagonism and yet demonstrates
a questioning attitude toward the marriage institution.

But whether Mrs. Pontellier represents the author or not is more
or less immaterial. While her rare note of pessimism in *The Awakening* may signify that she had given Edna certain of her own traits,
it is more important that the publisher's acceptance of the novel inspired the supremely relaxed attitude of "The Storm." No doubt
sensing how success engendered her growth as a writer, she must have
awaited the public's reception of her book with an intensity which is
found only in natures as deep as her own.

3. *The Awakening Banned*

The Awakening was published on April 22, 1899.[19] Twelve days
later Frances Porcher set the pattern for what was shortly to become
a general condemnation of the book by the reviewers. Writing about
it in Reedy's *Mirror,* she declared that Edna ought to have been satis-

fied with her marriage since Léonce had given her everything, including all the freedom a woman could desire. Even so, she would not have judged the heroine overharshly if she had "awakened to the gentle touch of Love, pure and simple," but her love was of such a "sensual and devilish" kind that the reviewer wished Kate Chopin had not written the novel. It made her wonder, though, whether all women were like Edna, and she sighed: "One would fain beg the gods, in pure cowardice, for sleep unending rather than to know what an ugly, cruel, loathsome monster Passion can be when, like a tiger, it slowly stretches its graceful length and yawns and finally awakens." Mrs. Porcher had to grant the artistic excellence of the book, but she ended with these words: "It leaves one sick of human nature and so one feels – *cui bono!*" [20]

Two St. Louis newspapers quickly joined the *Mirror* in censuring the novel. The *Globe-Democrat* conceded that the book dealt with existing conditions, but called it morbid because the author had failed to teach a moral lesson. The *Republic* put it even more strongly when it declared that *The Awakening,* like "most" of Mrs. Chopin's work, was "too strong drink for moral babes, and should be labeled 'poison'." [21]

Meanwhile, Kate Chopin received letters from her friends voicing more favorable reactions. A man found the tale to be a moral one with its "sermon against un-naturalness and Edna's marriage." A woman friend regretted that both fiction and life defeated those who dared to defy "the trammels of conventionalism," but admitted that a happy ending would be foreign to the school of Realism, and hence also to Kate Chopin, who was "as realistic as Zola." "I wish you believed that the Ednas will . . . somehow grow into a spiritual harmony to which the splendor of their frailty will contribute beauty," another lady sighed, while welcoming the novel's "revelation of a potential woman by a woman." And Sue V. Moore called the book *"great"* and said she was "so proud to know 'the artist with the courageous soul that dares & defies'." [22]

Some of these letters suggest that Kate Chopin's friends realized that she was hurt by the unfavorable reviews. Although she had seen how the critics of Mrs. Freeman's *Pembroke* had treated that novel, she was evidently unprepared for the strong attacks on *The Awakening.* She was also becoming concerned about its chances for success: "What are the prospects for the book?" she asked Herbert S. Stone.

At the same time she sent him C. L. Deyo's review in the *Post-Dispatch* with these words: "It seems so able and intelligent by contrast with some of the drivel I have run across that I thought I should like to have you read it when you have the time." [23]

Even this critic took strong issue with the book for displaying "positively unseemly" truths. "A fact ... which we have all agreed shall not be acknowledged, is as good as no fact at all," he declared. "And it is disturbing – even indelicate – to mention it as something which, perhaps, does play an important part in the life behind the mask." What made Deyo's review acceptable to Mrs. Chopin was that he went on, a little illogically, to accept the spirit of the work with its "searching vision into the recesses of the heart" and to praise the mastery with which the difficult subject had been treated. With a new "power born of confidence," the author had created not only an unusual, but a "unique" novel, he wrote, and the "integrity of its art" had brought about a perfect whole.[24]

While Deyo tried to set aside his prejudices, Alexander DeMenil was more representative of the St. Louis literati when he refused to review the book in his magazine. Some of the many who openly attacked *The Awakening* were no doubt genuinely horrified by what they considered an indecent novel, while others who had envied Kate Chopin her success – "there was a lot of jealousy," it has been said – welcomed the pretext to fall upon her.[25] The public outcry against the book quickly led the city's libraries to ban it.[26] According to C. E. Miller, then an apprentice at the Mercantile Library and later its head, Kate Chopin came in one day with a woman companion and asked politely for her novel. She probably just wanted to prove to her friend that they had banned it, for when Miller told her it was taken from circulation, she simply walked away without anger.[27] (In a later comment she was more sarcastic: "The libraries! Oh, no, they don't keep it.") On top of this, social acquaintances began to shun her, and she was cut even by some of her friends. In short, she was nothing less than "persecuted," as a man who knew her has put it.[28] As a final humiliation she apparently was refused membership in the St. Louis Fine Arts Club.[29]

The author's real friends of course were eager that she should justify her novel and defend herself against these reactions to it. It is typical of Mrs. Chopin that when she finally gave in and published a rejoinder, she did it in a national rather than a local periodical.

"Having a group of people at my disposal," she wrote, "I thought it might be entertaining (to myself) to throw them together and see what would happen. I never dreamed of Mrs. Pontellier making such a mess of things and working out her own damnation as she did. If I had had the slightest intimation of such a thing I would have excluded her from the company. But when I found out what she was up to, the play was half over and it was then too late." [30]

Kate Chopin's insistence that Edna's development was unknown to her when she started the novel and her suggestion that she would have excluded the heroine had she foreseen it, obviously represent minor concessions to the public. This is apparent when we consider the finished form in which her other tales had come to her, and the moral unconcern of "The Storm." While Flaubert had allowed his lawyer to present *Madame Bovary* as basically moral when it was tried, there is no suggestion of such an attitude here; the word "damnation" is equivocal, and the lightness of her tone, particularly where she uses the casual expression "a mess of things," shows that she refuses to bow to her censors' view that her heroine should be condemned. In fact, we might even say that she indirectly indicates her disapproval of the whole guild of literary critics.

Her statement appeared in the August issue of *Book-News*. By that time, *The Awakening* had already been nationally condemned. From Boston to Los Angeles the reviewers called it a morbid and unwholesome book. *Literature* even found it an "essentially vulgar story" and thought the end quite appropriate for "one who has drifted from all right moorings, and has not the grace to repent." When the *Critic* devoted a page to Kate Chopin – she was evidently "news" – without even mentioning the novel, and when, for example, the *Atlantic* never reviewed it, the conclusion is inescapable that this was because the editors considered the book scandalous. [31]

Though the commentators praised the author's artistic genius and even called the work a brilliant piece of writing, they could only accept the fictional use of extra-marital affairs, as one of them said, if it led to better conditions. "There is throughout the story an undercurrent of sympathy for Edna, and nowhere a single note of censure of her totally unjustifiable conduct," the New Orleans *Times-Democrat* complained, and according to another paper the author had even hinted "her belief that the heroine had the right of the matter." Most of the critics deplored that Mrs. Chopin had left behind the "agreeable short stories" of the local color tradition which they considered her proper field. "The real Miss Chopin . . . is at her best as a creator of sweet and lovable characters," the Chicago *Times Herald* declared, adding that "it was not necessary for a writer of so great refinement and poetic grace to enter the overworked field of sex fiction." [32]

While these critics complained of too much sex in literature, there were others who were less squeamish. In St. Louis, we recall, William Schuyler clamored for a French openness in American letters, and W. M. Reedy published shocking stories by Maupassant and his European successors in his *Mirror*. Reedy did not object to sinful Continental heroines, and he was also broadminded enough to accept a woman sinner on American soil if she was a "foreigner," such as the gipsy girl in Kate Chopin's tale "A Vocation and a Voice." But that Edna Pontellier, a real American lady, should be allowed to disrupt the sacred institutions of marriage and American womanhood and to disregard moral concepts even without repenting it, was totally unacceptable to him. A woman should devote herself to her "holy office" of a wife and a mother, Reedy declared, and he might have pointed to his sub-editor Frances Porcher who hid her very strong ambition under a mantle of eminently respectable domesticity. [33]

Though American feminists in general tried to improve the morals of men, something their European sisters rarely attempted, a good number of them demanded the right to free love. While Reedy laughed off the demand of the American Purity Alliance for a single standard, retorting that "the men won't have such a standard for themselves and that settles it," he was frightened about the females who wanted to be as promiscuous as the males; it would be a sacrilege in "the women who are dear to us," he asserted, because "the woman who is polyandric commits a sin against Nature," whereas "the man who is polygamic does not." [34] The fact that Schuyler never commented on *The Awakening* suggests that he, too, made a sharp distinction between what could be permitted in the men and in the women of America.

The nation was thus not ready to wake up to the unsparing truth about feminine passion, and it was inevitable that the reviews of the novel should take the form of violent attacks on it. A poem entitled "Life," written May 10, 1899, thus a few days after Mrs. Porcher's criticism appeared in the *Mirror,* suggests that this first attack had not been able to disturb the author's philosophical calm:

> A day with a splash of sunlight,
> Some mist and a little rain.
> A life with a dash of love-light,
> Some dreams and a touch of pain.
> To love a little and then to die!
> To live a little and never know why!

But as the reviews went from bad to worse, she became "stunned and bewildered," and even broken-hearted, at the reaction to *The Awakening*. In general, adversity could not easily put her down. Her great sense of humor, and the fact that she felt eminently socially secure, made her a master of herself against all prejudice. But this time nothing could save her from becoming deeply hurt; how deeply is seen in the fact that she refused to discuss the subject with anyone.[35]

One reason the matter affected her so strongly was that she believed the scandal had blocked her chances for literary success; another was that the St. Louis censure of her made her feel she was looked upon as morally suspect and even as a "social disgrace," to quote one of her friends.[36] Perhaps the chief reason was that she was deeply committed to her novel and now had to realize that she could never write as she wanted to. "It was unbelievable how she was crushed as it was truth as she saw it and people would not see," as another friend has put it; or, in the words of John Dillon: "She had poured herself – thoughts and feelings – into the novel with utmost honesty."[37]

When Kate Chopin spent part of October in Wisconsin, it may well have been to escape the unpleasantness of St. Louis. Here she received unexpected encouragement from two Londoners. A Lady Janet Scammon Young wrote to her, enclosing a letter sent her by a Dr. Dunrobin Thomson, whom she termed "the great consulting physician of England" and "one of the purest and best of men." Agreeing with the Doctor that *The Awakening* was the novel of the year and with the Dutch poet Maarten Maartens – then popular with English readers – that it ought to be translated, Lady Janet asked the author to write a book in which a Dr. Mandelet should tell Pontellier to assist the birth of his wife's "deeper womanliness" by trusting her, because "trusted she will never fail you." The London Doctor stated that he had helped many men and many women in this way:[38]

The essence of the matter lies in the accursed stupidity of men. They marry a girl, she becomes a mother. They imagine she has sounded the heights and depths of womanhood. Poor fools! She is not even awakened. She, on her part is a victim of the abominable prudishness which masquerades as modesty or virtue. ... The law, spoken or implied, which governs the upbringing of girls is that passion is disgraceful. It is to be assumed that a self respecting female has it not. In so far as normally constituted womanhood *must* take account of *something* sexual, it is called "love." It was inevitable, therefore, that *Edna* should call her feeling for *Robert* love.

[A wife] ... should be taught by her husband to distinguish between passion and love. ... It is inevitable, natural, and therefore clean and harmless, that a normal, healthfully constituted married woman will be stirred in her passional being by ... [many men]. If she knows perfectly well that it is passion ... [and not "love,"] she is safe. She knows that the thing *is*. She is no more ashamed of it than of her responsiveness to any other great appeal. She knows that it does not touch her wife-life, her mother-life, her true self-hood. It is not "naughty."

We do not know whether Kate Chopin ever reacted to Lady Janet's offer to help her with "publishers, translators, &c." (Most of her uncollected items already were included in the collection then being considered by Herbert S. Stone.) Although this offer makes the letters seem genuine, it is strange that the two Londoners fail to appear, as they should do, for example, in the lists of gentry and the Medical Registry, respectively,[39] and we cannot quite exclude the possibility that they may have been falsifications.

Mrs. Chopin's closest friends realized that the scandal had frozen the author's creativity and hurt her to the core of her being. They were also convinced that she had much more to say and could go beyond *The Awakening*. "She knew so much about life. She was an original genius," one of them observed.[40] It would not be unthinkable, therefore, that her friends wished to rehabilitate her. Dr. Kolbenheyer, for example, may have suggested the letters to London relations in the hope that they would restore her self-confidence and her desire to write.

However this may be, they did have an effect: She showed them to her friends, and she agreed to write a personal essay for the *Post-Dispatch*. When it appeared on November 26, 1899, it was accompanied by three pictures of her and one of her palatial childhood home, the latter perhaps intended as a reminder of her distinguished background. There was also a glowing description of what the heading called the "St. Louis woman who has won fame in literature ...

and whose latest novel has been recommended by . . . Maarten Maartens, for translation into European languages."

The *Post-Dispatch's* comments on the author came very close to describing her own view of what literature should be: "Mrs. Chopin has been called a southern writer, but she appeals to the universal sense in a way not excelled by any other American author," the commentator observed. "She is not sectional or provincial, nor even national, which is to say that she is an artist, who is not bound by the idiosyncrasies of place, race, or creed." And he went on to say that she sacrificed "all else, even pecuniary profit, to her artistic conscience." In her own statement, Kate Chopin asked herself a question which suggests that there were subjects she might have written about had she lived in a more tolerant literary milieu: "What do I write? Well, not everything that comes into my head." It was here, too, that she complained about her friends not taking her books seriously and about the libraries not accepting them. At the same time, she managed to evade all mention of *The Awakening*. The author's characteristic blend of insouciance and involvement is evident in the final question: [41]

"Do you smoke cigarettes?" is a question which I consider impertinent, and I think most women will agree with me. Suppose I do smoke cigarettes? Am I going to tell it out in meeting? Suppose I don't smoke cigarettes? Am I going to admit such a reflection upon my artistic integrity, and thereby bring upon myself the contempt of the guild?

In answering questions in which an editor believes his readers to be interested, the victim cannot take herself too seriously.

If the ladies of the elite Wednesday Club had known what serious, unorthodox, almost revolutionary ideas the author hid behind this urbane, detached, and lightly humorous form, it is doubtful that they would have included her, as they did, in their special program on November 29, 1899. Here, some of her songs, set to music by William Schuyler, were performed, whereupon she read her new story "Ti Démon." [42] Although this minor triumph in a way must have marked Mrs. Chopin's re-entry into social favor, it could not undo the harmful effects of the previous censure. "A Reflection," a short piece written at this time, can be read as saying that the "crushing feet" and the "stifling breath" of the critics who refused to see "the significance of things" had helped to kill the vital creative energy in her and to give her the feeling of being banned from the procession of literary life, where she would have liked to play a leading part: [43]

Some people are born with a vital and responsive energy. It not only enables them to keep abreast of the times; it qualifies them to furnish in their own personality a good bit of the motive power to the mad pace. They are fortunate beings. They do not need to apprehend the significance of things. They do not grow weary nor miss step, nor do they fall out of rank and sink by the wayside to be left contemplating the moving procession.

Ah! that moving procession that has left me by the roadside! Its fantastic colors are more brilliant and beautiful than the sun on the undulating waters. What matter if souls and bodies are falling beneath the feet of the ever-pressing multitude! It moves with the majestic rhythm of the spheres. Its discordant clashes sweep upward in one harmonious tone that blends with the music of other worlds – to complete God's orchestra.

It is greater than the stars – that moving procession of human energy; greater than the palpitating earth and the things growing thereon. Oh! I could weep at being left by the wayside; left with the grass and the clouds and a few dumb animals. True, I feel at home in the society of these symbols of life's immutability. In the procession I should feel the crushing feet, the clashing discords, the ruthless hands and stifling breath. I could not hear the rhythm of the march.

Salve! ye dumb hearts. Let us be still and wait by the roadside.

4. The Last Years

What Kate Chopin had in mind when she wrote this was that her fighting spirit had been stifled and that she had little hope it would ever live again. Not that she was ashamed of herself or the novel; her remarks in "Confidences" and "The Haunted Chamber" and in her rejoinder in *Book News* leave no doubt on this point.[44] But the social disapproval had crippled her courage. Had *The Awakening,* like *Madame Bovary,* become a *succès de scandale* and in a manner vindicated her, it might have given her the strength not only to weather the storm, but also to go beyond her previous work and disregard ever more openly the trammels hindering free expression in American literature. Instead, she had received little real encouragement outside the letters from London, and even some of those nearest to her had let her down. True, Reedy's *Mirror* said of her that she stood "among the first writers of the day," but she knew that Edna was unacceptable to him. That Alexander DeMenil no longer boosted her is not surprising, but it is significant that only two of her many other friends were ever to write of her later, a fact which suggests that they somehow were ashamed of the author of *The Awakening*.[45]

As the new century opened, Kate Chopin's life went on seemingly almost unchanged. The faithful continued to fill her home, and she was as genial a hostess as ever, graceful, attractive, and fascinating. But she was a little less sparkling and scintillant than before, and she drew the curtain a little tighter around her privacy and integrity. Having too much in herself ever to be bored, she welcomed solitude for quiet reflection; yet while becoming more reserved, she was still full of sympathy and interest. She remained a loving mother, and she also liked to talk to the young men – friends of her sons – who came to the house. Her children adored her, and she was glad that most of them still lived with her.

We may guess that Mrs. Chopin had a particular need to feel herself appreciated at this time, since the year 1900 started with two events which may well have confirmed her suspicion that her writings were no longer welcome. The first was that the *Atlantic* returned "Ti Démon," which they found too "sombre, . . . the sad note . . . [being] too much accented." This was the only tale she had written since the debacle. It deals with Marianne, a young woman who insists on her right to flirt with others although she is engaged to Ti Démon. On discovering her with an admirer, her fiancé beats the man half to death.[46] The story reflects the author's view of passions as having an imperative disregard of moral precepts. Even so, it is tame compared to its predecessors, and its rejection must have made Mrs. Chopin's courage sink even further.

The second disheartening event was that Herbert S. Stone in February, 1900, returned the collection "A Vocation and a Voice," giving no reason. Not knowing that Stone had decided to reduce the number of titles to be published by his company, nor that he had been unafraid of censorship when he brought out, for example, Garland's *Rose of Dutcher's Coolly*, Kate Chopin may have thought that the rejection meant that she had become a literary outcast.[47] This setback seems to have dealt a final blow to her audacious creativity. Marianne was to remain the last in her gallery of independent women who really act as they please, and though one or two of the few heroines she was still to create show a certain strength, they live it out well within the limits stipulated by genteel magazines.

Yet Mrs. Chopin permitted herself to fight back one last time at the male censors who had killed her literary creativity. In April, 1900, she wrote "Charlie," a long story named after its seventeen-year-old heroine. On the surface, it is something in between a *Youth's Companion* and a *Century* story – she offered it to both – about a boyish hoyden turning into a young lady so as to attract a young man, who proceeds to marry her older sister. On closer examination, however, the real story turns out to be the inverted one: It is about a young woman who acts the role of a man, but who is forced to give it up. Charlie is accused of being "wholly devoid of a moral sense"; she wears boots, spurs, leggings, and trousers like a boy, and she shoots with a revolver, once even threatening to use it to get the men on her father's Louisiana plantation to work. One day she hits the young man in the arm. Now in disgrace, she is made to deliver her firearm and her ammunition and to discard her male attire, in short, to behave like a woman, and for a time she does so.[48]

Not once in her career had Kate Chopin in any way emasculated her fictional men as some American women writers had done, depict- ing – as Crane did in *Maggie* – the heroine as basically blameless while bringing the villainous seducer to a pitiful end. In fact, though her particular theme is female self-assertion, her only example of what might be seen as antagonism toward men is her indirect sarcasm against R. W. Gilder in "Confidences." In "Charlie" she allows herself to disable a man, even a good man, thus subtly hitting back at the males who had labeled her a disgrace and silenced her literary gun because she had represented a woman taking the liberties of a man. One day Charlie's father loses an arm in an accident. At about the same time, the young man marries her older sister, and Charlie is freed from her infatuation with him. She resumes wearing her boots and trousers, and from now on she manages the plantation like a man, functioning as her father's lost arm. In short, she again assumes that self-assertive posture which men like to see as their prerogative; now it is her spurs which jangle like those of Athénaïse's husband.

There is a strong affinity between Charlie and her father. (A Freudian would call it a fixation and point to the secret outing of the two where they feel "like a couple of bees in clover," and recall Kate Chopin's early loss of all her male relatives.) Throughout the story there is an interplay of the strong and the weak, the masculine and the feminine, the active and the passive sex. This duality again is employed in her next work, "The White Eagle." The male bird follows the heroine of this sketch all through her life as an alter ego. (Since he is in cast-iron, he is never allowed to take flight, exert his independence and strength, and reach the heights.) The tension between the masculine and feminine principle is never released: "No mate came to seek her out." But sexual imagery may be involved when the dying woman imagines the bird pecking at her with its beak, and particularly when some children later, in what seems like a priapic rite, throw "wreaths of clover-blossoms" over the eagle, which now serves as her tombstone.[49]

The first thing Kate Chopin wrote after "The White Eagle" was an awkward piece of verse entitled "Alone." Like her first poem and so many later ones it is about the hoped-for reunion with the lost beloved. (The other of her two main poetic themes — that of the forceful urge of love in spring — had disappeared with the disaster in 1899.) While the speaker of "An Ecstasy of Madness," for example, can be seen as preferring the earthly to the celestial, the author here presents a speaker's "Love not born to die" whose object is "my distant Star":

> . . . .
> Bright is the light that lightens The Light
>   That shines from my heart to *you* afar:
> Lovely the Life that shall live in The Life
>   When the Distance no longer my Kisses bar.[50]

A month later, Mrs. Chopin wrote a poem which she called "To the Friend of My Youth: To Kitty." Here she seems to be once more seeking solace in recalling a close relationship of the past.

> It is not all of life
> To cling together while the years glide past.
> It is not all of love
> To walk with clasped hands from first to last.
> That mystic garland which the spring did twine
> Of scented lilac and the new-blown rose,
> Faster than chains will hold my soul to thine
> Thro' joy, and grief, thro' life — unto its close.[51]

These two poems suggest that Kate Chopin was now fully attuned to death. Nevertheless, she did make another attempt to place her third collection of stories, but nothing came of it.[52] At the end of 1901, she had a last, minor burst of energy, which resulted in four stories, all intended for the *Youth's Companion*. The heroines of the two extant ones – Léontine and Polly – both hold positions, one as a teacher, the other as a bookkeeper; but they are more than happy to marry and exchange their work for the "labor of loving" which Paula von Stoltz, Mrs. Chopin's early heroine, had refused. "Polly" was the last of the author's writings to reach print, and it is ironic that her final words to the public were these: "Polly, put the kettle on!"[53]

Meanwhile, though only just past fifty, Kate Chopin was ailing. She moved in 1903 to 4232 McPherson Avenue, and from this time on she seems to have been so weak that she often had to rest. Once she told her children: "I hope I will die first so that *I* will not lose any one of you." It seems that the fallen-away Catholic felt a need to make up with God; there is a family story – possibly apocryphal – of the author being seen just before her death coming out of a church which was then a fashionable place to go to confession.[54]

In spite of failing strength, Kate Chopin was ecstatic about the 1904 St. Louis World's Fair. This enormous exposition included a truly impressive display of every facet of the world's achievement, in industry, science, literature, and the arts. Also the daily life of various civilizations was represented here. Mrs. Chopin could inspect a replica of Robert Burns' birthplace; tour canals on gondolas manned by Venetian oarsmen, and study Malayan villages, complete with thatched huts and lightly clad natives. In short, the whole world was brought before her, and with her boundless curiosity about human nature, she was so excited about the Fair that she visited it every day. She was enraptured with the aspects of real life it displayed, and also felt uplifted, as she reportedly expressed it, "when her eye caught the Fair *ensemble* in a certain magical, semi-mystical light."[55] Both the moving procession of mankind and its individuals occupied her mind till the end.

On August 20, 1904, after a strenuous day at the exposition, Kate Chopin was stricken with a hemorrhage of the brain. Two days later, she died. Funeral services were held at the New Cathedral Chapel, and it seemed quite natural that what a newspaper called the author's "young friends" should be her pallbearers, and that a lilac bush, her favorite flower, should be planted at her grave.[56]

IX

The Long-Neglected Pioneer

1. *Oblivion and Rediscovery*

During her career, Kate Chopin had been regarded as a Louisiana local colorist. When she died in 1904, regional literature was out of fashion and she was practically forgotten. A book published in 1905 on *Southern Writers* does not even mention her.[1] Her death attracted little attention from the press, and in the few obituaries that can be found, she is generally referred to as a local colorist. True, at her death, the St. Louis *Globe-Democrat* recalled *The Awakening* as a fascinating book, and W. M. Reedy included it among the works which display what he calls her remarkable talent and rare intellect; the St. Louis *Post-Dispatch,* meanwhile, the newspaper which in 1899 had tried to counteract the condemnation of the novel, now nearly disregarded it, declaring that Mrs. Chopin's best work is found in her two collections of short stories.[2] For nearly half a century, this was to be the predominant attitude toward the author, that is, to the degree the critics were to recall her at all: To date, she has been seriously dealt with by fewer than twenty commentators of any importance.

For a moment, however, *The Awakening* seemed headed for a revival when it was reprinted in 1906 and Leonidas R. Whipple the following year included excerpts from it in the *Library of Southern Literature.* In his comments, Whipple pays tribute to the novel's honest descriptions of feminine psychology, but declares that it "fails of greatness because its theme and its persons . . . do not appeal to a wide audience." Mrs. Chopin's lasting fame will depend upon the artistry and universality of her shorter tales, he writes, where she is superior even to Cable, particularly in "Désirée's Baby," which he calls one of the most perfect short stories in English.[3]

The next critic of note to discuss Kate Chopin was Percival Pollard. He was known for his attacks on the puritanism of American literature, and it is therefore startling to read his diatribe of 1909 against

The Awakening, the more so because he thought the novel to be "utterly forgotten." The reason for this belated attack appears to be that Mrs. Pontellier transgresses into fields which the patriarchs reserve for men. Edna feels desire, and accepts it; *she* kisses her suitors, and she is aware that it is "merely Man, not Robert or Arobin" she desires. In short, she flouts the idea that "it was only the males who harbored thoughts fit only for the smoking-room," as Pollard expresses it. Of course, he did not know that Edna's creator was a smoker.[4]

Pollard's opinion of *The Awakening* was soon opposed by a member of the younger generation. In an article in the *Mirror* in 1911, Orrick Johns, the son of Mrs. Chopin's friend George S. Johns, praises the author for her candor about the complexities of the marriage relation. Calling her no less than "the most individual feminine talent America has produced," he recommends particularly that women read this author whose work would have been considered classic, he says, had she worked in France. Even in his view, however, she gave her best in her short stories and vignettes.[5]

This was also the attitude of Fred Lewis Pattee, who barely mentioned the novel in his *History of American Literature Since 1870,* and who left it out altogether in his treatment of Kate Chopin in the authoritative *Cambridge History of American Literature* (1918). Yet his discussion of her was important in that he for years did what he could to revive her, declaring that "no more exquisite work ... may be found in the whole range of the local color school" than in *Bayou Folk,* and that "she must be rated as a genius, taut, vibrant, intense of soul." She always strikes universal chords in her stories, he observes, adding that a few of them are "masterpieces before which one can only wonder."[6]

Dorothy Anne Dondore, the author of the entry on Mrs. Chopin in the *Dictionary of American Biography* (1930), agrees with Pattee that she ranks high among local colorists and that "Désirée's Baby," with its poignantly restrained ending, could hardly be excelled. But unlike Pattee, Miss Dondore views *The Awakening* as an important part of Kate Chopin's work; she commends its jewel-like polish and its subtle symbolism, and she calls it "one of the tragedies of recent American literature that Mrs. Chopin should have written this book two decades in advance of its time" and have been silenced by its adverse reception.[7]

Two years later, Rankin brought out his biography of Mrs. Chopin with his important material on how she had appeared to those who had known her. He included little criticism of his own, however, and his approach is suggested by the title: *Kate Chopin and her Creole Stories.* Regarding her as "an original genius" who belongs to the modern realism, he can accept the freedom and boldness she displays in the collection *A Night in Acadie,* particularly in "Athénaïse"; yet he condemns the "erotic morbidity" and "mental dissection" of *The Awakening.* This novel is not the real Kate Chopin, he seems to say, but a work inspired by the Decadents in general and Beardsley's "hideous . . . leer of sensuality" in particular. He concedes that she tells the truth without offense, but, like Frances Porcher, he asks: *cui bono?* In his view, Mrs. Chopin's efforts would have been better spent on further stories or vignettes of her bayou folk.[8]

Arthur Hobson Quinn echoes this attitude in his *American Fiction* (1936). Discussing Kate Chopin in his chapter on regional literature, he is lyric about her "brief, cameo-like stories," particularly "Désirée's Baby" which he, too, calls one of the greatest in the language. As for *The Awakening,* he first concedes that "the reality of the book is striking" and that it is admirably told, but then declares its standards to be "Continental rather than Creole" and the book itself to belong "rather among studies of morbid psychology than local color."[9]

A year later, Joseph J. Reilly devoted an article to Kate Chopin's artistry. With her "directness of approach, sureness of touch," and deep understanding, she is "incomparably the greatest American short story writer of her sex," he declares. He sees her women as homing birds, and though he commends her treatment of passion, he does not once refer to her novel about the passionate, home-fleeing Edna.[10]

In the *Literary History of the United States* (1948), Kate Chopin is once again discussed together with the local colorists. In the page Carlos Baker gives to her, he praises such qualities as her "intensity, courage, vigor, and independence"; her clean economy of line, and her Gallic finesse. "Her feeling for character was supported by an almost instinctive grasp of form and pace," he observes, adding, however, that "many of her stories fell short of excellence" because she refused to revise them. But he finds even her failures readable, and Mrs. Chopin's two collections, he seems to say, put the author almost on a par with Cable and Joel Chandler Harris, Miss Jewett and Mrs. Freeman. This makes it all the more surprising that such an authoritative history does not even mention *The Awakening.*[11]

But the novel was not entirely forgotten. In a 1946 essay, Cyrille Arnavon, a Frenchman, had been the first to discuss Kate Chopin together with such writers as Frank Norris and Theodore Dreiser rather than with the local colorists and to see *The Awakening* as a truly significant work in early American realism. He was also the first to compare it to *Madame Bovary* and to note its Maupassantian pessimism.[12]

As a further effort to revive and re-evaluate Kate Chopin, Arnavon in 1953 published a French translation of *The Awakening* together with an important discussion of its realism. Calling Mrs. Chopin a lucid and sensitive writer who still speaks to us, he points to the profundity and the mature judgment with which she treats the problems of sex and marriage. He sees the portrait of Edna as convincing, except that, as he says, her suicide is not sufficiently justified. In his view, the heroine's final swim is a neurotic woman's flight from sexual experience.[13]

Meanwhile, others were slowly becoming aware of the novel. In 1951, Clarence Gohdes wrote in *The Literature of the American People* that *The Awakening* is "as near to a *Madame Bovary* as the period produced" and that "it deserves a worthy place in the history of sterner realism in nineteenth-century America." In *The Confident Years: 1885–1915* (1952), Van Wyck Brooks calls it a "small perfect book that mattered more than the whole life-work of many a prolific writer." And he adds: "*The Awakening* was more mature than even the best of Cable's work, so effortless it seemed, so composed in its naturalness and grace . . . ." [14]

In 1956, two articles were devoted to *The Awakening*. In the first, Robert Cantwell declares the book to be "the finest novel of its sort written by an American"; in the second, Kenneth Eble calls it an "amazingly honest, perceptive and moving" book which recalls *Hippolytus* in the seriousness with which it treats the theme of sex. He adds that this French-influenced work is a "first-rate novel" and that we have few enough of its stature.[15]

In spite of this American championship of Kate Chopin, there was still no apparent interest in the author when the present writer started his work on her in 1961. But the year after, Edmund Wilson included some pages on her in his *Patriotic Gore;* here he discerningly points to "The Story of an Hour" as an example of the many unsatisfactory marriages in her fiction and calls *The Awakening* a "quite uninhibited and beautifully written [novel] which anticipates D. H. Lawrence in its treatment of infidelity." In 1964, Kenneth Eble's important article served as an introduction to a reprint of the book, the first reissue of the author's work (outside of anthologies) since *Bayou Folk* was last republished in 1911. The following year, Warner Berthoff gave a page to this "remarkable novel" in his study of *The Ferment of Realism.*[16]

In 1966, Larzer Ziff included in his study of *The American 1890s* a perceptive discussion of Mrs. Chopin's daring realism, which he in certain respects equates with that of Dreiser. He sees *The Awakening* as a novel of the first rank and observes that it "was the most important piece of fiction about the sexual life of a woman written to date in America," and he calls her later silence "a loss to American letters of the order of the untimely deaths of Crane and Norris."[17]

In a review of Ziff's book, Stanley Kauffmann suggests that Edna Pontellier speaks with a "lonely, existentialist voice out of the mid-20th century" and declares that her story "deserves a place in the line of major American fiction." In an article from 1967, George Arms agrees: "*The Awakening* seems likely to take a permanent place among the American novels of distinction" of its time, he observes. To his demonstration of how this work effectively makes use of a "complex sense of opposition," he adds a discussion of Kate Chopin's short stories. As if in answer to his treatment of them, *Bayou Folk* was reissued that same year, and *A Night in Acadie* in 1968.[18]

It would seem that the author is presently being revived in earnest. With the publication of *The Complete Works of Kate Chopin* (1969), the bulk of her writings is finally becoming available. This volume includes a large number of unpublished or uncollected stories, and the growing circle of her admirers can now for the first time fully judge of her range and importance.[19]

2. *Edna versus Maggie, Rose, Trina, and Carrie*

Cyrille Arnavon is thus no longer alone in elevating Kate Chopin from the group of local colorists to that of the American pioneer writers of the 1890's, the group which comprises such authors as Crane, Garland, Norris, and Dreiser. It is therefore fitting to look at works like *Maggie, Rose of Dutcher's Coolly, McTeague,* and *Sister Carrie,* all written in that formative decade of American literature, and compare their approach to certain fundamental issues with that of *The Awakening.*

If we turn to the treatment of sexuality in Garland's novel, for example, we find that his Rose, a farmer's daughter, views all aspects of animal reproduction as natural matters. We might then perhaps expect her to see sex in humans as equally natural, a view undoubtedly held by Edna. But though she is courted by "wholesome," "clean" men – one of them observes that human procreation is "not as yet a noble business" – she feels "revulsion" when she realizes how their presence stirs up desire in her "pure wholesome awakening womanhood." While men are "sordid and vicious, ... polygamous by instinct, insatiable as animals," women are virtuous by nature, Garland declares, and Rose sublimates her "brute passion" into a desire to become a great poet.[20]

That man's erotic and other drives are brutal is of course one of the tenets of naturalism, and Garland's illustration of it is mild compared to that of the others of the quartet. Norris, for example, whose theme in *McTeague* is how greed leads to murder, compares his hero to an evil beast who takes a "panther leap" and kisses Trina, the heroine, "grossly, full on the mouth," and who delights his wife and himself with biting and beating her. Though Kate Chopin saw brute selfishness as the dominant principle of the world, she rarely used the imagery of man as a warring animal, and, more specifically, she never attached anything brutish to physical passion. Moreover, she lets Edna make absolutely no attempt to suppress her amatory impulses.[21]

In fact, not only does Mrs. Chopin treat sex at least as amorally as any of the other four writers, but she also describes it more openly than they do. Their heroines – Maggie, Rose, Trina, and Carrie – are all rather sexless compared to Edna, and their descriptions of sexual matters in general are tame. This is perhaps most surprising in Dreiser, who is otherwise so elaborate and who wants us to believe that Carrie is dangerously attractive to men, and in Norris, who had made sex the main theme of his unfinished *Vandover and the Brute.* Garland is comparatively daring when he lets Rose feel desire and when he speaks of her "splendid curve of bust," but he allows her no more than a kiss on the hand. It is hard to understand that this book was locally banned; yet this reaction frightened the author, who thereafter fully adhered to R. W. Gilder's genteel literary code. *The Awakening,* meanwhile, is suffused with sex, and we witness how Alcée arouses

Edna and how she in turn sets Robert on fire with a voluptuous kiss. On this point of physical attraction and contact, Kate Chopin gave not only a fuller, but also a more convincing picture than any other serious American novelist had done.[22]

A fact which significantly sets off *The Awakening* from *Maggie, Rose, McTeague,* and *Sister Carrie,* is that Edna has children and the other heroines do not. This points to a fundamental difference in emphasis: Kate Chopin concentrates mainly on the biological aspects of woman's situation, while the other writers are more concerned with the socio-economic forces shaping her life. Where Edna stands back from society and questions its rules for woman's existence, the other women move with the procession in their fight for wealth, rank, or physical survival.

Common to all Edna's four counterparts is their admiration of those who are well dressed. Maggie and Carrie are more easily seduced because of their suitors' stylishness, which they equate with power and standing. Both Rose and Carrie are allured by the life of the rich, and their "imagination," as it is called, represents a desire to succeed and move up in the world. Dreiser speaks in one breath of Carrie's "emancipation" and her "more showy life." For Edna, who is the only one of these five women to start near the top, emancipation means something quite different; as she moves to a smaller house, she has "a feeling of having descended in the social scale, with a corresponding sense of having risen in the spiritual."[23]

When Carrie leaves Hurstwood, on the other hand, it is not her inner integrity she is thinking of, but her outer or material progress. She arrives at the attitude which long dominates Rose, that is, she does not want a husband and children to impede her climb on the ladder. As the two women rise, both judge themselves against their betters in society. Rose is particularly influenced by a woman doctor who tells her to think first of her career. Garland, who had once let a heroine demand "the right to be an individual human being first and a woman afterwards," is ostensibly in favor of female emancipation; the doctor leaves out the promise of obedience in her marriage ceremony, and Rose is told by her suitor that he expects her to be as "free and as sovereign" as himself and to follow her profession. But the author could not quite free himself from accepted ideas: The doctor insists that though she is ambitious in her career, she "could bear to give it all up a hundred times over, rather than [her] hope of being a mother," and Rose revels in "doing wifely things" for her friend the moment he has proposed, just as she suddenly finds it much more important that he appreciates her as a woman than that he praises her poetry.[24]

In Crane's version of the relationship between man and woman, Maggie's swaggering seducer asserts his "reassuring proprietorship" while she shows a dependent air: "Her life was Pete's." Norris' view is also uncomplicated when he lets Trina be subdued and conquered by McTeague's "sheer brute force" and declares that she "belongs" to him, body and soul, "forever and forever," because "the woman [worships] the man for that which she yields up to him." Norris here seems to have been influenced by the Darwinian idea of the female selecting the strongest suitor (which fits in with general male conceptions), and he also accepts the concomitant unromantic view of the love of an aroused heroine when he writes: "The Woman is awakened, and, starting from her sleep, catches blindly at what first her newly opened eyes light upon. It is a spell, a witchery, ruled by chance . . . ." *McTeague* thus for a moment parallels *The Awakening*, but Trina's "love of submission," on the other hand, is utterly unthinkable in the self-asserting Edna.[25]

Kate Chopin's novel stands up well when compared to these four important works in the canon of early American realism or naturalism. *Maggie* is a stereotype seduction-story which is only saved by Crane's irony and general artistic mastery; *Rose* has much of a moralistic, sentimental romance in spite of Garland's attempts to make it into a serious *Bildungsroman,* and *McTeague* has not a little of the melodramatic, particularly in the conclusion of its Zolaesque *motif.* *The Awakening,* on the other hand, has a fundamental seriousness which goes beyond that of these three works, and this and other qualities unite it more closely with *Sister Carrie* than with any of the other books.

Kate Chopin and Theodore Dreiser have in common a directness and a complete honesty in their descriptions of Edna's and Carrie's violations of what both writers considered society's "arbitrary scale" of morals. Unable to see their heroines as sinners, they braved public opinion by refusing to let the two repent, and they had the further audacity to present their stories with no trace of moralism and without apology. There are no villains in the two works. A seducer like Arobin appeals to the reader; Hurstwood achieves a certain dignity even in his downfall, and Adèle, who represents everything that Edna opposes, is portrayed with sympathy and understanding.[26]

We have here two unillusioned authors each writing about a heroine pursuing a chimera; the magnet drawing Carrie is the golden radiance on the distant hill tops, and the illusion firing Edna is the idea that she can achieve the ecstasy of an all-encompassing love. Both writers see their protagonists as wisps in the wind among the forces that move us, but with a difference. Though Dreiser at one point speaks in terms of evolutionary optimism and Kate Chopin sees man as basically unimprovable, there are greater changes, certainly a greater spiritual evolution, in Edna than in Carrie.[27]

The reason is that Dreiser, reflecting a mostly socio-economic determinism, endows Carrie with less free will than that found in Edna. What freedom Carrie has she uses to act out the changing roles which she copies from those one step ahead of her. True, she achieves outer independence, but she is unthinkable without the society which provides her with models. As symbolized by the rocking-chair, she has scarcely moved at the end of the novel; she is basically unchanged, ever looking to the next hill, her eyes still largely unopened to the real emptiness of her longings.

Edna, meanwhile, is awakened to a spiritual independence in general and to a realization of the nature of reality in particular. Of these two solitary souls, the outwardly successful Carrie gains little more than the finery without which she, like her first lover, is merely "nothing"; when the apparently defeated Edna takes off her clothes, on the other hand, it symbolizes a victory of self-knowledge and authenticity as she fully becomes herself.[28]

Carrie's blind, irresistible fight to get ahead has an unquestionable universality, and there is a similar quality in Edna's open-eyed choice to defy illusions and conventions. Different as these two novels are in form and theme – one terse in its concentration on inner reality, the other full of details on the outer show – both give a sense of tragic life, conveying something of the human condition.

What unites these five works from the 1890's is that they all, in one way or another, represent their authors' will to renew American literature. In subject matter or approach, they had enough of the new realism or naturalism to shock the Iron Madonnas. Refusing to idealize life in the old manner, these writers all took a step forward in what Howells called truthful treatment of material.

Kate Chopin parallels the naturalists in her view of basic urges as imperative, but differs from them in that she lets Edna decide her own destiny in an existentialist way. *The Awakening* also differs from *Maggie* and *McTeague* in that there is nothing of the sordid in it. Yet we note that while Norris and Crane became less iconoclastic in their subsequent work, Mrs. Chopin moved on to the increased openness of "The Storm." After science had robbed her of some of her early beliefs, she may at times have wanted to join one of her heroines who decided to "go back into the dark to think" because "the sight of things" confused her. However, whereas Maupassant's reaction to the new knowledge was sadness rather than exhilaration – "tous ces voiles levés m'attristent," as he expressed it – Kate Chopin was sad only at the thought of woman's position, while being exhilarated at the opportunity of portraying life truthfully. Though she did not aim at exposing false respectability, her work is in certain respects a forerunner of such later eye-openers as *Spoon River Anthology, Winesburg, Ohio,* and *Main Street.*[29]

Mrs. Chopin was at least a decade ahead of her time. During the years following America's silencing of her, "Edith Wharton's genteel satire and Ellen Glasgow's moral searchings were the strongest fare that it could take," as Robert E. Spiller has observed.[30] Kate Chopin can be seen not only as one of the American realists of the 1890's, but also as a link in the tradition formed by such distinguished American women authors as Sarah Orne Jewett, Mary E. Wilkins Freeman, Willa Cather, and the two just mentioned. One factor uniting these writers is their emphasis on female characters. Another is their concern with values, but here we see a difference between the St. Louisian and the others in that she is less interested than they are in preserving these values. As exemplified in Mrs. Todd of *The Country of the Pointed Firs,* for instance, woman is a rock guarding the old qualities, the men being either weak or dead. To Mrs. Chopin, woman is no more of a rock than is man, being neither better nor worse than he. Mrs. Wharton and Miss Glasgow may have attacked certain aspects of the aristocracies they sprang from, but they also wanted to preserve some of their values. Kate Chopin, on the other hand, was no celebrant of the aristocratic qualities of her own distinguished background.

The one value that really counted with her was woman's opportunity for self-expression. She knew that there are many *Woman's Kingdoms.* She was sensitive, intelligent, and broad enough in her outlook to see the different basic needs of the female and the various sides of her existence and to represent them with impartiality. Her work is thus no feminist plea in the usual sense, but an illustration – rather than an assertion – of woman's right to be herself, to be individual and independent whether she wants to be weak or strong, a nest-maker or a soaring bird.

3. An American Pioneer Writer

The work of Kate Chopin was apparently unknown to Dreiser, even though he began writing *Sister Carrie* just when *The Awakening* was being loudly condemned. Also Ellen Glasgow, who was at this time beginning to describe unsatisfactory marriages, seems to have been unaware of the author's existence. Indeed, we can safely say that though she was so much of an innovator in American literature, she was virtually unknown by those who were now to shape it and that she had no influence on them.[31]

Had *The Awakening* been tried like a *Lady Chatterley's Lover,* it would no doubt have permanently established the author's fame. As it was, she received support from practically no one. The number of her readers was small. Though she had remarkably little of the provincial, it probably hampered her development that she had no contact with the nationally important writers and critics. While her friends encouraged her, they did not understand or accept what she was really trying to do, not even W. M. Reedy who told Dreiser that *Sister Carrie* was "damned good" and who was later to defend a work like *The Genius.* Whereas Crane, Garland, and Norris all enjoyed the moral support of Howells, and Dreiser was helped by Norris, Kate Chopin stood virtually alone as she became more and more outspoken in her truthful descriptions of life as she saw it.[32]

She took her writing seriously. While she had the commercial instinct and wanted her work to succeed even financially, literary integrity was her paramount concern. She was one of the utterly few who wrote to suit their own taste, and she made practically no concessions to the public and did not aspire to reaching beyond the group who would be in sympathy with her. Partly because she did not write in self-justification as Mmes. de Staël and Sand had done, she could do away with both their militancy in the portrayals of female emancipation and their protestations that the works were moral. Her courage is even more remarkable when we consider that she did not have her predecessors' influential friends and that she lived in a country where intellectual genius – even in a man – did not count for much.[33]

Kate Chopin had much of the Gaul in her individualism, her frankness and freedom, and her combination of serious thought and subtle humor. Having been exposed to a French skepticism from childhood, she was removed from traditional Yankee optimism. In short, she reflected much of the Creole tradition to which she was born. With Dreiser, she was one of the first writers of a Continental, Catholic background to enter the American literary scene, which was still largely dominated by Anglo-Saxon Protestants; but unlike him, she felt entirely secure with her heritage and was happily free from all need to prove herself for ethnic or social reasons.

As a result of her background, she could also draw fully on the rich French literary traditions. That she had so much of the Gaul and leaned toward the French school in literature did not mean that she had any Gallic bias, however. In a relaxed, unambivalent way she was both a Creole and an American, and though she was foreign to all extreme Yankee nationalism, she shared Howells' feeling that American literature should and could stand on its own.

She agreed with him, for example, that United States authors should employ Americanisms. Terming it "a matter which [touched her] closely concerning the use and misuse of words," she answered a critic who had objected to her speaking in At Fault of a "depot" rather than a "railway station" that the latter was an unacceptable Briticism. (Supposing for a moment that Howells had been willing to let "nudities" enter New World fiction, he ought to have applauded Mrs. Chopin who refused to follow the American habit of blurring them by giving them a French garb.) Obviously thinking not only of herself who had a tradition to fall back upon and who, furthermore, was interested in the timeless rather than in her own very usable past, she felt that her country offered its authors enough literary material. This is evident from what she told William Schuyler: "Americans, in their artistic insight and treatment, are," he reports her as saying, "well up with the French; and, with the advantage which they enjoy of a wider and more variegated field for observation, would, perhaps, surpass them," were it not for the bans on free literary expression.[34]

This was thus a major point: To arrive at true art, American authors would have to insist on depicting true life. In this attitude, Kate Chopin did of course reflect the French writers, as she did in her themes and technique. She was also influenced by the general emphasis of the 1890's on sexuality and feminism. But her perspective was wider than that. She drew on both the Greeks and the Bible, on science as well as modern fiction. In a manner combining the ideas of Euripides and Darwin, she had formed her independent and entirely personal view of passion and woman.

Mrs. Chopin had the vision, the originality and independence, and the sense of artistic form which are needed to give us the great novel. She also had remarkable courage. She hid her ambition and her goal somewhat, knowing that men do not readily accept what Mme. de Staël had called "superiority" in a progressive woman. But she was unable to keep her inclinations in check, and the tensions she felt between Paul and Paula, between the dictates of the Biblical male and the urges of the female artist, resulted in unheard of illustrations of woman's spiritual and sensuous self-assertion. No wonder that she was shipwrecked, like another Margaret Fuller, with her cargo of iconoclastic views.

The great achievement of Kate Chopin was that she broke new ground in American literature. She was the first woman writer in her country to accept passion as a legitimate subject for serious, outspoken fiction. Revolting against tradition and authority; with a daring which we can hardly fathom today; with an uncompromising honesty and no trace of sensationalism, she undertook to give the unsparing truth about woman's submerged life. She was something of a pioneer in the amoral treatment of sexuality, of divorce, and of woman's urge for an existential authenticity. She is in many respects a modern writer, particularly in her awareness of the complexities of truth and the complications of freedom. With no desire to reform, but only to understand; with the clear conscience of the rebel, yet unembittered by society's massive lack of understanding, she arrived at her culminating achievements, *The Awakening* and "The Storm."

From "The Poor Girl" to her last novel she was praised for her artistry, but criticized for her subject matter. She obviously does not come near the breadth and stature of Dreiser, but among the American authors of second rank she occupies an important and distinctive position. In her best writings within her particular field, she not only equals Dreiser's courage, but shows an independence, a directness of purpose, a deep understanding, and a sensitive artistry which make them into minor masterpieces. With *The Awakening* and a handful of her stories, such as "Regret," "Athénaïse," and "The Storm," she deserves to be permanently included, not only in her country's literary history, but also in its body of living fiction.

Kate Chopin is a rare, transitional figure in modern literature. In her illustrations of the female condition she forms a link between George Sand and Simone de Beauvoir. In her descriptions of the power of sexuality she reflects the ideas of such a work as *Hippolytus* and foreshadows the forceful 20th-century treatments of Eros.

She was of course too much of a pioneer to be accepted in her time and place. True, Henry Adams asked himself in 1900 whether he knew of any American artist besides Whitman "who had ever insisted on the power of sex, as every classic had always done." Had he looked into *The Awakening*, he would have found more than he may have asked for. D. H. Lawrence would not have accepted Edna, either, since she would not have renounced her sovereignty to achieve his type of man-dictated transcendence. Indeed, in the field of spiritual assertion, Mrs. Pontellier will for a long time to come be faced with male condescension and prejudice – "l'homme que je pourrais aimer n'est pas né, et il ne naîtra peut-être que plusieurs siècles après ma mort," as George Sand lets Lélia observe – and she will also be up against preconceived ideas in a number of women. Most female readers, however, are likely to take to their heart this deeply moving portrait of a woman's growth into self-awareness, just as the author had done with Maupassant's pictures of awakening *Françaises*.[35]

Mrs. Chopin had a daring and a vision all her own, a unique pessimistic realism applied to woman's unchangeable condition. When the storm over *The Awakening* hit her, it showed that she was truly a solitary soul, and indeed, in 1900 she was, with Dreiser, the most isolated, the least recognized of the important American realists of that era. As the old century came to an end, these two writers introduced a belated freedom from all moral preconceptions into American literature. Though they did not openly attack the codes of society, their supreme unconcern with the sacredness of marriage and morals was considered so dangerous that they were forced into silence.

The blow dealt her by the prudish boycott discouraged Kate Chopin from delving as deeply as she could have done into the psychology of her women. She had started out like the animal in "Emancipa-

Notes and References

Abbreviations:

BF   Kate Chopin, *Bayou Folk* (Boston, 1894).
CW   *The Complete Works of Kate Chopin,* ed. Per Seyersted (Baton Rouge, 1969).
MHS   Missouri Historical Society, St. Louis.
NA   Kate Chopin, *A Night in Acadie* (Chicago, 1897).
PS   Per Seyersted, "Kate Chopin: An Important St. Louis Writer Reconsidered," Missouri Historical Society *Bulletin,* XIX (Jan. 1963), 89–114.
Rankin   Daniel S. Rankin, *Kate Chopin and Her Creole Stories* (Philadelphia, 1932).
Schuyler William Schuyler, "Kate Chopin," *Writer,* VII (Aug. 1894), 115–117.

Note: With only a few exceptions, Kate Chopin's own spelling and punctuation have been kept throughout this book.

Chapter One

[1] Mark Twain, *Life on the Mississippi,* Ch. XXII.
[2] *Biographical and Historical Memoirs of Northwestern Louisiana* (Nashville, 1890), p. 333.
[3] Rankin, pp. 13–14.
[4] William Hyde and Howard L. Conard, *Encyclopedia of the History of St. Louis,* I (New York, 1899), p. 358; Rankin, Chs. I, II.
[5] Hyde and Conard, I, p. 358.
[6] Ibid.; Schuyler, pp. 116–117.
[7] Rankin, pp. 12, 19, 105.
[8] As quoted in Rankin, pp. 28–29.
[9] Felix Chopin, as quoted in Rankin, pp. 29–31.
[10] See T. A. Post, *Truman Marcellus Post, D. D. A Biography* (Boston, 1891), pp. 222–228.
[11] Kate Chopin's children, as quoted in Rankin, pp. 33–34.
[12] Rankin, pp. 33–35.

[13] Rankin, pp. 35–36.

[14] Rankin, pp. 13, 36, 174.

[15] See John Francis McDermott, *The Early Histories of St. Louis* (St. Louis, 1952), pp. 5–6, and "Pierre de Laclède and the Chouteaus," MHS *Bulletin,* XXI (July 1965), 279–283. Ernest Kirschten, *Catfish and Crystal* (Garden City, N. Y., 1960), pp. 53–55. In *Glimpses of Creole Life in Old St. Louis* (St. Louis, 1933, p. 9), Eugénie Berthold maintains that Mme. Chouteau was a very active woman and that her share in the development of the village cannot be overestimated.

[16] J. Thomas Scharf, *History of St. Louis City and County,* I (Philadelphia, 1883), pp. 175–176, 179.

[17] Rankin, pp. 13, 15, 28.

[18] The fragment is at MHS. See p. 48.

[19] Sister Garesché, as quoted in Rankin, p. 37.

[20] *Histoire des Grandes Familles Françaises du Canada ou Aperçu sur le Chevalier Benoist et Quelques Familles Contemporaines* (Montréal, 1867), pp. 110–113.

[21] Alexander DeMenil, "Kate Chopin," *Hesperian,* IV (Oct. 1904), 383–384.

[22] Sister Garesché, as quoted in Rankin, p. 37.

[23] Sister Garesché, as quoted in Rankin, p. 40; CW, p. 716.

[24] As quoted in Rankin, p. 38.

[25] Ibid.

[26] CW, p. 716; Sister Garesché, as quoted in Rankin, p. 43. The flag episode is mentioned in a letter written in 1863 by Anne E. Lane to Sarah L. Glasgow, now at MHS.

[27] Rankin, p. 45.

[28] Schuyler, p. 116. See Hyde and Conard, I, p. 358.

[29] Quoted in Louise Callan, *The Society of the Sacred Heart in North America* (New York, 1937), p. 666.

[30] Ibid., pp. 727, 741, 745.

[31] Ibid., p. 662. Sister Garesché, as quoted in Rankin, p. 46.

[32] Schuyler, p. 116; Alexander DeMenil, "A Century of Missouri Literature," *Missouri Historical Review,* XV (Oct. 1920), 117–119.

[33] As quoted in Rankin, p. 52.

[34] Sister Garesché, as quoted in Rankin, p. 48.

[35] Hyde and Conard, I, p. 358.

[36] [Lady Blessington,] *Conversations of Lord Byron with the Countess of Blessington* (London, 1834), pp. 31–33.

[37] CW, p. 717.

[38] CW, p. 709.

[39] [Dinah Maria Mulock Craik,] *The Woman's Kingdom* (New York, 1869), p. 89.

40 Interview with Felix Chopin, 1949, by the then Director of MHS.

41 Felix Chopin, as quoted in Rankin, p. 58.

Chapter Two

1 Bernard DeVoto, "Victoria Woodhull," *Saturday Review of Literature,* V (Dec. 29, 1928), 552. A full treatment of this early part of Mrs. Woodhull's career is found in Emanie Sachs, *The Terrible Siren: Victoria Woodhull, 1838–1927* (New York, 1928), pp. 27–106.

2 Interview with Miss Gladys Breazeale (daughter of Phanor Breazeale; see p. 43), New Orleans, 1964; Rankin, p. 84.

3 Succession Papers of Julia Chopin, CDC, New Orleans; Phanor Breazeale, "Denies Uncle Tom's Cabin is Tale of Louisiana," New Orleans *States,* Dec. 29, 1929.

4 The legend would have it that McAlpin had treated his slaves with exceptional cruelty and that a brother of Harriet Beecher Stowe had visited him and taken notes which later formed the basis for the final episode of *Uncle Tom's Cabin.* Some commentators have even maintained that the author herself visited McAlpin. On McAlpin and Legree, see D. B. Corley, *A Visit to Uncle Tom's Cabin* (Chicago, 1892), and Breazeale, "Denies Uncle Tom's Cabin ... ." Corley quotes a letter from Charles Beecher, who did visit the general area. Because of the lack of evidence to back up the legend, however, the Natchitoches Parish Chamber of Commerce in 1960 decided against declaring the plantation an historic site.

5 A recent booklet on the parish is *Natchitoches. Oldest Settlement in the Louisiana Purchase* (Natchitoches, 1958). Other treatments are found in Germaine Portré-Bobinsky and C. M. Smith, *Natchitoches, the Up-to-date Oldest Town in Louisiana* (Natchitoches, 1936), and James Fair Hardin, *Northwestern Louisiana,* I–III (Louisville, Ky., [1937?]).

6 Herman de Bachellé Seebold, *Old Louisiana Plantation Homes and Family Trees,* I (New Orleans, 1941), pp. 367, 370.

7 Interview with Miss Breazeale; CW, p. 954.

8 Rankin, pp. 85–86.

9 On the heavy Civil War destruction along the Cane River, see John D. Winters, *The Civil War in Louisiana* ([Baton Rouge,] 1963), pp. 365–366.

10 Rankin, p. 95.

11 CW, p. 81.

12 Interview with Miss Breazeale; Rankin, p. 81; CW, p. 938.

13 Interview with Mrs. John S. Tritle, St. Louis, 1965; statement by

Mrs. L. Tyler, as quoted in Rankin, p. 89; obituary on Kate Chopin, *Picayune* (New Orleans), Aug. 23, 1904.

[14] Rankin, pp. 81–82, 195. She could mimic anything: clergy, animals, etc. (interview with Rankin, Paris, 1962).

[15] Interview with Miss Breazeale; Mrs. Tyler, as quoted in Rankin, p. 89.

[16] Rankin, p. 83; CW, p. 940. When Kate Chopin observes in her honeymoon diary: "Had one of my fearful headaches, which took me directly to bed – knowing that sleep alone would come to my relief," it seems to indicate that such attacks were then not infrequent.

[17] Rankin, p. 80; interview with Miss Breazeale.

[18] Rankin, p. 83. The diary is at MHS. Besides stories and poems, the notebook contains about thirty-five pages of diary entries, a considerable part of which is quoted in the present book.

[19] Interview with Miss Breazeale; Mrs. Tyler, as quoted in Rankin, pp. 89–90. Kate Chopin's children were: Jean (1871–1911); Oscar (1873–1933); George (1874–1952); Frederick (1876–1953); Felix (1878–1955); Lelia (1879–1962).

[20] Schuyler, p. 116; CW, p. 990.

[21] In speaking of this notebook, Rankin reports (p. 93) that an entry in it describing a visit to a café was used, "with variations," in Ch. XXXVI of *The Awakening*.

[22] Edward L. Tinker, *Lafcadio Hearn's American Days* (New York, 1924), pp. 91–96.

[23] Elizabeth B. Wetmore, *The Life and Letters of Lafcadio Hearn,* I (Boston, 1906), pp. 206, 226; Twain, *Mississippi,* Ch. XLV.

[24] See John Smith Kendall, *History of New Orleans,* II (Chicago, 1922), pp. 731–740; Tinker, pp. 60, 67–70, 150, 156; Arlin Turner, *George W. Cable. A Biography* (Durham, N. C., 1956), pp. 39, 102. Kate Chopin may have known such a New Orleans newspaper editor as Marion A. Baker, who was a friend of Cable and Hearn, but there is nothing to indicate that she ever met these authors.

[25] Alcée Fortier, *A History of Louisiana,* IV: 2 (New York, 1904), pp. 112, 192–193. See Turner, p. 73; Stuart Omer Landry, *The Battle of Liberty Place* (New Orleans, 1955), pp. 113–114, 235; H. Oscar Lestage, "The White League in Louisiana and Its Participation in Reconstruction Riots," *Louisiana Historical Quarterly,* XVIII (July 1935), 685.

[26] Wetmore, *Hearn,* I, p. 215.

[27] CW, p. 892.

[28] Kate Chopin's notebook, as quoted in Rankin, pp. 94–95. Rankin maintains (interview) that Oscar Chopin paid what he could of his debts, "even though he did not have to."

[29] Breazeale's report is in the possession of Miss Breazeale. See also

Biographical ... Louisiana, p. 304; Lestage, "The White League ...,"
pp. 685–689.
[30] Colfax *Chronicle,* April 3, 1880.
[31] CW, pp. 105, 108. Kate Chopin's house has now been restored and
turned into a "Bayou Folk Museum." According to "Succession of
Oscar Chopin," Natchitoches Parish Court Records No. 1941, dated
March 30, 1883, some $12,000 in accounts outstanding had to be
written off at that time.
[32] A Cloutierville lady and Mrs. Lelia Hattersley (Kate Chopin's daughter), as quoted in Rankin, pp. 102–103. The records of the St. John
the Baptist Church, Cloutierville, show that Lelia was born in that
village on Dec. 31, 1879; the packet was frequently mentioned in the
Colfax *Chronicle* in 1880.
[33] L. R. Whipple, "Kate Chopin," in Edwin A. Alderman and Joel
Chandler Harris, eds., *Library of Southern Literature,* II (New
Orleans, 1907), p. 864. Natchitoches *Vindicator,* Sept. 3 and Oct. 8,
1881. Lelia Chopin (Kate Chopin's grand-daughter), "Kate Chopin,"
Maryville Magazine (St. Louis), VIII (May 1933), 25. Oscar apparently died on Jan. 10, 1883.
[34] CW, p. 741; Schuyler, p. 116.
[35] Schuyler, p. 116.
[36] Rankin, p. 105.

Chapter Three

[1] Rankin, pp. 41–42. The handwriting shows that the fragment – which
is clearly part of a larger whole – must have been written shortly
before 1887, thus not "toward the end of her life," as Rankin declares
(p. 42). The fragment is in MS at MHS. Lelia Hattersley in letter of
Nov. 12, 1907, as quoted in Rankin, p. 35.
[2] Rankin, p. 89.
[3] Interview with Mrs. Marjorie McCormick (Kate Chopin's grand-
daughter), St. Louis, 1964; interview with Felix Chopin.
[4] Obituary on Kolbenheyer, St. Louis *Post-Dispatch,* April 10, 1921;
Don C. Seitz, *Joseph Pulitzer. His Life & Letters* (New York, 1924),
pp. 57, 104.
[5] Schuyler, p. 116.
[6] Rankin, pp. 105, 107; Schuyler, p. 116; Whipple, "Kate Chopin," p.
864. After Mrs. O'Flaherty's death, Kate Chopin supported her family
on the modest yield of the Cloutierville plantations and some St. Louis
real estate inherited from her mother. In 1891, Mrs. Chopin apparently made a brief, unsuccessful attempt to make money through

translating popular articles, probably from the French, for the news-papers. (The following were published: "The Shape of the Head"; "Revival of Wrestling"; "How to Make Manikins." They appeared in the St. Louis *Post-Dispatch,* Jan. 25, 1891; March 8, 1891, and April 5, 1891.) Her notebooks show that she earned a total of $2,300 on her writings. Rankin declares (p. 107) that the impecunious heroine of "A Pair of Silk Stockings" is a picture of the author, but all family reports suggest that while her funds were never ample (and she was too honest to pretend they were), there was no lack.

[7] A Kate Chopin letter to Marie Breazeale is dated Cloutierville, June 21, 1887.

[8] The poem was probably written in 1890.

[9] Kate Chopin's notebook.

[10] CW, pp. 700–701.

[11] It has proved impossible to identify the volume she refers to. The stories she translated are listed in the Bibliography.

[12] [Sue V. Moore,] "Mrs. Kate Chopin," *St. Louis Life,* X (June 9, 1894), 11–12. An entry in Mrs. Chopin's 1894 diary seems to prove that Mrs. Moore was the author of this "authorized sketch," as Rankin calls it (p. 136).

[13] Schuyler, pp. 116–117. "Crude and unformed" apparently represent Mrs. Chopin's actual words.

[14] Julian S. Rammelkamp, *Pulitzer's Post-Dispatch 1878–1883* (Princeton, 1967), pp. 13–16, 294.

[15] Schuyler, p. 117. Schuyler writes that she "even gave away" some stories to local periodicals so as to see them in print.

[16] According to Rankin (p. 129; interview), Kate Chopin's appreciation of Howells was "attested by the number of his novels, comedies, and books of criticism in her library," and her marginal notes in them, such as "good," "excellent," etc. We know nothing more specific about this library, except that it contained mostly fiction; all that remains of it is a few issues of the *Yellow Book* and [Mary Anette Russel,] *Elizabeth and Her German Garden* (London, 1898). The reading of Howells' comedies remained a lasting pleasure to her, says Rankin (p. 132), and they inspired her one effort in this genre, "An Embarrassing Situation," which she wrote for a New York *Herald* "Dramatic Contest."

[17] St. Louis *Post-Dispatch,* Oct. 5, 1890.

[18] *Fashion and Fancy,* V (Dec. 1890), 60. See also the *Spectator,* XI (Oct. 4, 1890), 55; *St. Louis Life,* II (Oct. 11, 1890), 8; St. Louis *Republic,* Oct. 18, 1890.

[19] *Nation,* LIII (Oct. 1, 1891), 264.

[20] Schuyler, p. 117.

[21] CW, p. 152; Rankin, p. 132. I am indebted to George Arms for the information that Howells apparently never commented on Kate Chopin.

[22] CW, p. 314.

[23] Undated MS at MHS; written before June 8, 1893.

[24] Hamlin Garland, *Roadside Meetings* (New York, 1930), p. 335. The letter to the *Century,* dated July 12, 1891, also contains Gilder's outline for the answer, which is lost.

[25] Letter to Gilder, dated [New York,] May 10, 1893. Rankin maintains (p. 31) that Kate Chopin's love for St. Louis is illustrated by "an experience she submitted to after the publication of her first collection of short stories. Friends and the publisher advised her to go to Boston where the atmosphere was supposed to be literary. She went, and after three days fled home to St. Louis." Whatever the basis for this story, it seems to have been changed underway. *Bayou Folk* was not published until 1894, and there is no indication that she ever repeated her 1893 trip to the East. Furthermore, her own letters to Gilder make it clear that the paramount reason for a possible visit to Boston would have been her wish to find a publisher for her books.

[26] For a discussion of an interesting earlier Natchitoches writer, see James S. Patty, " A Woman Journalist in Reconstruction Louisiana: Mrs. Mary E. Bryan," *Louisiana Studies,* III (Spring 1964), 77–104. *Nation,* LVIII (June 28, 1894), 488; St. Louis *Post-Dispatch,* April 8, 1894. For further reviews, see e. g. St. Louis *Republic,* May 20, 1894, and the *Critic,* XXIV (May 5, 1894), 299–300.

[27] *Sunday Mirror,* IV (April 15, 1894), 4, and IV (Sept. 30, 1894), 4; *Atlantic Monthly,* LXXIII (April 1894), 558–559.

[28] CW, pp. 352–354.

[29] CW, pp. 695, 722.

[30] Kate Chopin apparently showed "Young Dr. Gosse" to Schuyler, and possibly also other items, but nothing indicates that she ever asked his advice.

[31] Mrs. Hattersley, as quoted in Rankin, p. 116, and as quoted by her son, Mr. Robert C. Hattersley (interview, New York, 1961).

[32] CW, p. 597; interviews with Mrs. Tritle and Rankin.

[33] CW, p. 708; Schuyler, p. 117.

[34] Interviews with Mrs. Tritle and Miss Breazeale; Dorothy Anne Dondore, "Kate O'Flaherty Chopin," *Dictionary of American Biography,* IV (New York, 1930), pp. 90–91.

[35] Mrs. Sommers in "A Pair of Silk Stockings."

[36] CW, p. 700.

[37] Rankin, interview, and pp. 106, 107. A partially preserved letter at MHS, written by a member of Kate Chopin's entourage, suggests that her admirers were jealous of each other.

[38] Rankin, pp. 106, 107; Reedy, "Death of Mrs. Chopin," *Mirror,* XIV (Aug. 25, 1904), 1; interview with Mrs. George Chopin, St. Louis, 1964.

[39] Diary. Interviews with Felix Chopin and Robert C. Hattersley. The composition, "Lilia. Polka for Piano," was "published for the author by H. Rollman & Sons, St. Louis," 1888.

[40] A sketch of the room (by Oscar Chopin, the author's son) is found in St. Louis *Post-Dispatch,* Nov. 26, 1899.

[41] "Is There an Interesting Woman in St. Louis?" St. Louis *Republic,* Sept. 11, 1910 (probably written by Vernon – "Bunny" – Knapp or some other member of the Knapp family, owners of the paper); letter to Mrs. Chopin from Sue V. Moore at MHS; CW, p. 712.

[42] Max Putzel, *The Man in the Mirror: William Marion Reedy and His Magazine* (Cambridge, Mass., 1963), pp. 53, 135; Orrick Johns (son of George S. Johns; see p. 64), *Time of Our Lives* (New York, 1937), p. 88; Herbert Howarth, *Notes on Some Figures Behind T. S. Eliot* (Boston, 1964), pp. 55–63. For a recent discussion of the Society, see Loyd D. Easton, *Hegel's First American Followers* (Athens, Ohio, 1967). For William Schuyler's links with the Society, see his article "German Philosophy in St. Louis," *Bulletin of the Washington University Association,* II (1904), 62–84.

[43] St. Louis *Star-Times,* Feb. 13, 1948, quoting itself from "50 Years Ago." For a discussion of DeMenil, see Putzel, pp. 52–53. Interview with Felix Chopin.

[44] Rammelkamp's book deals at length with these *Post-Dispatch* campaigns. How greatly the members of Kate Chopin's group admired her is seen in a number of letters at MHS, e. g. in one from George S. Johns to the poet William Vincent Byars, which shows how they deferred to her literary judgment.

[45] Interview with Felix Chopin; Putzel, pp. 70, 136; Reedy, "Death of Mrs. Chopin."

[46] CW, pp. 706–720. A French translation by Dumay of "The Story of an Hour" is in MS at MHS. Fired from the *Criterion* early in 1898, Dumay became a newspaper editor, first of the New York *World,* and later of the Paris *Quotidien.*

[47] Interviews with Robert C. Hattersley and Mrs. McCormick. In a perhaps apocryphal report, a lady is quoted as saying that she had the most interesting conversations with Kate Chopin while the author was in a hot bath, smoking a big black cigar.

[48] Orrick Johns, *Time of Our Lives,* p. 201; Alexander DeMenil, *The Literature of the Louisiana Territory* (St. Louis, 1904), pp. 258–259. (DeMenil here practically repeats what Sue V. Moore had said in "Mrs. Kate Chopin.") A woman reports that, when a young girl, she

was not allowed to meet Kate Chopin "because she sat with legs crossed and smoked a cigarette."

49 Interviews with Miss Breazeale and Rankin.

50 Schuyler, p. 117. [Sue V. Moore,] "Mrs. Kate Chopin," p. 11.

51 "Constitution and By-Laws. List of Officers and Members. Wednesday Club of St. Louis. 1890–1891" (St. Louis, 1890), p. 3. See also the club's yearly Programmes, and Hyde and Conard, IV, pp. 2479–2484. The paper is undoubtedly identical with "Typical German Composers," an article which Mrs. Chopin offered in Jan. 1899 to the *Atlantic,* which had just published another essay of hers.

52 Howarth, pp. 22–28. Diary.

53 CW, p. 702.

54 Ibid.

55 There were no women in the group of acquaintants whom Kate Chopin's children suggested that Rankin consult.

56 Diary; CW, p. 706.

57 Diary.

58 When Kate Chopin later published a slightly changed version of this diary entry (CW, p. 366), she called it "The Night Came Slowly."

59 *Vogue,* too, refused "The Story of an Hour," in April 1894, but accepted it when Kate Chopin re-submitted it – apparently unchanged – after her success with *Bayou Folk.*

60 For discussions of Gilder, see Arthur W. John, "A History of *Scribner's Monthly* and *The Century Illustrated Monthly Magazine,* 1870–1900," and Herbert F. Smith, "The Editorial Influence of Richard Watson Gilder, 1870–1909" (unpublished doctoral dissertations, Harvard University, 1951, and Rutgers University, 1961, respectively). Smith describes the refusal of *Maggie* on p. 351.

61 Letters of July 12, 1891, and Jan. 5, 1897.

62 CW, p. 498. The original ending has not survived.

63 Letters from Page, dated Oct. 9 and 23, 1896. The first version of the essay is lost; the second, called "Confidences," is in MS at MHS, while the third was published in Jan. 1899 as "In the Confidence of a Story-Writer." CW, p. 700.

64 CW, p. 718; letter from Scudder of July 12, 1895. Part of the *Criterion* essay quoted here is very likely derived from the first version of "Confidences."

65 CW, p. 463.

66 MS, dated Dec. 1895, at MHS. CW, p. 472.

67 Interview with Rankin. The poem is dated Aug. 16, 1895.

68 "Good Night" is undated. It was published in the *Times-Democrat,* New Orleans, July 22, 1894, and was probably newly written.

69 Two other poems possibly bearing on the author's own situation might

be quoted. Both are in MS at MHS; the first is dated Aug. 18, 1895, while the second is undated.

Under My Lattice

. . . . . .

There are flowers to gather and with them the dew,
Take them or leave them or trample a few.
Some – to pluck them I would not care;
And others – to touch them I would not dare.

. . . . . .

A Fancy

Happily naught came of it.
   'Twas but a fancy born of fate and wishing.
   But I thought all the same of it.
Now that the wishing's dead,
   I find that naught remains of it.
   Fancy and fate are fled.

[70] CW, pp. 475, 477. Maupassant's "Lui" (see Bibliography) may have furnished the starting point for this story.

[71] As quoted by Rankin (interview).

[72] CW, pp. 712, 713. Mrs. Stuart, on her part, seems never to have mentioned Kate Chopin, not even in an article in which she enumerated the authors who had written about Louisiana (Ruth McEnery Stuart, "American Backgrounds for Fiction, VI – Arkansas, Louisiana and the Gulf Country," *The Bookman*, XXXIX (Aug. 1914), 620–630.

[73] *Vogue*, IV (Dec. 6, 1894), 380. The letter, dated Jan. 2, 1896, cannot be located, but it was quoted in part by a dealer who in 1942 offered it to Herbert S. Stone, Jr.

[74] Letters from Houghton Mifflin dated March 13 and July 12, 1895, and Jan. 20, 1897. Apart from the title story, "A Vocation and a Voice" was to contain (Rankin, p. 195): "Elizabeth Stock's One Story; Two Portraits; An Idle Fellow; A Mental Suggestion; An Egyptian Cigarette; The White Eagle; Story of an Hour; Two Summers and Two Souls; Sketches (The Night Came Slowly, and Juanita); The Unexpected; Her Letters; The Kiss; Suzette; Fedora; The Recovery; The Blind Man; A Morning's Walk; Lilacs; Ti Démon; The Godmother." (This list, which is now lost, was probably made in 1900.) "Mad Stories" is the title Kate Chopin used in her notebook. Very likely it was these stories she had in mind in "Confidences" (see p. 51). According to a letter from Houghton Mifflin (dated June 21, 1968), *Bayou Folk* was reprinted in 1895 (500 copies), 1906 (150), and 1911 (150). (The original printing was 1,250 copies.)

[75] *Nation,* LXVI (June 9, 1898), 447; *Critic,* XXXII (April 16, 1898), 266; *Mirror,* VII (Nov. 25, 1897), 5–6; *Hesperian,* II (Jan.–March 1898), 171–172.

Chapter Four

[1] For more recent treatments of Natchitoches, see e. g. Ada Jack Carver, "Redbone," *Harper's Magazine,* CL (Feb. 1925), 257–270, and Lyle Saxon, *Children of Strangers* (New Orleans, 1948).

[2] CW, p. 711.

[3] CW, pp. 219, 223.

[4] Ibid.

[5] CW, p. 561.

[6] CW, p. 201.

[7] CW, pp. 82, 84.

[8] CW, p. 844.

[9] CW, pp. 137, 319, 320, 323.

[10] CW, pp. 323, 324.

[11] John H. Nelson, *The Negro Character in American Literature* (Lawrence, Kansas, 1926), p. 23, as quoted in Seymor L. Gross and John Edward Hardy, eds., *Images of the Negro in American Literature* (Chicago, 1966), p. 5; CW, p. 413.

[12] CW, p. 110.

[13] CW, p. 350.

[14] CW, p. 832.

[15] Ruth McEnery Stuart, "American Backgrounds for Fiction: VI . . . ," p. 624.

[16] Cyrille Arnavon, Introduction to Kate Chopin, *Edna* (Paris, 1953), p. 8. Documents in the Russel Library, Northwestern State College of Louisiana, show that she subscribed to Natchitoches papers for a number of years after her move to St. Louis. Cable, *Picayune* (New Orleans), Feb. 25, 1872, as quoted in Turner, *George W. Cable,* p. 41.

[17] Rankin, p. 15. The story was written for a *Youth's Companion* "Folklore Contest."

[18] CW, p. 704.

[19] According to Rankin (p. 119), *At Fault* constitutes "the first definite mention in American fiction" of the supposed Legree-McAlpin relationship. In the original version of "The Return of Alcibiade" (see CW, Appendix), McFarlane was actually called McAlpin.

[20] CW, p. 720.

[21] Kate Chopin, as quoted by Rankin (interview).

[22] James L. Weygand, *Winona Holiday. The Story of the Western Association of Writers* (Nappanee, Indiana, 1948), pp. 11, 44.

[23] CW, pp. 691–692. When the *Critic* accepted Mrs. Chopin's diary

entry (it was published on July 7, 1894) and gave her a year's sub-
scription for it, she commented: "not bad when I expected nothing
for it, and hardly thought it would be used."

[24] See e. g. the retort in Minneapolis *Journal*, July 21, 1894. Rankin,
p. 142.

[25] Diary; Schuyler, p. 117. Kate Chopin here carries to its logical conclusion George Eliot's complaint that women writers show "an amaz-
ing ignorance, both of science and of life" ("Silly Novels by Lady
Novelists," in Nathan Sheppard, ed., *The Essays of George Eliot;* New
York, 1883, p. 188).

[26] Leonard Huxley, *Life and Letters of Thomas Henry Huxley,* II
(London, 1900), p. 268.

[27] CW, pp. 727, 733. The couplet is entitled "I Wanted God," and subtitled "Lines Suggested by Omar."

[28] Thomas H. Huxley, *Collected Essays,* III (London, 1893), p. 397.

[29] "Because" was written between 1895 and 1899, probably in the latter
year.

[30] Practically all the information we have concerning Kate Chopin's
reading of, and views on, the authors which were active in the second
half of the nineteenth century, has been included in the present book.
Rankin (interview); [Sue V. Moore,] "Mrs. Kate Chopin," pp. 11–12.
According to Rankin (interview), his statement on pp. 174–175 of his
book that Kate Chopin was indebted to Schopenhauer, Flaubert, Tur-
genev, Tolstoy, D'Annunzio, Maupassant, and Bourget, was based on
a surmise only.

[31] According to Professor Henry Murray of Harvard University, the
"French savant" whom Kate Chopin quotes in an essay of Nov. 17,
1894 (CW, p. 698), is undoubtedly Le Bon. The quotation was probably taken from an article of that year, and it is found nearly unchanged in Le Bon's *Psychologie des Foules* (Paris, 1895), p. 15. CW,
p. 718.

[32] CW, p. 693. Hamlin Garland, *Crumbling Idols* (Chicago, 1894), pp.
79, 100, 102.

[33] CW, pp. 693–694.

[34] CW, pp. 697, 698.

[35] CW, p. 698.

[36] CW, p. 714; Schuyler, p. 117.

[37] Thomas Hardy in his Preface to *Jude the Obscure* (London, 1895);
CW, p. 714.

[38] CW, pp. 709, 713; Schuyler, p. 117.

[39] CW, p. 710; Diary.

[40] CW, pp. 711, 712. When Kate Chopin did not object to the sentimentality of this novelette, it was perhaps because she agreed that the

young heroine should be freed from the unnatural obligation to her old fiancé so that she could marry a man her own age.

[41] The diary entry reads as follows: "Last night Mr. Deyo spoke of the ecstatic pleasure which he finds in reading Plato. He seems to have reached the sage by stages: through Browning then Pater. He feels that there is nothing for him beyond that poetic height. And when Plato begins to pall – as he will in a few years, he wonders what life will have to offer him, and shudders already in anticipation of the nothingness. This is to me a rather curious condition of mind. It betokens a total lack of inward resource, and makes me doubt the value of the purely intellectual outlook. Here is a man who can only be reached through books. Nature does not speak to him, notwithstanding his firm belief that he is in sympathetic touch with the true – the artistic. He reaches his perceptions through others' minds. It is something, of course that the channel which he follows is a lofty one; but the question remains, has such perception the value of spontaneous insight, however circumscribed." *Harper's Magazine,* LXXXVIII (May 1894), 926–940.

[42] Schuyler, p. 117.

[43] CW, p. 1013.

[44] Alphonse Daudet, as quoted in Murray Sachs, *The Career of Alphonse Daudet* (Cambridge, Mass., 1965), pp. 152, 219.

[45] Letter, at MHS, from Anna L. Moss, dated June 25, 1899.

[46] Mrs. Eliot's poem with these expressions is quoted in Howarth, *Eliot,* p. 24.

[47] Emile Zola in his Preface to *L'Assomoir* (Paris, 1877). An article by Lewis Leary (see Bibliography) – so recent that it has not reached me when this is going to press – is apparently the first to be devoted entirely to *At Fault.*

[48] The statement by D. A. Dondore in "Kate Chopin," *Dictionary of American Biography,* IV (New York, 1930), p. 90, that Thérèse represents Mrs. Eliza O'Flaherty, was possibly based on information from Mrs. Chopin's daughter, but nothing can be found to substantiate it.

[49] CW, p. 769.

[50] CW, pp. 746, 777.

[51] CW, p. 841.

[52] CW, p. 872.

[53] CW, p. 786.

[54] CW, p. 764. In his *Divorce and the American Divorce Novel 1858–1937* (Philadelphia, 1939), James Harwood Barnett appears to be unfamiliar with the works of Kate Chopin, even though *At Fault* would have been No. 6 on his chronological list of divorce novels, preceded only by *A Modern Instance,* which had a certain moral em-

phasis, and four others, all of which were either against divorce or against remarriage. Sachs, *Daudet,* pp. 157–158.

55 Alexander DeMenil, "Kate Chopin," *Hesperian,* IV (Oct.–Dec. 1904), 383; Felix Chopin in letter of Aug. 18, 1931, as quoted in Rankin (p. 4); Grace King, *Memories of a Southern Woman of Letters* (New York, 1932), p. 60. (It might be added that Miss King had been harshly treated by the Union commander of New Orleans.)

56 CW, p. 305.

57 CW, p. 245.

58 CW, p. 257.

59 Cable's story was published in his *Strange True Stories of Louisiana* (New York, 1889), pp. 192–232; Grace King, *History of Louisiana* (New York, 1897), p. 239.

60 CW, pp. 202, 203. This sketch was turned down by two New Orleans newspapers and two children's magazines; after that, Kate Chopin made no further attempt to place it.

61 CW, pp. 202, 203.

62 Since so many of Kate Chopin's friends were St. Louis *Post-Dispatch* editors, it is worth noting that this paper (according to Rammelkamp, *Post-Dispatch,* p. 120) "did not accept the position of the white supremacists that the Negro should remain in permanent subjection."

63 CW, pp. 205, 206. The Whisky Ring was a national scandal of the 1870's, centered in St. Louis.

64 Merle Mae T. Jordan, "Kate Chopin: Social Critic" (unpublished M. A. thesis, University of Texas, 1959). It is possible to see mild criticism of political favoritism in "Elizabeth Stock's One Story" (CW, pp. 586–591), and of the reckless businessman in "Alexander's Wonderful Experience" (MS, MHS). Rankin, p. 107.

65 Arlin Turner, ed., *Creoles and Cajuns. Stories of Old Louisiana by George W. Cable* (Garden City, N. Y., 1959), p. 14; Arthur W. John, *"Scribner's . . . ,"* p. 317; CW, p. 768; *Spectator* (St. Louis), XI (Oct. 4, 1890), 55.

66 CW, pp. 295, 539, 541.

67 William Schuyler, "The American Reading Public," *Criterion* (St. Louis), XV (Aug. 7, 1897), 6–7.

Chapter Five

1 For comments on this aspect of Mme. de Staël, see J. Christopher Herold, *Mistress to an Age. A Life of Madame de Staël* (London, 1959), pp. 222, 309–310. The de Staël quotations are taken from Morroe Berger, ed., *Madame de Staël on Politics, Literature, and National Character* (Garden City, N. Y., 1965), pp. 218, 219.

[2] Berger, *Madame de Staël,* pp. 143, 148, 245, 263.

[3] Perry Miller, ed., *Margaret Fuller. American Romantic. A Selection from Her Writings and Correspondence* (Garden City, N. Y., 1963), pp. xxviii, 150, 180.

[4] George Sand as quoted in André Maurois, *Lélia. The Life of George Sand* (London, 1953), pp. 374, 433.

[5] Maurois, *Sand,* p. 435.

[6] Ibid., pp. 265, 266, 325.

[7] Interview with Mr. Hattersley.

[8] Craik, *The Woman's Kingdom,* pp. 69, 71. See Maurois, *Sand,* p. 155.

[9] Frank O'Connor, *The Lonely Voice. A Study of the Short Story* (Cleveland and New York, 1965), p. 64; Diary.

[10] Edward Foster, *Mary E. Wilkins Freeman* (New York, 1956), p. 107.

[11] *Webster's New World Dictionary of the American Language. College Edition* (Cleveland and New York, 1956).

[12] Smith, "Gilder," p. 374; Thomas Beer, *The Mauve Decade* (New York, 1926), p. 187; Sarah Grand, *The Heavenly Twins* (New York, 1893).

[13] Simone de Beauvoir, *The Second Sex* (New York, 1960), p. 451.

[14] A copy of the sermon is in the Bayou Folk Museum, Cloutierville.

[15] CW, pp. 401, 631. Simone de Beauvoir, *A History of Sex* (New York, 1961), p. 209; Mme. de Staël, *Corinne ou l'Italie,* III (Bruxelles, 1832), p. 129 (translation mine).

[16] CW, pp. 80–103, 1005.

[17] CW, pp. 45, 46.

[18] Beauvoir, *The Second Sex,* p. 451, and *A History of Sex,* p. 21.

[19] CW, p. 46.

[20] St. Louis *Post-Dispatch,* May 14, 1895.

[21] CW, p. 50.

[22] CW, pp. 48, 49.

[23] CW, p. 54.

[24] CW, pp. 54, 58.

[25] CW, pp. 47, 48, 50.

[26] CW, pp. 51, 53, 55.

[27] CW, p. 49.

[28] *Webster's New World Dictionary . . .* ; CW, pp. 51, 53.

[29] CW, pp. 146, 304.

[30] Ella Wheeler Wilcox, *Poems of Passion* (Chicago, 1883), pp. 11, 47; Laura Daintrey, *Eros* (Chicago, 1888), p. 10; Gertrude Atherton, *Patience Sparhawk and Her Times* (New York, 1908), pp. 177, 178, 179.

[31] CW, pp. 134, 135.

[32] CW, p. 136.

[33] CW, p. 114.

[34] CW, p. 164.

[35] CW, pp. 335, 336.

[36] CW, p. 381.

[37] "Ti Frère" is in MS at MHS.

[38] CW, p. 124.

[39] See CW, p. 720, for another example of this mental energy. Felix Chopin recalled (interview) that his mother once stood up in the middle of a theater performance, saying: "Something has happened to Lelia," rushed home, and found that her daughter had caught fire from a spark, but had been able to save herself.

[40] CW, pp. 431, 433, 434.

[41] CW, pp. 431, 438.

[42] CW, pp. 434, 444, 450.

[43] CW, pp. 433, 451, 454.

[44] *Mirror,* VII (Nov. 25, 1897), 6; CW, p. 432.

[45] When Kate Chopin wrote "Athénaïse," the function of the tree as a symbol of fertility had recently been discussed by Sir James G. Frazer in *The Golden Bough* (London, 1890, Vol. I). In *The Faith of Our Feminists. A Study in the Novels of Edith Wharton, Ellen Glasgow, Willa Cather* (New York, 1950), Josephine Lurie Jessup draws on another set of Athena's many qualities. This goddess "not only managed without a husband, she scarcely acknowledged a father," she reminds us (p. 9), equating her (and the three authors) with "the spirit of woman disjunct and triumphant in her separateness" (p. 13).

[46] Examples of such pairs: April, 1891, "The Going Away of Liza" (a wife giving up her attempt at emancipation) and "The Maid of Saint Phillippe" (a heroine making her own life); August, 1892, "A Visit to Avoyelles" (a wife devoting herself to her demanding husband) and "Ma'ame Pélagie" (a girl wanting to live her own life); April-May, 1894, "The Story of an Hour" and the diary entry about rejoining Oscar Chopin.

[47] "Madame Célestin's Divorce" was written May 24-25, 1893, and "An Idle Fellow" June 9, 1893. CW, pp. 280-281.

[48] 1 *Cor.* 14.34; *Col.* 3.18; 1 *Tim.* 2.14-15.

Chapter Six

[1] Felix Chopin, in a letter of Aug. 11, 1925, to Amy Elizabeth Taggart, as quoted in her M. A. thesis, "Mrs. Kate O'Flaherty Chopin: Her Life and Writing" (Tulane University, 1928), p. 11; Schuyler, p. 117; Kate Chopin, letter to Waitman Barbe, Oct. 2, 1894.

[2] Letter to Barbe. (In the letter, Kate Chopin clearly tries to flatter the

editor; even so, the article never materialized.) [Sue V. Moore,] "Mrs. Kate Chopin," p. 11. When the author noted in her diary regarding "Lilacs": "I cannot recall what suggested it," it seems to indicate that she sometimes may have been aware of an outer stimulus that led to a story.

3 *Natchitoches. Oldest Settlement* ..., p. 57. One informant suggests that some Cloutierville people felt Kate Chopin ridiculed them in her writings, but Schuyler reports (p. 117) that "the people of Natchitoches ... thoroughly endorse her artistic presentation of their locality and its population."

4 CW, p. 722. Rankin writes (pp. 92, 134) that the sketch "Dr. Chevalier's Lie" and *The Awakening* were based on actual incidents, but nothing can be found to prove this. In addition to what the alert Mrs. Chopin observed herself, she was furnished with material by such raconteurs as Phanor Breazeale and Dr. Kolbenheyer. Even so, it is only in the case of four items that we today have proofs or indications that her writings were taken more or less directly from life. Three of them were originally diary entries. Two of these were published together as "A Scrap and a Sketch," the first ("The Night Came Slowly") dealing with herself (see pp. 67–68), and the second ("Juanita") with the daughter of the local postmaster (see *History of Franklin, Jefferson, Washington, Crawford & Gasconade Counties, Missouri;* Chicago, 1880, p. 444). The third is "Cavanelle," and the last "Vagabonds." As the MS at MHS of this latter sketch indicates, it describes an actual incident in the life of Kate Chopin, the Cloutierville widow. Very few further items are written in the first person.

5 CW, p. 722.

6 Letter to Barbe.

7 CW, pp. 704–705.

8 CW, pp. 40, 44, 45, 46.

9 CW, pp. 43, 44.

10 Ibid.

11 CW, p. 778.

12 CW, pp. 845–846. Kate Chopin is quoting verbatim from Alban Butler's *The Lives of the Fathers, Martyrs, and other Principal Saints,* I (London and Dublin, 1833), p. 566.

13 CW, pp. 792, 846.

14 CW, p. 872.

15 CW, pp. 819, 820, 858.

16 CW, pp. 833, 852.

17 Alexander DeMenil, "A Century of Missouri Literature," *Missouri Historical Review,* XV (Oct. 1920), 119; Schuyler, p. 117.

18 Brander Matthews' essay "The Philosophy of the Short-story" first

appeared in 1884. Guy de Maupassant, *Romans* (texte définitif établi et augmenté de notices introductives par Albert-Marie Schmidt; Paris, 1959), pp. 833, 841.

[19] "Miss Witherwell's Mistake," CW, pp. 59–66.

[20] CW, p. 265.

[21] CW, p. 241.

[22] CW, pp. 276, 279.

[23] CW, p. 382.

[24] CW, pp. 382, 383.

[25] Mamie Bowman Tarlton, "Modern Notes in the Portrayal of the Louisiana Negro 1870–1900," *Narrative: A Literary Bi-Monthly* (Natchitoches, La.), I (Dec. 1947), 7–18. For the reasons I have indicated, I cannot agree with this critic that Ozème should be a free-mulatto. (She bases her statement on the facts that Velcour is a typical free-mulatto name on L'Isle des Mulâtres and that there are Velcours among Ozème's associates.) CW, pp. 212–213 ("Loka").

[26] CW, p. 383.

[27] CW, pp. 384, 385.

[28] CW, pp. 385–386.

[29] CW, p. 387.

[30] Guy de Maupassant, *Contes et Nouvelles* (textes présentés, corrigés, classés et augmentés de pages inédites, par Albert-Marie Schmidt), II (Paris, 1960), pp. 829–836.

[31] CW, p. 375.

[32] Ibid.

[33] CW, p. 376.

[34] Ibid.; Robert Burton Bush, "Louisiana Prose Fiction, 1870–1900" (unpublished Ph. D. dissertation, State University of Iowa, June 1957), p. 250. In his chapter on Kate Chopin (pp. 232–276), Bush gives what is possibly the most perceptive of the unpublished treatments of the author.

[35] MS, MHS. Other examples of changes: *yonder* instead of the original *back* in "Where was Ti Nomme? Yonder in the shed" – hardly an improvement, and *see* instead of the ambiguous *follow* in "She could no longer see the cart" (CW, p. 378).

[36] CW, p. 376.

[37] CW, p. 377.

[38] CW, pp. 376–377.

[39] CW, pp. 377, 378.

[40] Edward D. Sullivan, *Maupassant: The Short Stories* (London, 1962), p. 23.

[41] Maupassant, *Contes et Nouvelles*, II, p. 836 (translation mine).

[42] Robert Burton Bush, "Louisiana Prose Fiction . . . ," p. 254.

[43] Maupassant in *Le Gaulois,* July 20, 1882, as quoted in Paul Ignotus, *The Paradox of Maupassant* (London, 1966), p. 142.

[44] Mrs. Hattersley in letter of Nov. 12, 1907, to Leonidas Rutledge Whipple, as quoted in Rankin, p. 116.

[45] CW, pp. 355, 412, 416, 444.

[46] CW, pp. 426, 439, 451.

[47] CW, pp. 428, 447, 452.

[48] George Arms, "Kate Chopin's *The Awakening* in the Perspective of Her Literary Career," in Clarence Gohdes, ed., *Essays in American Literature in Honor of Jay B. Hubbell* (Durham, N. C., 1967), p. 222; CW, p. 450.

[49] CW, p. 453.

[50] Letter to Waitman Barbe, dated Oct. 2, 1894.

[51] In her decision to use the theme in a novel, Kate Chopin may have been inspired not only by H. E. Scudder's observation, but also by Kolbenheyer's prodding. It is not inconceivable that her decision to use the theme at all was prompted by the fact that her grandmother, Mme. Athénaïse Charleville Faris – the last remaining relative whose feelings she may have wanted to spare – died on Jan. 27, 1897.

[52] CW, p. 572.

Chapter Seven

[1] CW, pp. 888, 899.

[2] CW, p. 889.

[3] CW, p. 898.

[4] CW, p. 927.

[5] CW, pp. 931, 948.

[6] CW, p. 946.

[7] CW, pp. 963, 966.

[8] CW, p. 967.

[9] CW, p. 993.

[10] CW, pp. 995, 996, 997; Euripides, *Hippolytus,* in *Greek Tragedies,* I (translated by David Grene; Chicago, 1960), lines 420–424.

[11] CW, p. 999.

[12] Rankin, p. 92. Miss Breazeale never heard her father mention any original for the novel. Rankin's observation (p. 114) that "it is quite possible" that the unfinished Grand Isle story of 1888–89 may refer to what became a decade later the story of Edna is beyond checking; nothing is known that possibly bears on this question, except the fact that not only *The Awakening,* but also "At Chênière Caminada" (written in 1893) are set in part on Grand Isle.

[13] Guy de Maupassant, *Contes et Nouvelles,* I (Paris, 1959), pp. 877–882

(translation mine). Rankin (p. 174) appears to see D'Annunzio's *Triumph of Death,* and perhaps also Maeterlinck's *Pélléas et Mélisande* and Tolstoy's *Anna Karenina,* as possible "literary influences that engendered *The Awakening.*" Their importance as such, however, seems negligible compared to that of "Réveil" and *Madame Bovary.*

[14] Gustave Flaubert, *Madame Bovary* (translated by Francis Steegmuller; New York, 1957), p. 39; CW, p. 898.

[15] George R. Stewart, *American Ways of Life* (Garden City, N. Y., 1954), p. 174.

[16] CW, p. 715; W. D. Howells, *Criticism and Fiction* (New York, 1891), p. 128; *Scribner's Magazine,* X (Sept. 1891), 394.

[17] [Mary Anette Russel,] *Elizabeth and Her German Garden* (London, 1898), the only book from Kate Chopin's library which has survived, throws an interesting sidelight on her obvious occupation with the woman's position in society. It deals with an English lady who protests (p. 67) against the *Kirche, Küche, und Kinder*-attitude of her German husband: "What nonsense it is to talk about the equality of the sexes when the women have the babies!" He acknowledges that she is right: "Nature, while imposing this agreeable duty on the woman, weakens and disables her for any serious competition with man." (The book is in the possession of Mr. Hattersley.)

[18] Miller, ed., *Margaret Fuller,* p. 188; CW, pp. 888, 890.

[19] CW, pp. 893, 908.

[20] CW, pp. 938, 953.

[21] CW, p. 939.

[22] CW, p. 959.

[23] CW, p. 967.

[24] Ibid.

[25] CW, pp. 972, 977–978.

[26] CW, p. 987.

[27] CW, pp. 929, 990; Jean-Paul Sartre, *Action,* Dec. 29, 1944, as quoted in François Denoeu, ed., *Sommets Littéraires Français* (Boston, 1957), p. 529.

[28] CW, pp. 991, 992.

[29] Victoria C. Woodhull, *A Speech on the Principles of Social Freedom Delivered in Steinway Hall, Monday, Nov. 20, 1871* (New York, 1874), p. 23.

[30] Kenneth Eble, "A Forgotten Novel: Kate Chopin's *The Awakening,*" *Western Humanities Review,* X (Summer 1956), 261–269. Euripides, *Hippolytus,* lines 247, 442–443, 469, 506, 1433–1434. How intimately Robinson was attuned to *Hippolytus* is shown in Sigmund Skard, "E. A. Robinson: 'Eros Turannos.' A Critical Survey," in *Americana Norvegica. Norwegian Contributions to American Studies,* I (Sigmund

Skard and Henry H. Wasser, eds.; Philadelphia, 1966), pp. 295–304.

31 George Sand, *Lélia* (texte établi, présenté et annoté par Pierre Reboul; Paris, 1960), p. 56; Euripides, *Hippolytus,* lines 561–562.

32 George Sand, *Valentine* (Bruxelles, 1832), II, p. 23 (translation mine).

33 Henrik Ibsen, *Samlede Verker. Hundreårsutgave,* XI (Oslo, 1934), p. 508; CW, p. 996.

34 CW, p. 1000.

35 CW, p. 996.

36 CW, pp. 457, 537, 599, 996, 999. For an entirely different reading of Kate Chopin – as an author who "upholds the Creole belief in the purity of womanhood" – see Marie Fletcher, "The Southern Woman in the Fiction of Kate Chopin," *Louisiana History,* VII (Spring 1966), 117–132.

37 Guy de Maupassant, "Suicide," St. Louis *Republic,* June 5, 1898, and "Solitude," *St. Louis Life,* XIII (Dec. 28, 1895), 30 (both translated by Kate Chopin).

38 According to a review of *The Awakening* in the St. Louis *Republic* (Rankin quotes it on p. 173, giving the date as May 20, 1899, but it cannot be found in that issue), it was rumored that the publishers had furnished "the title page." This cannot be checked. If the publishers were dissatisfied with "A Solitary Soul," it is not unlikely that Kate Chopin herself suggested the new – equally appropriate – title, possibly inspired by Maupassant's "Réveil." The fact that the author, in her notebook, later added "The Awakening" on top of "A Solitary Soul" without canceling the original title as was her normal practice may mean that she would have liked to retain it as a subtitle.

39 Jean-Paul Sartre, *Being and Nothingness* (translated and with an introduction by Hazel E. Barnes; New York, 1956), p. 439.

40 CW, pp. 548, 951; George Sand, *Indiana* (Bruxelles, 1832), I, p. 6, and II, p. 107; Sand as quoted in Maurois, *Lélia,* p. 156.

41 Beauvoir, *A History of Sex,* p. 13.

42 CW, p. 1000.

43 CW, pp. 719, 720; Eble, "A Forgotten Novel . . . ," p. 265.

44 The fact that Kate Chopin dropped chapter titles in *The Awakening* may be an indication that she was trying to get away from the more episodic technique of *At Fault.*

45 CW, pp. 893, 907. Cyrille Arnavon, Introduction to *Edna,* p. 10. In *Chita,* Lafcadio Hearn deals with these same localities; much in the manner of the naturalists, he makes the Gulf into a malevolent ravager of the land.

46 Bush, "Louisiana Prose Fiction . . . ," pp. 268–269; Eble, "A Forgotten Novel . . . ," p. 266.

[47] James E. Miller makes this point about Whitman in his *Walt Whitman* (New York, 1962), p. 146; Whitman, "Song of Myself," Section 28.

[48] Freud as quoted in William York Tindall, *The Literary Symbol* (Bloomington, Ind., 1955), p. 131; W. H. Auden, *The Enchafèd Flood or the Romantic Iconography of the Sea* (London, 1951), p. 26; Gaston Bachelard, *L'Eau et les Rêves* (Paris, 1960), pp. 219, 225.

[49] CW, p. 892.

[50] CW, pp. 896, 897, 906.

[51] CW, pp. 890, 963, 967.

[52] CW, pp. 956, 980.

[53] George Arms, "Kate Chopin's *The Awakening* . . . ," p. 221; CW, p. 978.

[54] CW, p. 978.

[55] CW, p. 889.

[56] CW, pp. 888, 893, 916.

[57] CW, pp. 905, 964.

[58] CW, p. 910.

[59] CW, pp. 882, 894.

[60] CW, pp. 935, 955.

[61] CW, pp. 903, 956.

[62] CW, pp. 900, 952, 953, 956, 957, 988; Flaubert, *Madame Bovary,* p. 147.

[63] CW, pp. 970, 972, 973. In *At Fault* (CW, p. 803), Melicent transforms her lover likewise: she "bedecked him with garlands and festoons . . . till he looked a very Satyr."

[64] CW, p. 973.

[65] CW, p. 972.

[66] CW, pp. 979, 994, 997; Euripides, *Hippolytus,* lines 162–163.

[67] CW, p. 934.

[68] CW, p. 999.

[69] Cf. the entry on "mockingbird" in *Webster's New World Dictionary* . . .; CW, pp. 906, 968.

[70] Bush, "Louisiana Prose Fiction . . . ," p. 271; CW, pp. 966, 1000.

[71] CW, p. 1000.

[72] Ibid.

[73] The "Solitude"-picture evoked in Edna by Mlle. Reisz' music is accompanied by another which resembles that of the young girl walking through the meadow, her field of vision limited; it shows a young woman "taking mincing dancing steps as she came down a long avenue between tall hedges" (CW, p. 906).

[74] Edmund Wilson, *Patriotic Gore* (New York, 1962), p. 590.

[75] CW, pp. 911, 971.

[76] Flaubert, *Madame Bovary,* pp. 364, 367; CW, p. 956. In *The Gates of*

Horn: A Study of Five French Realists (New York, 1963), Harry Levin points (p. 264) to two Flaubert terms – "cette corruption" at the end of Pt. 3, Ch. V, and "ses pauvres mains" in Ch. VIII – as samples of a stigmatizing or a pitying of Emma. In B. F. Bart, ed., *"Madame Bovary" and the Critics* (New York, 1966, p. 105), Bart makes the case that Flaubert's change of aesthetic distance at Emma's deathbed is so abrupt that "we are unprepared for our new attitude toward her."

77 In dealing with Edna's earliest infatuations, Kate Chopin tells us that she "was nothing, nothing, nothing to the engaged young man," the second of the men who had attracted her (CW, p. 898). While this gives the effect of irony, it is no more than a faithful reproduction of Edna's own childish attitude.

78 CW, p. 996; Cyrille Arnavon, Introduction to *Edna,* pp. 7, 9.

79 CW, p. 981.

Chapter Eight

1 Letter from Gilder, March 8, 1898.

2 The MS of "The Storm" is at MHS; CW, p. 592. When Kate Chopin put together the MS for her third collection, she excluded not only such early efforts as "Wiser than a God" and "A Point at Issue," but also "The Storm" and "A Shameful Affair," undoubtedly because she thought they would make the publishers turn down the book.

3 CW, p. 594.

4 CW, pp. 594–595.

5 CW, p. 596.

6 Ibid.

7 Maupassant, *Romans,* p. 419, and *Contes et Nouvelles,* I, pp. 379–381.

8 *Song,* 4.3, and 4.5; CW, p. 595; Henry James, *Partial Portraits* (London, 1888), p. 249.

9 CW, pp. 592, 593, 595. The author's use of shrimps may represent a conscious allusion to the potency often denoted by sea foods. Marie-quita in *The Awakening* also carries a basket of shrimps, and in "Athénaïse," the heroine eats shrimps together with Gouvernail.

10 CW, pp. 594, 595; see, for example, D. H. Lawrence, *Women in Love* (Penguin, 1960), p. 197.

11 Flaubert, *Novembre,* in *Oeuvres Complètes,* I (Paris, 1964), p. 257. According to *L'Express,* 28 Oct.–3 Nov., 1968, p. 42, Zola once wrote: "Tout geste sexuel qui n'a pas pour but la procréation est une infamie." Mary McCarthy in a TV interview, New York, Sept. 7, 1964.

12 André Malraux, Preface to *L'Amant de Lady Chatterley* (Paris, 1932); Charlotte Brontë, *Jane Eyre,* Ch. XII; Virginia Woolf, *A Room of One's Own* (New York, 1929), pp. 120, 121, 181, 182.

[13] MS, dated Oct. 24, 1898, at MHS.

[14] MS, dated July 10, 1898, at MHS.

[15] Sidney Kramer's *History of Stone & Kimball and Herbert S. Stone & Co.* (Chicago, 1940), reports (pp. 114, 298) that Stone reissued *A Night in Acadie* in 1899. See CW, p. 1003.

[16] "Come to Me," undated MS, MHS. Kate Chopin spoke of "the delight which Madison Cawein [had given her] in his poems" (inscription, dated Aug. 17, 1899, in a book now in the Widener Library, Harvard University), and "the pleasure" she took in her friend Robert E. Lee Gibson's poems (letter to Gibson, Oct. 13, 1901). It is difficult to judge to what extent she really liked their conventional poetry or was trying to please.

[17] Written June 27, 1893; CW, p. 729.

[18] Schuyler, p. 116.

[19] Kramer, p. 297. *The Awakening* was distributed (not published, as Kramer says) in England, by Stone, in July 1899.

[20] *Mirror,* IX (May 4, 1899), 6.

[21] St. Louis *Globe-Democrat,* May 13, 1899. The St. Louis *Republic* review is quoted from Rankin, p. 173 (see Ch. VII, n. 38).

[22] All these letters are at MHS.

[23] Letter dated June 7, 1899. A letter of Aug. 24, 1899, to the Hon. Richard B. Shepard, who had asked what she had published, shows how eagerly she attended to her public relations.

[24] St. Louis *Post-Dispatch,* May 20, 1899.

[25] Unnamed contemporary, as quoted by Rankin (interview), There was also a commotion at this time concerning Tolstoy's *Awakening* (in book-form called *Resurrection),* then being serialized in the *Cosmopolitan.*

[26] St. Louis *Post-Dispatch,* July 5, 1953, quotes Felix Chopin to the effect that the book was "withdrawn from the Mercantile and St. Louis Public Libraries, later being restored to the Central Public Library in a 1906 reprint edition."

[27] Interview with Miller, St. Louis, 1961. He ascribed the ban to the "bigoted people on the book-committee." There is still no copy of *The Awakening* in the Mercantile Library.

[28] CW, p. 722. Orrick Johns, "The 'Cadians," *Mirror,* XX (July 20, 1911), 5.

[29] Rankin, p. 173. No single document from such a club has come down to us, but this is no proof it did not exist. Rankin's informant may possibly have been thinking of the St. Louis Artists' Guild, which according to [Holmes Smith et al.,] *The Story of the St. Louis Artists' Guild, 1886–1936* [St. Louis, 1936], in 1902 was thoroughly overhauled by George S. Johns and William Schuyler. We might add that

the Western Association of Writers, for example, admitted as members only those "of good moral character." The Wednesday Club left her out of the "American Prose Writers" series which the club started in Sept. 1899, while including lesser authors. This may well have represented another affront to her.

30 *Book News*, XVII (July 1899), 612; the statement, dated May 28, appeared on a page with "Aims and Autographs of Authors."

31 *Literature*, I N. S. (June 23, 1899), 570; *Critic*, XXXV (Aug. 1899), 677.

32 New Orleans *Times-Democrat*, June 18, 1899; Los Angeles *Times*, June 25, 1899; *Nation*, LXIX (Aug. 3, 1899), 96; Chicago *Times Herald*, June 1, 1899. See also *The Congregationalist*, LXXXIV (Aug. 24, 1899), 256; Boston *Herald*, Aug. 12, 1899; Baltimore *News*, June 24, 1899; Indianapolis *Journal*, Aug. 14, 1899; *Public Opinion*, XXVI (June 22, 1899), 794; *The Dial*, Aug. 1, 1899, and Boston *Beacon*, XVI (June 24, 1899), 4.

33 *Mirror*, V (Jan. 16, 1896), 2–3.

34 Ibid., and VI (June 11, 1896), 7.

35 Rankin, p. 173; interviews with Miss Breazeale, Mrs. Tritle, and Felix Chopin; Rankin (interview).

36 Unnamed informant, as quoted by Rankin (interview).

37 Unnamed informant, and Dillon, as quoted by Rankin (interview).

38 These letters (and the envelope) are at MHS. I am indebted to the Maartens-expert, Professor W. van Maanen of Amsterdam, for the information that this author was indeed in London in Oct. 1899, but that he apparently never referred to Kate Chopin in writing.

39 Letters to the present writer from Mr. R. A. Christopher, of the British Museum, dated June 1, 1962, and Nov. 24, 1966. Nothing at all can be found to verify the existence of these two persons.

40 John Dillon, as quoted by Rankin (interview).

41 CW, pp. 722, 723.

42 The program for this so-called "Reciprocity Day: An Afternoon with St. Louis Authors," is at MHS. The songs – "In Spring," "You and I," and "The Song Everlasting" – were quite popular for some time. The first of these was published in 1913, as "The Joy of Spring," by John Church Co., New York and Cincinnati, with music by C. B. Hawley.

43 Written Nov. 1899; CW, p. 622.

44 In "A Century of Missouri Literature," *Missouri Historical Review*, XV (Oct. 1920), 119, Alexander DeMenil describes *The Awakening* as "a novel with an unfortunate chapter that [the author] agreed with me later on, should have been omitted." The present writer is convinced that the genteel, self-important DeMenil made this up in a well-meant attempt to whitewash an author he considered to have

strayed from the right path, just as he later made great efforts to rehabilitate Mme. Chouteau's honor.

[45] Rankin declares (p. 195) that "the novel sold well," but Mrs. Chopin's notebooks show that she only received $102 in royalties in 1899, $40 in 1900, and $3 in 1901. *Mirror,* IX (Nov. 30, 1899), 10. The 1910 St. Louis *Republic* article on the author (see Ch. III, n. 41) does not mention *The Awakening*; Orrick Johns (see Ch. III, n. 42) belonged to the next generation.

[46] Letter of Jan. 16, 1900.

[47] See Kramer, p. 298. *The Awakening* was later transferred to Duffield & Co., who republished it in 1906.

[48] CW, p. 643.

[49] CW, pp. 662, 672, 673. In "Art as Symbolic Speech" (in Ruth Nanda Anshen, ed., *Language: An Enquiry into its Meaning and Function;* New York, 1957), Margaret Naumburg discusses how the Maoris, for example, saw the "sacred Beak" as a "male Life-Symbol." In *The Golden Bough* (London, 1890), Sir James G. Frazer shows how the use of garlands and maypoles goes back to ancient fertility rites.

[50] Poem dated July 6, 1900; MS at MHS. This is the only Kate Chopin MS which is not in her hand. Its heavy reliance on a stereotyped syntactic formula is somewhat atypical of her, but the theme, tone, and imagery make it very probable that the poem is hers.

[51] The poem, apparently written Aug. 24, 1900, is in MS at MHS. It is undoubtedly addressed to Kitty Garesché.

[52] We do not know whom she approached. On August 22, 1904, the St. Louis *Post-Dispatch* wrote: "The announcement was made some time ago that another volume of short stories was to be issued this year."

[53] CW, p. 684.

[54] Interviews with Mr. Hattersley and Mrs. McCormick.

[55] Frances Hurd Stadler, *St. Louis* (St. Louis, 1962), pp. 74–79. Interview with Mrs. McCormick. Unnamed informant, as quoted by Rankin (p. 196).

[56] St. Louis *Post-Dispatch,* Aug. 22, 1904. While this lengthy obituary reports that Mrs. Chopin's children and her doctor were with her (she was unconscious except for one brief moment), no mention is made of a priest having been at her bedside. Unidentified clipping at MHS. Rankin, p. 196. Kate Chopin was buried in the Calvary Cemetery. No trace of her grave remains today.

Chapter Nine

1 W. P. Trent, *Southern Writers* (New York, 1905).
2 *Globe-Democrat,* Aug. 23, 1904; *Mirror,* XIV (Aug. 25, 1904), 1; *Post-Dispatch,* Aug. 22, 1904. For further obituaries, see e. g. *Hesperian,* IV (Oct.–Dec. 1904), 383–384; *Picayune* (New Orleans), Aug. 23, 1904; Boston *Evening-Transcript,* Aug. 26, 1904.
3 Leonidas Rutledge Whipple, "Kate Chopin," in Edwin Anderson Alderman and Joel Chandler Harris, eds., *Library of Southern Literature,* II (New Orleans, 1907), pp. 863–866.
4 Percival Pollard, *Their Day in Court* (New York, 1909), pp. 40–45.
5 Orrick Johns, "The 'Cadians," *Mirror,* XX (July 20, 1911), 5–6.
6 Fred Lewis Pattee, *A History of American Literature Since 1870* (New York, 1915), pp. 364–365; "The Short Story," in *The Cambridge History of American Literature,* II (New York, 1918), pp 390–391; *The Development of the American Short Story* (New York, 1923), pp. 324–327.
7 Dorothy Anne Dondore, "Kate O'Flaherty Chopin," *Dictionary of American Biography,* IV (New York, 1930), pp. 90–91.
8 Rankin, pp. 140, 162, 170, 174–177.
9 Arthur Hobson Quinn, *American Fiction* (New York, 1936), pp. 354–357.
10 Joseph J. Reilly, "Stories by Kate Chopin," *Commonweal,* XXV (March 26, 1937), 606–607.
11 Carlos Baker, "Delineation of Life and Character," in Robert E. Spiller and others, eds., *Literary History of the United States,* I (New York, 1948), pp. 858–859.
12 Cyrille Arnavon, "Les Débuts du Roman Réaliste Américain et l'Influence Française," in Henri Kerst, ed., *Romanciers Américains Contemporains* (Paris, 1946), pp. 9–35.
13 Kate Chopin, *Edna* (translated, and with an introduction, by Cyrille Arnavon; Paris, 1953), pp. 1–22.
14 Clarence Gohdes, "Exploitation of the Provinces," in Arthur Hobson Quinn, ed., *The Literature of the American People* (New York, 1951), p. 654; Van Wyck Brooks, *The Confident Years: 1885–1915* (New York, 1952), p. 341.
15 Robert Cantwell, "*The Awakening* by Kate Chopin," *Georgia Review,* X (Winter 1956), 489–494; Kenneth Eble, "A Forgotten Novel: Kate Chopin's *The Awakening,*" pp. 262, 263.
16 Edmund Wilson, *Patriotic Gore* (New York, 1962), pp. 587–593; Kate Chopin, *The Awakening* (with an introduction by Kenneth Eble; New York, 1964); Warner Berthoff, *The Ferment of Realism. American Literature 1884–1919* (New York, 1965), pp. 88–89.

[17] Larzer Ziff, *The American 1890s. Life and Times of a Lost Generation* (New York, 1966), pp. 296–305.

[18] Stanley Kauffmann, "The Really Lost Generation," *The New Republic*, CLV (Dec. 3, 1966), 22, 38; George Arms, "Kate Chopin's *The Awakening* in the Perspective of Her Literary Career," pp. 215, 222; Kate Chopin, *Bayou Folk* (Ridgewood, N. J., 1967), and *A Night in Acadie* (New York, 1968).

[19] Per Seyersted, ed., *The Complete Works of Kate Chopin* (Baton Rouge, 1969).

[20] Hamlin Garland, *Rose of Dutcher's Coolly* (Chicago, 1895), pp. 59, 62, 121, 147, 288, 294, 364.

[21] Frank Norris, *McTeague* (New York, 1899), pp. 30–31, 300, 310.

[22] Garland, *Rose*, p. 245.

[23] Ibid., p. 299; Theodore Dreiser, *Sister Carrie* (New York, 1900), pp. 58, 126; CW, p. 977. Jessie Ogden of Henry B. Fuller's *The Cliff-Dwellers* (New York, 1893), is an example of a contemporary American heroine who has a child; when she neglects it, it is in order to rise socially, not spiritually.

[24] Hamlin Garland, *A Spoil of Office*, in *Arena*, V (March 1892), 515; *Rose*, pp. 330, 380, 395.

[25] Stephen Crane, *Maggie: A Girl of the Streets* [New York, 1893], pp. 106, 107; Norris, *McTeague*, pp. 84, 88, 89, 183, 309.

[26] Dreiser, *Sister Carrie*, p. 101.

[27] Ibid., p. 83.

[28] Ibid., p. 4.

[29] CW, p. 483; Maupassant, as quoted in Sullivan, *Maupassant: The Short Stories*, p. 57.

[30] Robert E. Spiller and others, eds., *Literary History of the United States*, II (New York, 1948), p. 1197.

[31] Margaret Deland may have been aware of Kate Chopin's novel when she wrote – or when she named – *The Awakening of Helena Richie* (New York, 1906). In the short story "Typhoon" (in Theodore Dreiser, *Chains. Lesser Novels and Stories;* New York, 1927), Dreiser describes a suicide in water quite similar to the one in *The Awakening*, but Ida Zobel's reason for taking her life is very different from that of Edna Pontellier.

[32] Reedy, as quoted in Max Putzel, "Dreiser, Reedy, and De Maupassant, Junior," *American Literature*, XXXIII (Jan. 1962), 471; Putzel, *Reedy*, p. 261.

[33] For an example of such protestations, see George Sand's *Indiana*, I, p. 4.

[34] When the St. Louis *Republic* criticized Kate Chopin's use of the words *store* and *depot* instead of *shop* and *railway station*, she replied (St.

Louis *Republic,* Oct. 25, 1890) that Howells used *depot* and that she was "hardly ready to believe the value of 'At Fault' marred by following so safe a precedent." This is her only reference to Howells. For an example of the use of French, see George W. Cable, *The Grandissimes* (New York, 1880), p. 182. Schuyler, p. 117.

[35] Henry Adams, *The Education of Henry Adams,* Ch. XXV. We might add that Adams felt "unwell," as he termed it, after reading Maupassant (Worthington Chauncey Ford, ed., *Letters of Henry Adams,* I; Boston, 1930, p. 534). George Sand, *Lélia,* p. 529.

Selected Bibliography

Primary Sources

Nearly all the material Kate Chopin left behind is at the Missouri Historical Society. This collection includes: MSS of some twenty stories and forty poems (in the list below, only those poems are included which were published during the author's lifetime); clippings of magazine versions of her stories; translations from Maupassant; an album; a commonplace book; an 1894 diary; two notebooks recording the fate of her writings; photographs; letters from friends, etc. The Society also holds two Kate Chopin letters, one to Mrs. Walter B. Douglas, and another to Robert E. Lee Gibson.

Only a few further items are known to exist: the MS of "Charlie" and a letter to the Hon. Richard B. Shepard (Mr. Robert C. Hattersley, New York); part of the MS of "Nég Créol" (Per Seyersted, Oslo); five letters to the *Century* and a copy of one of the editor's to her (Century Collection, New York Public Library); two letters to Herbert S. Stone (Mr. Herbert S. Stone, Jr., Guilford, Conn.); one letter to Waitman Barbe (West Virginia University, Morgantown); two letters to Marie Breazeale (Miss Gladys Breazeale, New Orleans); and copies of twelve Houghton Mifflin (and *Atlantic*) letters to Mrs. Chopin (Houghton Library, Harvard University).

Kate Chopin's Writings

Arranged in order of composition; for abbreviations, see p. 201. The listings include: final title; date of composition; first appearance in print; inclusion in collections.

If It Might Be (poem). Undated. *America* (Chicago), I (Jan. 10, 1889), 9. CW.

"Unfinished Story – Grand Isle." 1888–89. Destroyed.

A Poor Girl. May, 1889. Destroyed.

Wiser Than a God. June 1889. *Philadelphia Musical Journal,* IV (Dec. 1889), 38–40. CW.

A Point at Issue. Aug. 1889. St. Louis *Post-Dispatch,* Oct. 27, 1889. CW.

Miss Witherwell's Mistake. Nov. 18, 1889. *Fashion and Fancy* (St. Louis), V (Feb. 1891), 115–117. CW.

With the Violin. Dec. 11, 1889. *Spectator* (St. Louis), XI (Dec. 6, 1890), 196. CW.

At Fault (novel). July 5, 1889–April 20, 1890. Published for the author by Nixon-Jones Printing Co., St. Louis, Sept. 1890. CW.

Monsieur Pierre (translation from Adrien Vely). April 1890. St. Louis *Post-Dispatch,* Aug. 8, 1892.

Young Dr. Gosse (novel). May 4–Nov. 27, 1890. Destroyed.

A Red Velvet Coat. Dec. 1–8, 1890. The MS is now lost.

Mrs. Mobry's Reason. Jan. 10, 1891. New Orleans *Times-Democrat,* April 23, 1893. CW.

A No-Account Creole. 1888; rewritten Jan. 24, 1891–Feb. 24, 1891. *Century,* XLVII (Jan. 1894), 382–393. BF, CW.

Roger and His Majesty. March 1, 1891. Destroyed.

For Marse Chouchoute. March 14, 1891. *Youth's Companion,* LXIV (Aug. 20, 1891), 450–451. BF, CW.

The Going Away of Liza. April 4, 1891. "Syndicated – American Press Association," Dec. 1892. CW.

The Maid of Saint Phillippe. April 19, 1891. *Short Stories* (New York), XI (Nov. 1892), 257–264. CW.

A Wizard from Gettysburg. May 25, 1891. *Youth's Companion,* LXV (July 7, 1892), 346–347. BF, CW.

A Shameful Affair. June 5, 7, 1891. New Orleans *Times-Democrat,* April 9, 1893. CW.

A Rude Awakening. July 13, 1891. *Youth's Companion,* LXVI (Feb. 2, 1893), 54–55. BF, CW.

A Harbinger. Sept. 11, 1891. *St. Louis Magazine,* XII N. S. (apparently Nov. 1, 1891; no copies can be found of the issues of this period). CW.

Dr. Chevalier's Lie. Sept. 12, 1891. *Vogue,* II (Oct. 5, 1893), 174, 178. CW.

A Very Fine Fiddle. Sept. 13, 1891. *Harper's Young People,* XIII (Nov. 24, 1891), 79. BF, CW.

Boulôt and Boulotte. Sept. 20, 1891. *Harper's Young People,* XIII (Dec. 8, 1891), 112. BF, CW.

Love on the Bon-Dieu. Oct. 3, 1891. *Two Tales* (Boston), II (July 23, 1892), 148–156. BF, CW.

An Embarrassing Position. Comedy in One Act. Oct. 15–22, 1891. *Mirror* (St. Louis), V (Dec. 19, 1895), 9–11. CW.

Beyond the Bayou. Nov. 7, 1891. *Youth's Companion,* LXVI (June 15, 1893), 302–303. BF, CW.

Typical Forms of German Music. Paper read at the Wednesday Club, St. Louis, Dec. 23, 1891. Probably identical with Typical German Composers, an essay offered in 1899 to the *Atlantic.* Destroyed or lost.

After the Winter. Dec. 31, 1891. New Orleans *Times-Democrat,* April 5, 1896. NA, CW.

The Bênitous' Slave. Jan. 7, 1892. *Harper's Young People,* XIII (Feb. 16, 1892), 280. BF, CW.

A Turkey Hunt. Jan. 8, 1892. *Harper's Young People,* XIII (Feb. 16, 1892), 287. BF, CW.

Old Aunt Peggy. Jan. 8, 1892. First published in BF. CW.

The Lilies. Jan. 27–28, 1892. *Wide Awake,* XXXVI (April 1893), 415–418. NA, CW.

The Mittens. Feb. 25, 1892. Destroyed.

Ripe Figs. Feb. 26, 1892. *Vogue,* II (Aug. 19, 1893), 90. NA, CW.

Croque-Mitaine. Feb. 27, 1892. First published in PS. CW.

A Little Free-Mulatto. Feb. 28, 1892. First published in PS. CW.

Miss McEnders. March 7, 1892. *Criterion* (St. Louis), XIII (March 6, 1897), 16–18, signed La Tour. CW.

Loka. April 9–10, 1892. *Youth's Companion,* LXV (Dec. 22, 1892), 670–671. BF, CW.

Bambo Pellier. May (?) 1892. Destroyed or lost.

At the 'Cadian Ball. July 15–17, 1892. *Two Tales* (Boston), III (Oct. 22, 1892), 145–152. BF, CW.

A Visit to Avoyelles. Aug. 1, 1892. *Vogue,* I (Jan. 14, 1893), 74–75. BF, CW.

Ma'ame Pélagie. Aug. 27–28, 1892. New Orleans *Times-Democrat,* Dec. 24, 1893. BF, CW.

Désirée's Baby. Nov. 24, 1892. *Vogue,* I (Jan. 14, 1893), 70–71, 74. BF, CW.

Caline. Dec. 2, 1892. *Vogue,* I (May 20, 1893), 324–325. NA, CW.

The Return of Alcibiade. Dec. 5–6, 1892. *St. Louis Life,* VII (Dec. 17, 1892), 6–8. BF, CW.

In and Out of Old Natchitoches. Feb. 1–3, 1893. *Two Tales,* V (April 8, 1893), 103–114. BF, CW.

Mamouche. Feb. 24–25, 1893. *Youth's Companion,* LXVII (April 19, 1894), 178–179. NA, CW.

Madame Célestin's Divorce. May 24–25, 1893. First published in BF. CW.

An Idle Fellow. June 9, 1893. First published in CW.

A Matter of Prejudice. June 17–18, 1893. *Youth's Companion,* LXVIII (Sept. 25, 1895), 450. NA, CW.

Azélie. July 22–23, 1893. *Century,* XLIX (Dec. 1894), 282–287. NA, CW.

A Lady of Bayou St. John. Aug. 24–25, 1893. *Vogue,* II (Sept. 21, 1893), 154, 156–158. BF, CW.

La Belle Zoraïde. Sept. 21, 1893. *Vogue,* III (Jan. 4, 1894), 2, 4, 8–10. BF, CW.

At Chênière Caminada. Oct. 21–23, 1893. New Orleans *Times-Democrat,* Dec. 23, 1894. NA, CW.

A Gentleman of Bayou Têche. Nov. 5–7, 1893. First published in BF. CW.

In Sabine. Nov. 20–22, 1893. First published in BF. CW.

A Respectable Woman. Jan. 20, 1894. *Vogue,* III (Feb. 15, 1894), 68–69, 72. NA, CW.

Tante Cat'rinette. Feb. 23, 1894. *Atlantic Monthly,* LXXIV (Sept. 1894), 368–373. NA, CW.

A Dresden Lady in Dixie. March 6, 1894. *Catholic Home Journal* (March 3, 1895). (No copy of this issue can be found.) NA, CW.

Bayou Folk (collected stories). Published March 1894, by Houghton Mifflin & Co., Boston.

The Story of an Hour. April 19, 1894. *Vogue,* IV (Dec. 6, 1894), 360. CW.

Lilacs. May 14–16, 1894. New Orleans *Times-Democrat,* Dec. 20, 1896. CW.

Good Night (poem). Undated. New Orleans *Times-Democrat,* July 22, 1894. CW.

The Western Association of Writers (criticism). June 30, 1894. *Critic,* XXII N. S. (July 7, 1894), 15. CW.

A Divorce Case (translation from Maupassant's Un Cas de Divorce). July 11, 1894. MS.

The Night Came Slowly. July 24, 1894. *Moods.* (Philadelphia), II (July 1895), n. p. CW.

Juanita. July 26, 1894. *Moods* (Philadelphia), II (July 1895), n. p. CW.

Cavanelle. July 31–Aug. 6, 1894. *American Jewess,* I (April 1895), 22–25. NA, CW.

Mad? (translation from Maupassant's Fou?). Sept. 4, 1894. MS.

Regret. Sept. 17, 1894. *Century,* L (May 1895), 147–149. NA, CW.

The Kiss. Sept. 19, 1894. *Vogue,* V (Jan. 17, 1895), 37. CW.

Ozème's Holiday. Sept. 23–24, 1894. *Century,* LII (Aug. 1896), 629–631. NA, CW.

'Crumbling Idols.' By Hamlin Garland (criticism). Undated. *St. Louis Life,* X (Oct. 6, 1894), 13. CW.

The Real Edwin Booth (criticism). Undated. *St. Louis Life,* X (Oct. 13, 1894), 11. CW.

Emile Zola's 'Lourdes' (criticism). Undated. *St. Louis Life*, X (Nov. 17, 1894), 5. CW.

A Sentimental Soul. Nov. 18–22, 1894. New Orleans *Times-Democrat*, Dec. 22, 1895. NA, CW.

Her Letters. Nov. 29, 1894. *Vogue*, V (April 11, 18, 1895), 228–230, 248. CW.

Odalie Misses Mass. Jan. 28, 1895. Shreveport *Times*, July 1, 1895. NA, CW.

It? (translation from Maupassant's Lui?). Feb. 4, 1895. *St. Louis Life*, XI (Feb. 23, 1895), 12–13.

Polydore. Feb. 17, 1895. *Youth's Companion*, LXX (April 23, 1896), 214–215. NA, CW.

Dead Men's Shoes. Feb. 21–22, 1895. *Independent* (New York), XLIX (Feb. 11, 1897), 194–195. NA, CW.

Solitude (translation from Maupassant's Solitude). March 5, 1895. *St. Louis Life*, XIII (Dec. 28, 1895), 30.

Night (translation from Maupassant's La Nuit). March 8, 1895. MS.

Athénaïse. April 10–28, 1895. *Atlantic Monthly*, LXXVIII (Aug., Sept., 1896), 232–241, 404–413. NA, CW.

A Lady of Shifting Intentions. May 4, 1895. Destroyed or lost. (Pp. 6–10 of what may well be a first draft of this story are at MHS.)

Two Summers and Two Souls. July 14, 1895. *Vogue*, VI (Aug. 7, 1895), 84. CW.

The Unexpected. July 18, 1895. *Vogue*, VI (Sept. 18, 1895), 180–181. CW.

Two Portraits. Aug. 4, 1895. First published in Rankin. CW.

Fedora. Nov. 19, 1895. *Criterion* (St. Louis), XIII (Feb. 20, 1897), 9, signed La Tour. CW.

Vagabonds. Dec.(?) 1895. First published in Rankin. CW.

Suicide (translation from Maupassant's Suicides). Dec. 18, 1895. St. Louis *Republic*, June 5, 1898.

Madame Martel's Christmas Eve. Jan. 16–18, 1896. First published in CW.

The Recovery. Feb. 1896. *Vogue*, VII (May 21, 1896), 354–355. CW.

A Night in Acadie. March 1896. First published in NA. CW.

A Pair of Silk Stockings. April 1896. *Vogue*, X (Sept. 16, 1897), 191–192. CW.

Nég Créol. April 1896. *Atlantic Monthly*, LXXX (July 1897), 135–138. NA, CW.

Aunt Lympy's Interference. June 1896. *Youth's Companion*, LXXI (Aug. 12, 1897), 373–374. CW.

The Blind Man. July 1896. *Vogue*, IX (May 13, 1897), 303. CW.

In the Confidence of a Story-Writer (essay). Oct. 1896. *Atlantic Monthly*, LXXXIII (Jan. 1899), 137–139. An earlier version, written

Sept. 1896, is entitled Confidences. Both versions are published in CW, Confidences for the first time.

Ti Frère (unfinished children's story). Sept. 1896. MS.

For Sale (translation from Maupassant's A Vendre). Oct. 26, 1896. MS.

A Vocation and a Voice. Nov. 1896. *Mirror* (St. Louis), XII (March 27, 1902), 18–24. CW.

A Mental Suggestion. Dec. 1896. First published in CW.

Suzette. Feb. 1897. *Vogue,* X (Oct. 21, 1897), 262–263, 266. CW.

As You Like It (a series of six essays). Undated. *Criterion* (St. Louis), XIII:

    I "I have a young friend ..." (Feb. 13, 1897), 11. CW.

    II "It has lately been ..." (Feb. 20, 1897), 17. CW.

    III "Several years ago ..." (Feb. 27, 1897), 11. CW.

    IV "A while ago ..." (March 13, 1897), 15–16. CW.

    V "A good many of us ..." (March 20, 1897), 14. CW.

    VI "We are told ..." (March 27, 1897), 10. CW.

The Locket. March 1897. First published in CW.

A Morning Walk. April 1897. *Criterion* (St. Louis), XV [sic] (April 17, 1897), 13–14. CW.

An Egyptian Cigarette. April 1897. *Vogue,* XV (April 19, 1900), 252, 254. CW.

A Night in Acadie (collected stories). Published Nov. 1897, by Way & Williams, Chicago.

The Awakening (novel). June (?) 1897–Jan. 21, 1898. Published April 22, 1899, by Herbert S. Stone & Co., Chicago & New York. CW.

A Family Affair. Dec.(?) 1897. "Syndicated – American Press Association," Jan. 1898; *Saturday Evening Post,* CLXXII (Sept. 9, 1899), 168–169. CW.

Elizabeth Stock's One Story. March 1898. First published in PS. CW.

A Horse Story (unfinished children's story). March 1898. MS.

Father Amable (translation from Maupassant's Le Père Amable). April 21, 1898. MS.

The Storm. July 19, 1898. First published in CW.

In Spring (poem). Undated; Jan. 1899(?) *Century,* LVIII (July 1899), 361.

The Godmother. Jan.–Feb. 6, 1899. *Mirror* (St. Louis), XI (Dec. 12, 1901), 9–13. CW.

A Little Country Girl. Feb. 11, 1899. First published in CW.

A Reflection. Nov. 1899. First published in Rankin. CW.

"On certain brisk, bright days ..." (untitled essay). Undated, but undoubtedly Nov. 1899. St. Louis *Post-Dispatch,* Nov. 26, 1899. CW.

Ti Démon. Nov. 1899. First published in CW.

A December Day in Dixie. Jan. 1900. Published in part in Rankin. CW.

Alexander's Wonderful Experience (unfinished children's story). Jan. 23, 1900. MS.

The Gentleman from New Orleans. Feb. 6, 1900. First published in CW.

Charlie. April 1900. First published in CW.

The White Eagle. May 9, 1900. *Vogue*, XVI (July 12, 1900), 20, 22. CW.

Millie's First Party. Oct. 16, 1901. Lost.

The Wood-Choppers. Oct. 17, 1901. *Youth's Companion*, LXXVI (May 29, 1902), 270–271. CW.

Toot's Nurses. Oct. 18, 1901. Destroyed or lost.

Polly. Jan. 14, 1902. *Youth's Companion*, LXXVI (July 3, 1902), 334–335. CW.

The Impossible Miss Meadows. Undated; probably 1903. First published in CW.

The Complete Works of Kate Chopin, ed. Per Seyersted (Louisiana State University Press, Baton Rouge, 1969).

Secondary Sources

Arranged in order of publication.

[Moore, Sue V.,] "Mrs. Kate Chopin," *St. Louis Life,* X (June 9, 1894), 11–12.

Schuyler, William, "Kate Chopin," *Writer,* VII (Aug. 1894), 115–117.

Whipple, Leonidas Rutledge, "Kate Chopin," in Edwin Anderson Alderman and Joel Chandler Harris, eds., *Library of Southern Literature,* II (New Orleans, 1907), pp. 863–866.

Pollard, Percival, *Their Day in Court* (New York, 1909), pp. 40–45.

[Knapp?, Vernon,] "Is There an Interesting Woman in St. Louis?" St. Louis *Republic,* Sept. 11, 1910.

Johns, Orrick, "The 'Cadians," *Mirror* (St. Louis), XX (July 20, 1911), 5–6.

Pattee, Fred Lewis, *A History of American Literature Since 1870* (New York, 1915), pp. 364–365.

Pattee, Fred Lewis, *The Development of the American Short Story* (New York, 1923), pp. 324–327.

Dondore, Dorothy Anne, "Kate O'Flaherty Chopin," *Dictionary of American Biography,* IV (New York, 1930), pp. 90–91.

Rankin, Daniel S., *Kate Chopin and Her Creole Stories* (Philadelphia, 1932).

Quinn, Arthur Hobson, *American Fiction* (New York, 1936), pp. 354–357.

Reilly, Joseph J., *Of Books and Men* (New York, 1942), pp. 130–136.

Arnavon, Cyrille, "Les Débuts du Roman Réaliste Américain et l'Influence Française," in Henri Kerst, ed., *Romanciers Américains Contemporains* (*Cahiers des Langues Modernes*, I, Paris, 1946), pp. 9–35.

Baker, Carlos, "Delineation of Life and Character," in Robert E. Spiller and others, eds., *Literary History of the United States*, I (New York, 1948), pp. 858–859.

Gohdes, Clarence, "Exploitation of the Provinces," in Arthur Hobson Quinn, ed., *The Literature of the American People* (New York, 1951), p. 654.

Brooks, Van Wyck, *The Confident Years: 1885–1915* (New York, 1952), p. 341.

Arnavon, Cyrille, Introduction to Kate Chopin, *Edna* (Paris, 1953), pp. 1–22.

Cantwell, Robert, "*The Awakening* by Kate Chopin," *Georgia Review*, X (Winter 1956), 489–494.

Eble, Kenneth, "A Forgotten Novel: Kate Chopin's *The Awakening*," *Western Humanities Review*, X (Summer 1956), 261–269.

Bush, Robert Burton, "Louisiana Prose Fiction, 1870–1900" (unpublished Ph. D. dissertation, State University of Iowa, 1957), pp. 232–276.

Jordan, Merle Mae T., "Kate Chopin: Social Critic" (unpublished M. A. thesis, University of Texas, 1959).

Wilson, Edmund, *Patriotic Gore* (New York, 1962), pp. 587–593.

Seyersted, Per, "Kate Chopin: An Important St. Louis Writer Reconsidered," Missouri Historical Society *Bulletin*, XIX (Jan.1963), 89–114.

Berthoff, Warner, *The Ferment of Realism. American Literature, 1884–1919* (New York, 1965), pp. 88–89.

Fletcher, Marie, "The Southern Woman in the Fiction of Kate Chopin," *Louisiana History*, VII (Spring 1966), 117–132.

Ziff, Larzer, *The American 1890s. Life and Times of a Lost Generation* (New York, 1966), pp. 296–305.

Arms, George, "Kate Chopin's *The Awakening* in the Perspective of Her Literary Career," in Clarence Gohdes, ed., *Essays in American Literature in Honor of Jay B. Hubbell* (Durham, N. C., 1967), pp. 215–228.

Leary, Lewis, "Kate Chopin's Other Novel," *The Southern Literary Journal*, I (Autumn 1968), 60–74.

Index

Publications of
the American Institute
University of Oslo

Halvdan Koht: *The American Spirit in Europe. A Survey of Trans-atlantic Influences.* IX, 289 pp. Out of print.
(Philadelphia, Pa. 1949.)
Einar Haugen: *The Norwegian Language in America. A Study in Bilingual Behavior.* Out of print.
Vol. I: The Bilingual Community. XIV, 317 pp.
Vol. II: The American Dialects of Norwegian. VII, 377 pp.
(Philadelphia, Pa. 1953.)
Sigmund Skard: *American Studies in Europe. Their History and Present Organization.*
Vol. I: The General Background, The United Kingdom, France, and Germany. Pp. 1–358.
Vol. II: The Smaller Western Countries, The Scandinavian Countries, The Mediterranean Nations, Eastern Europe, International Organization, and Conclusion. Pp. 359–736.
(Philadelphia, Pa. 1958.)
Americana Norvegica. Norwegian Contributions to American Studies.
Vol. I. Editors: Sigmund Skard and Henry H. Wasser. 340 pp.
(Philadelphia, Pa. 1966.)
Vol. II. Editor: Sigmund Skard. Editorial Committee: Ingvald Raknem, Georg Roppen, Ingrid Semmingsen. 357 pp.
(Philadelphia, Pa. 1968.)
Jan W. Dietrichson: *The Image of Money in the American Novel of the Gilded Age.* 418 pp.
(Oslo and New York, 1969.)
Per Seyersted: *Kate Chopin. A Critical Biography.* 247 pp.
(Oslo and Baton Rouge, La. 1969.)